THE THEATRE OF TENNESSEE WILLIAMS

Volume II

By TENNESSEE WILLIAMS

THE THEATRE OF
TENNESSEE WILLIAMS

Volume II

The Eccentricities of a Nightingale

Summer and Smoke

The Rose Tattoo

Camino Real

A NEW DIRECTIONS BOOK

Manufactured in the United States of America.
New Directions Books are printed on acid-free paper.
First published clothbound in 1976 (ISBN 0-8112-0418-9) and as
New Directions Paperbook 695 in 1990.
Published simultaneously in Canada by Penguin Books Canada Limited.

Library of Congress Cataloging-in-Publication Data

Williams, Tennessee, 1911-1983.
     The theatre of Tennessee Williams.
          p.   cm.
     Contents: v. 1. Battle of the angels. The glass menagerie. A streetcar named
Desire   —v. 2. The eccentricities of a nightingale. Summer and smoke. The
rose tattoo. Camino Real   —v. 5. The milk train doesn't stop here anymore.
Kingdom of Earth (The seven descents of Myrtle). Small craft warnings. The two-
character play.
     ISBN 0-8112-1136-3 (v. 2: pbk.: alk. paper)
     I.   Title.
PS3545.I5365A19   1990
812'.54—dc20   90-5998
                                                                CIP

New Directions Books are published for James Laughlin
by New Directions Publishing Corporation,
80 Eighth Avenue, New York 10011

SECOND PRINTING

Contents

THE ECCENTRICITIES OF A NIGHTINGALE

CHARACTERS

ALMA WINEMILLER

THE REVEREND WINEMILLER, her father

MRS. WINEMILLER, her mother

JOHN BUCHANAN, JR.

MRS. BUCHANAN, his mother

ROGER DOREMUS

VERNON

MRS. BASSETT

ROSEMARY

A TRAVELING SALESMAN

SCENES

The entire action of the play takes place in Glorious Hill, Mississippi. The time is shortly before the First World War.

AUTHOR'S NOTE

Aside from the characters having the same names and the locale remaining the same, I think *The Eccentricities of a Nightingale* is a substantially different play from *Summer and Smoke,* and I prefer it. It is less conventional and melodramatic. I wrote it in Rome one summer and brought it with me to London the fall that *Summer and Smoke* was about to be produced there. But I arrived with it too late. The original version of the play was already in rehearsal.

This radically different version of the play has never been produced on Broadway. I hope that its publication in this volume may lead to its production and that the production may confirm my feeling that it is a better work than the play from which it derived.

ACT ONE

THE FEELING
OF A SINGER

SCENE ONE

It is the evening of July 4th of a year shortly before the First World War.

The exterior set is part of a public square in the small Southern town of Glorious Hill, Mississippi. Two stone steps ascend, at the rear, to a public fountain which is in the form of a stone angel (Eternity), in a gracefully crouching position with wings lifted and hands held together in front to form a cup from which water flows. Near the fountain is a small bench. Framing the set above are mossy branches. Behind is a sky with stars beginning to appear.

Before and for a few minutes after the curtain rises, a somewhat-better-than-typical church soprano is heard singing a semisecular song such as "O That We Two Were Maying."

The Reverend and Mrs. Winemiller, an Episcopal clergyman and his wife, in their early sixties, are on the bench. Sitting on the steps to the fountain is John Buchanan.

The song ends, there is a burst of applause, and while it continues, Miss Alma Winemiller enters from the right. At the same moment a rocket explodes in the sky, casting a momentary white radiance beneath it.

ALMA [*excitedly calling to her parents*]:
The first skyrocket! Oh, look at it burst into a million stars!

[*There is a long-drawn "Ahhh" from unseen spectators. After the brief glare the stage seems very dark. Barely visible figures, laughing, chattering, sweep about the fountain like a sudden passage of birds. Alma cries out as if frightened.*]

11

ALMA:

Oh, I'm blinded, I can't see a *thing*! Father, Father, where *are* you?

[*A child imitates her mockingly.*]

REV. WINEMILLER:

Here we are, Alma, we're down here on the bench.

ALMA:

Oh . . . [*She rushes breathlessly down to them.*]

[*The stage lightens again. Alma is dressed in pale yellow and carries a parasol to match.*]

ALMA:

The words flew out of my mind. I sang the same verse twice. Was it noticeable? Please open my bag for me, Father. My fingers are frozen stiff. I want my handkerchief. My face and my throat are drenched with perspiration. Was that— Oh, I'm talking too loudly! [*She lowers her voice to a shrill whisper.*] Is that John Buchanan up there by the fountain? I rushed right by him but I think he spoke! Don't look now, he'll know we're talking about him. But I think it is!

REV. WINEMILLER:

Suppose it is! What of it? Sit down, Alma.

ALMA:

Oh, the Gulf wind is blowing, what a relief! . . . Yes . . . yes, that *is* John Buchanan. . . . [*Her voice quivers over the name. Her father hands her the handkerchief.*] Oh, thank you, Father. Yesssss—that's John Buchanan, he's been home for a week but hasn't called or dropped ove\
. . . I wonder *why*! Don't you think it's *peculiar*?

REV. WINEMILLER:

Why "peculiar"?

[*A stout dowager in black lace and pearls approaches John Buchanan and takes his arm.*]

ALMA:

His mother stands guard over him like an old dragon! Look at her, keeping time to the music with her lorgnette, one arm hooked through John's, terrified that someone will snatch him from her!

REV. WINEMILLER:

Alma, sit still for a minute. Just sit here quietly and listen to the music until you get back a little composure.

ALMA [*in a shrill rapid whisper, staring straight out*]:

She'll pretend not to see me. I remember the last time John came home from college, no, the time before last, two, two summers ago, while he was still at Johns Hopkins, I was sitting on the front porch one evening. I nodded to him as he went by the house and he lifted his hat and started to come up to me to say hello. Do you know what she did? She immediately stuck her head out of their window and shouted to him, literally shouted to him as if the house had caught fire. "John! John! Come here right this minute! Your father wants you *immediately* in his office!"

REV. WINEMILLER:

Do you want them to overhear you?

ALMA:

Oh, they're not *there* any more, she's dragged him out of danger!

REV. WINEMILLER:

Mrs. Buchanan is always friendly and I don't think it's reasonable of you to blame her for his failure to pay you as much attention as you would like. Now where is your mother gone?

13

MRS. WINEMILLER [*wistfully, at a distance*]:
Where is the ice cream man?

ALMA:
Mother, there *isn't* any ice cream man!

REV. WINEMILLER:
I'll have to take her right home. She's on her bad behavior.

ALMA:
Has she been talking about the Musée Mécanique?

REV. WINEMILLER:
Babbling about it to everybody we meet!

ALMA:
Let her go home. She can get home by herself. It's good for her. Oh, I see where she's headed, she's going across the Square to the White Star Pharmacy to treat herself to an ice cream sundae.

REV. WINEMILLER:
What a terrible cross to have to bear!

ALMA:
The only thing to do with a cross is *bear* it, Father.

REV. WINEMILLER:
The failure of a vocation is a terrible thing, and it's all the more terrible when you're not responsible for the failure yourself, when it's the result of a vicious impulse to destroy in some other person.

ALMA:
Mother isn't responsible for her condition. You know that.

REV. WINEMILLER:
Your mother has *chosen* to be the way she is. She isn't out of her mind. It's all deliberate. One week after our mar-

14

riage a look came into her eyes, a certain look, a look I can't describe to you, a sort of a cold and secretly spiteful look as if I, who loved her, who was *devoted* to her, had done her some, some—*injury!*—that couldn't be—*mentioned.* . . .

ALMA:

I think there are women who feel that way about marriage.

REV. WINEMILLER:

They ought not to marry.

ALMA:

I know, but they do, they *do! They* are the *ones* that marry! The ones that could bring to marriage the sort of almost— *transcendental! tenderness* that it calls for—what do they do? Teach school! Teach singing! Make a life out of little accomplishments. Father . . . *Look! Mrs. Buchanan is making another entrance!*

[*The dowager approaches her son again.*]

ALMA:

She looks so sweet and soft, but under the black lace and pearls is something harder and colder than the stuff that stone angel is made of! And something runs in her veins that's warm and sympathetic as—mineral water! She's come to take her son home. He's too exposed in this place. He might meet a girl without money! A girl who was able to give him nothing but love!

REV. WINEMILLER:

Alma, you're talking wildly. I don't like this kind of talk!

ALMA:

Oh, yes, oh, yes. She told Miss Preston, who works at the public library, that she was determined that John should make the right kind of marriage for a young doctor to make, a girl with beauty and wealth and social position somewhere in the East!—the Orient where the sun rises! *Ha ha ha!*

[*Mrs. Buchanan calls "John? John? John?" with idiotic persistence, like a bird.*]

REV. WINEMILLER:

Alma, I think you had better come home with me, you're not yourself. You're talking almost as wildly as your mother. . . .

ALMA:

I'm sorry, Father. Singing in public always leaves me feeling overexcited. You go, you go on home, I'll be all right in a moment or two. I have to wait for Roger. . . .

REV. WINEMILLER:

I'm not sure I like you being seen so much and associated in people's minds with that, that—well—that rather *peculiar* young man. . . .

ALMA:

You make me think of that story about the Quakers. One Quaker met another Quaker and he said, "Everybody is mad in this world but thee and me, and thou art a little peculiar!" *Ha ha ha!*

REV. WINEMILLER:
Why do you laugh like that?

ALMA:
Like what, Father?

REV. WINEMILLER:
You throw your head back so far it's a wonder you don't break your neck!—Ah, me . . . Hmmm . . . [*He strolls away with a slight parting nod.*]

[*A skyrocket goes off. There is a long "Ahhh!" from the crowd.*]

[*In dumb play, John's mother tries to lead him from the square, but he protests. Somebody calls her. She reluctantly goes, passing in front of Miss Alma.*]

ALMA [*overbrightly*]:
Good evening, Mrs. Buchanan.

MRS. BUCHANAN:
Why, Miss Alma! I want to congratulate you. I heard you sing and I've never heard anyone sing with quite so much . . . *feeling*! No wonder they call you "the Nightingale of the Delta."

ALMA:
It's sweet of you to fib so, I sang so badly.

MRS. BUCHANAN:
You're just being modest! [*She simpers, as she goes off.*]

[*Alma had risen from the bench. She now sits down again and closes her eyes, unfolding a fan suspended about her throat.*]

[*John glances down at her, then notices an unexploded firecracker. He picks it up, lights it, and tosses it under the bench. It goes off and Alma springs up with a sharp outcry. He laughs and descends the steps and comes over to the bench.*]

JOHN:
Hello, Miss Alma.

ALMA:
Johnny Buchanan, did you throw that firecracker?

JOHN:
Ha ha!

ALMA:

It scared me out of my wits! Why, I'm still breathless.

JOHN:

Ha ha!

ALMA:

Ha ha ha! I think I needed a little shock like that to get me over the shock of my fiasco—on the bandstand!

JOHN:

I heard you sing. I liked it.

ALMA:

Ha ha ha ha ha! You liked both verses of it? I sang *one twice*! Ha ha ha . . .

JOHN:

It was good enough to sing three or four times more.

ALMA:

Chivalry! Chivalry still survives in the Southern states!

JOHN:

Mind if I sit down with you?

ALMA:

Oh, please, please *do*! There's room enough for us both. Neither of us is terribly large—in *diameter*! Ha ha ha!

[*He sits down. There is an awkward pause.*]

JOHN:

You sang with so much feeling, Miss Alma.

ALMA:

The feeling was panic!

JOHN:

It sounded O.K. to me.

ALMA:

Oh, I can't hear myself sing, I just feel my throat and tongue working and my heart beating fast!—a *hammer* . . .

JOHN:

Do you have palpitations when you sing?

ALMA:

Sometimes I'm surprised that I don't just drop dead!

JOHN:

Then maybe you shouldn't.

ALMA:

Oh, afterward I feel I've done something, and that's a different feeling from what one feels—most times. . . .

JOHN:

You seem to be still shaking?

ALMA:

That firecracker was a shock to my whole nervous system! Ha ha ha!

JOHN:

I'm sorry. I had no idea that you were so nervous.

ALMA:

Nobody has a right to be so nervous! You're—you're home for the holidays, are you? I mean home for the rest of the summer?

JOHN:

I've finished medical school. But I'm connected with a hospital now, doing laboratory work.

ALMA:

Oh, in *what*, how *thrilling*! How thrilling that sounds, in *what*?—Uh?

JOHN:
Bacteriology.

ALMA:
That's—[*She gasps.*]—that's something to do with, with, with a—*microscope?*—Uh?

JOHN:
Sometimes you have to look through a microscope.

ALMA:
I looked through a telescope once, at Oxford, Mississippi, at the state university when Father delivered the baccalaureate address there one spring. But I've never, never looked through a *microscope*! Tell me, what do you see, I mean, what is it like, through a microscope, if that question makes any sense?—Uh?

JOHN [*slowly*]:
Well—you see pretty much the same thing that you see through a telescope.

ALMA:
Ohhhh?

JOHN:
A—a cosmos, a—microcosmos!—part anarchy and—part order. . . .

[*Music is heard again.*]

ALMA:
Part anarchy and part order! Oh, the *poetry* of science, the *incredible* poetry of it! Ha ha ha!

JOHN [*vaguely*]:
Yes . . .

ALMA:

Part anarchy and part order—the footprints of God!—Uh?

JOHN:

His footprints, maybe, yes . . . but not—God!

ALMA:

Isn't it strange? He never really, *really*—exposes Himself!
Here and there is a footprint, but even the footprints are
not very easy to follow! No, you can't follow. In fact you
don't even know which way they're pointing. . . . Ha ha ha!

JOHN:

How did we get started on that subject?

ALMA:

Heaven knows, but we did!—So you're home for a while!
I bet your mother's delighted, she's so crazy about you,
constantly singing your praises, tells me you graduated
magna cum laude from Johns Hopkins last summer! What
are your—future plans?

JOHN:

I'm leaving tomorrow.

ALMA:

Oh, tomorrow? So soon! As soon as all that?!

JOHN:

Just got a wire from an old teacher of mine who's fighting
bugs in Cuba.

ALMA:

Fighting bugs! In Cuba?

JOHN:

Yes. Bugs in Cuba. *Fever* bugs.

ALMA:
Ohhhh, fever!—Ha ha ha . . .

JOHN:
There's a little epidemic down there with some unusual—aspects, he says. And I've always wanted to visit a Latin country. [*He spreads his knees.*]

ALMA:
Oh, those Latins. All they do is dream in the sun, dream, dream in the sun and indulge their senses!

JOHN [*smiling suddenly*]:
Well, I've heard that cantinas are better than saloons, and they tell me that señoritas are—caviar among females!

ALMA:
Be careful you don't get caught. They say that the tropics are a perfect quagmire. People go there and never are *heard* of again!

JOHN:
Well, it couldn't be hotter than here, that's one sure thing.

ALMA:
Oh, my, isn't it dreadful? Summer isn't the pleasantest time of year to renew your acquaintance with Glorious Hill, Mississippi.—The Gulf wind has failed us this year. It usually cools the nights off, but it has failed us this year.

JOHN:
Driving along the river cools you off.

ALMA:
How heavenly that sounds, driving along the river to cool off!

JOHN:
Does it sound good to you?

ALMA:
Almost too good to believe!

JOHN:
Why don't we take a drive.

ALMA:
What a *divine suggestion*! [*She springs up. But Mrs. Buchanan enters quickly.*]

MRS. BUCHANAN
John! John, darling!

JOHN:
What is it, Mother?

MRS. BUCHANAN:
Your father and I have been searching the whole Square for you!—Excuse us, Miss Alma!

ALMA:
Certainly, Mrs. Buchanan. [*She closes her eyes for a moment with a look of infinite desolation.*]

MRS. BUCHANAN [*continuing as she grabs hold of John's arm*]:
Your father's received a call from Mrs. Arbuckle, but I insist that he must go right to bed; he's about to collapse from exhaustion, and there's absolutely no reason why you can't go and give that woman—please excuse us, Miss Alma! —[*She is dragging him away.*]—the morphine injection, that's all that can be done. . . .

JOHN [*calling back*]:
Goodbye, Miss Alma.

ALMA:
Goodbye! Goodbye! [*She sinks back down on the bench.*]

[*A skyrocket goes up. The crowd cries "Ahhh!"*]

23

[*Roger Doremus, a young man with the little excitements of a sparrow, rushes on with his French horn in a case.*]

ROGER:
How did it go, my solo on the French horn?

ALMA:
I'm!—please get me some water, water, from the fountain, I—I—

ROGER:
You're not feeling well?

ALMA:
I have to take one of my tablets but my mouth is so dry that I can't swallow the tablet. [*She leans back, touching her throat as Roger crosses anxiously to the fountain.*]

[*The scene dims out.*]

SCENE TWO

The Rectory interior on Christmas Eve of the following winter. During the interval the soprano sings a traditional Christmas carol, one not too familiar.

Like all the sets, the Rectory interior is barely suggested, by window and doorframes and a few essential properties.

The Reverend and Mrs. Winemiller are seated on either side of a small round clawfoot table that supports a cut-glass bowl of eggnog with cups. Rev. Winemiller faces the fireplace, which is in the fourth wall and is indicated by a flickering red glow. (Every interior in the play has a fireplace indicated in this way in the same position.) Evidently the fire gives little warmth, for the minister has a lady's lavender woolen shawl wrapped about his hunched shoulders.

Mrs. Winemiller is never quite silent, although her interior monologue is never loud enough to be intelligible. She sounds like a small running brook or a swarm of bees and her face changes expression as her interior world falls under light and shadow.

Miss Alma is a little outside the lighted area as the scene begins and her responses to Rev. Winemiller's singsong elegiac ruminations come out of the shadow where the window frame is located. In this frame is a small candle.

REV. WINEMILLER [*as if continuing*]:
Actually we have about the same number of communicants we've had for the past ten years, but church attendance has dropped off about, hmmm, twenty per cent.

25

ALMA:

Just remember what old Doctor Hoctor announced to his congregation one year, he said to his congregation, "We haven't had any additions to the congregation this year but we've had a number of valuable subtractions."

REV. WINEMILLER:

In the old days before they had the church pension fund ministers stayed in the pulpit as long as they were able to crawl up the chancel.

ALMA:

Yes, poor old Doctor Hoctor, he hung on forever! Much longer than his congregation. They say it finally dwindled down to just a pair of old ladies, one widow and one spinster who hated each other so fiercely that one would sit in the front pew and the other so far in the rear that old Doctor Hoctor, who had lost his sight but still had a little hearing, was never quite certain whether she was there or not except when she had the hiccoughs. Ha ha!

REV. WINEMILLER:

A man must know when he's outlived his term of useful-ness and let go. I'm going to retire next year. . . .

ALMA:

But, Father, you won't come into the pension for five more years! What will we live on, what I make teaching singing?

REV. WINEMILLER:

The Bishop has hinted to me that if I don't feel able to continue, it might be arranged for me to come into my pension a little bit sooner than I'm due to get it.

ALMA:

Ah? [*She suddenly turns out a lamp and rushes back to the window.*] I have never seen anything so ridiculous! Mrs.

26

Buchanan has put on a Santie Claus outfit and is going out their front walk with a sack of presents. I wonder if—John's with her. Yes!—Perhaps they'll . . . Oh, we must get Mother upstairs! They'll come here first, I should think, since we're next door. Yes, they are, they're going to come here first! Mother! Mother! Go upstairs and I'll bring you a piece of fruitcake! Mother? A piece of—! Oh . . . No . . . They're *not* going to come here first. They're crossing the street. [*In a tone of desolation*] They've crossed the street, yes, they've—crossed—the street. . . . You don't suppose they'll—*overlook* us this year?

REV. WINEMILLER:

You're constantly at that window spying on the Buchanans.

ALMA:

*Spy*ing on the Buchanans? What a notion!

REV. WINEMILLER:

You come in the parlor, turn out the lamp, gravitate to that window as if you had to stand by that window to breathe.

ALMA:

Why, Father, I've been looking at the snow. I just happened to notice Mrs. Buchanan in her Santie Claus outfit coming out of the . . .

REV. WINEMILLER:

The house is surrounded by snow on all four sides and all four sides of the house have windows in them through which you could look at the snow if it is only the snow that holds such a fascination over you.

ALMA:

It does, it *does* fascinate me, why, it's the first snow that's fallen on Glorious Hill in more than a hundred years, and

27

when it started falling, they closed all the stores on Front Street and every office in town, even the bank. And all came out, just like overgrown boys, and had snow fights on the street!—Roger Doremus told me . . . No. I don't believe they're going to come here at all. They've gone in the other direction down the block. . . . [*She pours a cup of eggnog, sips it with one hand extended toward the glow of the fireplace.*] The snow reminds me of an old proverb. "Before you love, you must learn how to walk over snow— and leave no footprint. . . ."

[*A carol is heard at some distance.*]

The Methodist carolers have already gone out. I must get . . .

REV. WINEMILLER:
Alma. Sit down for a moment. There's something I want to talk to you about.

ALMA [*apprehensively*]:
I have to get ready to go out with the carolers, Father.

REV. WINEMILLER:
They're not going out until half past eight.

ALMA:
That's almost now.

REV. WINEMILLER:
Then let them start without you. This is more important.

ALMA:
That means it's something unpleasant?

REV. WINEMILLER:
Yes, extremely unpleasant and that's why it's important. Alma, I've had one heavy cross to bear. [*He nods toward*

Mrs. Winemiller.] One almost insufferable cross. A minister isn't complete without a family, he needs his wife and his family to make a—a social bond—with the parish!

ALMA:

Father, I do all I can. More than I have the strength for. I have my vocal pupils. I sing at weddings, I sing at funerals, I swear there's nothing I don't sing at except the conception of infants!

REV. WINEMILLER:

Alma, I won't endure that kind—!

ALMA:

Excuse me, Father, but you know it's true. And I serve on the Altar Guild and I teach the primary class at Sunday school. I made all their little costumes for the Christmas pageant, their angel wings and dresses, and you know what thanks I got for that! Mrs. Peacock cried out that the costumes were inflammable! Inflammable, she screamed! Exactly as if she thought it was my secret hope, my intention, to burn the children up at the Christmas pageant! No, she said, those costumes are inflammable, if they wear those costumes they can't march in with candles! [*She gasps.*]— And so the candles weren't lighted. They marched in holding little stumps of wax!—holding little dirty stumps of wax! The absurdity of it, as if a wind had blown all the candles out—the whole effect I'd worked so hard to create was destroyed by that woman, and I had to bite my tongue because I couldn't answer, I knew that *you* wouldn't want me to answer back. Oh, I've had to bite my tongue so much it's a wonder I have one left!

REV. WINEMILLER:

Please, more calmly, Alma. You're going to swallow your tongue from overexcitement some day, not bite it off from holding back indignation! I asked you to please sit down. Alma— Because of the circumstances, I mean your mother's condition, pitiable, and the never, never outlived notoriety of your Aunt Albertine and the Musée Mécanique . . .

ALMA:
Why can't we forget something that happened fifteen years ago?

REV. WINEMILLER:
Because other people remember!

ALMA:
I'm not going to elope with a Mr. Otto Schwarzkopf!

REV. WINEMILLER:
We must discuss this quietly.

ALMA:
Discuss what quietly? *What!*

REV. WINEMILLER:
Alma, someone, Alma—someone, Alma, who is—deeply devoted to you—who has your interests—very much at heart— almost as fond of you as her own daughter!

ALMA:
Oh, this is Mrs. Peacock—my bête noire!

REV. WINEMILLER:
She was deeply, deeply distressed over something that happened lately. It seems that she overheard someone giving an imitation of you at a young people's party. . . .

ALMA:
An imitation? An imitation, Father? Of what? Of what? Of *me*!

REV. WINEMILLER:
Yes, of you.

ALMA [*gasping*]:
What was it they imitated? What did they imitate about me, Father?

REV. WINEMILLER:
The point is, Alma—

ALMA:
No, please tell me, I want to, I *have* to be told, I must—know . . .

REV. WINEMILLER:
What they imitated was your singing, I think, at a wedding.

ALMA:
My voice? They imitated my voice?

REV. WINEMILLER:
Not your voice but your gestures and facial expressions . . .

ALMA:
Ohhh . . . This leaves me quite speechless!

REV. WINEMILLER:
You're inclined to—dramatize your songs a—bit too much! You, you get carried away by the, the emotion of it! That's why you choke sometimes and get hoarse when you're singing and Mrs. Peacock says that sometimes you weep!

ALMA:
That's not true. It's true that I feel the emotion of a song. Even an ordinary little song like "The Voice That Breathed O'er Eden" or "O Promise Me" or "Because"—why, even commonplace little songs like "I Love You Truly," they

31

have a sincere emotion and a singer must feel it, and when you feel it, you *show* it! A singer's face and hands are part of a singer's *equipment*! Why, even a singer's heart is part of her equipment! That's what they taught me at the Conservatory!

REV. WINEMILLER:

I'm sometimes sorry you went to the Conservatory.

ALMA [*in a stricken voice*]:
All right! I'll give up singing . . . *everything*!

REV. WINEMILLER:

The thing for you to give up is your affectations, Alma, your little put-on mannerisms that make you seem—well—slightly *peculiar* to people! It isn't just your singing I'm talking about. In ordinary conversations you get carried away by your emotions or something, I don't know what, and neither does anyone else. You, you, you—*gild the lily*! —You—express yourself in—fantastic highflown—phrases! Your hands fly about you like a pair of wild birds! You, you get out of breath, you—stammer, you—laugh hysterically and clutch at your throat! Now please remember. I wouldn't mention these things if I didn't know that they were just mannerisms, things that you could control, that you can correct! Otherwise I wouldn't mention them to you. Because I can see that you are upset, but you can correct them. All you have to do is *concentrate*. When you're talking, just watch yourself, keep an eye on your hands, and when you're singing, put them in *one* position and *keep* them there. Like *this*!

ALMA:

Make a steeple?—No, I'd rather not sing. . . .

REV. WINEMILLER:

You're taking altogether the wrong attitude about this.

ALMA:

I'll, I'll just give up my—social efforts, Father—all of them!

REV. WINEMILLER:

The thing for you to give up is this little band of eccentrics, this collection of misfits that you've gathered about you which you call your club, the ones you say will be meeting *here* next Monday!

ALMA:

What a cruel thing to say about a group of sweet and serious people that get together because of—interests in common—cultural interests—who want to create something—vital—in this town!

REV. WINEMILLER:

These young people are not the sort of young people that it's an advantage to be identified with! And one thing more—

ALMA:

What else, Father?

REV. WINEMILLER:

Is it true that you go to the Square with a sack of crumbs?

ALMA:

What, what, what?

REV. WINEMILLER:

Is it true that you go every day to the Square with a sack of crumbs which you throw to the birds?

ALMA:

I scatter breadcrumbs in the Square for the starving birds. *That's* true!

REV. WINEMILLER:

Have you thought how it might look to people?

ALMA:

I thought it only concerned myself and the birds.

REV. WINEMILLER:

Little things like that, an accumulation of them, Alma, little habits, little, little mannerisms, little—peculiarities of behavior—they are what get people known, eventually, as —*eccentrics*! And eccentric people are not happy, they are not happy people, Alma. Eccentrics are—what are you doing?

ALMA [*breathlessly*]:

I can't open the box, I can't open the box, I can't open the box!

REV. WINEMILLER:

Your Amytal tablets?

ALMA:

I can't open the box!

REV. WINEMILLER:

Give it to me.—Hysteria was the beginning of your mother's condition.

ALMA:

I can't breathe! [*She rushes out.*]

REV. WINEMILLER:

Alma! Don't leave the house till you get your mother upstairs! [*She has run out. He turns to his wife and shouts in her ear.*] Grace! This is Christmas Eve and we are going to have callers! You must go up to your bedroom and I will bring you up a piece of fruitcake!

MRS. WINEMILLER [*rousing slightly*]:

No, oh, no, not till you give me the letter, you've hidden it from me, Albertine's last letter! It's got the new address of the Musée Mécanique!

34

[*The "Valse Musette" fades in.*]

REV. WINEMILLER [*after a pause*]:
Grace, listen to me. Albertine has been dead for fifteen years. She and her paramour both died in a fire fifteen years ago, when Mr. Schwarzkopf set fire to the Musée Mécanique.

MRS. WINEMILLER:
Oh, I remember the address, Seven Pearl Street!—I must keep that in my mind, that's the new address of the Musée Mécanique, it's Seven Pearl Street—or was it—Seventeen Pearl Street?

[*The doorbell rings.*]

REV. WINEMILLER:
There, there now, visitors! And look at yourself, how you look! Go upstairs *quickly, quickly!* [*He claps his hands violently together.*]

MRS. WINEMILLER:
Yes . . .

[*She makes a confused turn. He leads her out of the lighted area.*]

[*The scene dims out.*]

35

SCENE THREE

A few minutes later. John and his mother and the Reverend Winemiller are seated in the Rectory parlor. Mrs. Buchanan is ludicrously attired as a female Santa Claus with the incongruous addition of a lorgnon on a silver chain.

She is spotted first before the light comes up on the others.

MRS. BUCHANAN:

The children say to me, You're not Santie Claus, Santie Claus has whiskers, and I say, No, I'm Santie Claus's *wife*! They're so surprised!

REV. WINEMILLER:

I know they must be delighted.

MRS. BUCHANAN:

Tickled to death! Having a wife gives him such a respectability! And how has Grace been lately?

REV. WINEMILLER:

A—uh—little disturbed.

MRS. BUCHANAN:

All the excitement in the air, don't you think? Mrs. Santie Claus has something for her, but if she's a little disturbed, we'll just put it under the tree. Is that Miss Alma? Oh, it *is*. how *lovely*!

[*Alma's high-pitched laughter is heard. John rises from a hassock before the fireplace.*]

ALMA:

Joyeux Noel! Ha ha!

36

MRS. BUCHANAN:

How pretty you look, Miss Alma! I was afraid we'd miss you.

ALMA:

I sang one carol and my throat felt scratchy. The combined church choirs are doing Handel's *Messiah*. [*She gasps.*] Such dreadful demands on the voice! That's Thursday. No, no, Friday, Friday evening, in the high school—goodness, I *am* getting hoarse!—auditorium!

MRS. BUCHANAN:

Let John give you a gargle.

ALMA:

Nasty gargles. . . . I hate them! The voice is such a delicate instrument. When was the last time I saw you? Last— last . . . ?

JOHN:

Fourth of July. The band concert in the Square.

ALMA:

Oh!—oh, dear, the recollection of that . . . !

JOHN:

I heard you sing.

ALMA:

Goodness, yes, I still shudder. The same verse twice!

JOHN:

Ha ha! And I threw a firecracker at you!

ALMA:

Goodness, yes, you *did*! Ha ha! That was so naughty of you! You always· did as a boy, I mean as a little boy, you always threw—firecrackers! Ha ha!—into the Rectory lawn! No Fourth of July was complete without— [*She gasps.*]

37

JOHN:
Ha ha! That's right. I had to keep up the tradition.

ALMA [*gasping*]:
That's right, that's right, you had to keep up the tradition! Let me give you some—oh, where is it?—eggnog!

JOHN:
We've already been served.

ALMA:
Have you? Why, yes, I'm *blind*! I have snow in my eyelashes. It makes rainbows in the light! What an adventure, just imagine, the first snow that's fallen on Glorious Hill in—how many years? Almost a century. Before it began to snow it rained for two days. Suddenly the temperature fell. The rain froze on the trees, on the lawns, on the bushes and hedges, on the roofs, the steeples, the telephone wires. . . . [*She pauses to gasp for breath.*]

REV. WINEMILLER:
Alma, sit down so John can sit down.

ALMA:
Yes, forgive me!—Till the whole town was literally sheathed in ice!—And when the sun rose that morning . . . you can't imagine how *dazzling*! It made you suddenly *see* how dull things *usually* are—the trees, oh, the trees, like huge crystal chandeliers!—turned upside down!

MRS. BUCHANAN:
It's just like fairyland.

ALMA:
Exactly like fairyland.

JOHN:
I wish I had five cents for every time someone has said that.

38

MRS. BUCHANAN:

Little John has been up North so long it's made him a cynic.

ALMA:

Have you lost patience with our romantic clichés?

MRS. BUCHANAN:

Little John, Little John, I can see that your shoes are still damp!—We call him Little John and his father we call *Big* John although Little John is almost twice as tall as Big John is!

ALMA:
How tall is Little John?

MRS. BUCHANAN:
As tall as Jack's beanstalk!

ALMA:
I don't think it's fair for a boy to have such curls!

MRS. BUCHANAN:
As a boy he was so indifferent to the ladies! But those days are all gone now. Every morning cards and letters this high, to the junior Doctor Buchanan in green pink and lavender ink with all the odors of springtime!

ALMA:
What a success he's going to have as a doctor.

MRS. BUCHANAN:
His waiting room will be large as a railroad station.

ALMA:
At least that large and probably with an annex.

MRS. BUCHANAN:
But his love is bugs! He's specializing in something I can't even pronounce.

39

ALMA:
Bacteriology! He told me last Fourth of July.

MRS. BUCHANAN [*turning to Rev. Winemiller*]:
Graduated *magna cum laude* from Johns Hopkins with the highest marks in the history of the college. Already—think of it—seven fine offers from staffs of various hospitals in the East, and one in California!

ALMA [*gasping*]:
All the gifts of the gods were showered on him!

MRS. BUCHANAN [*to Rev. Winemiller*]:
I wanted to have five sons but I only had one. But if I had had fifteen I don't think it would have been reasonable to expect that one of the lot would have turned out *quite* so *fine*!

ALMA:
Your mother is proud as a peacock.

MRS. BUCHANAN:
Don't you think it's excusable in a mother?

ALMA:
Not only excusable but . . . Your cup is empty, John, do let me—fill it!

MRS. BUCHANAN:
Don't make him tipsy! John, your shoes *are* damp, I can tell by just looking at them! [*Declining eggnog*] Oh, no, no more for me, I have to climb down some more chimneys!—That sounds like Grace!

[*Mrs. Winemiller is heard descending the stairs, imitating Alma's shrill laugh.*]

REV. WINEMILLER [*anxiously*]:
Alma, I think your mother is—

ALMA [*gasping*]:
Oh, excuse me!—I'll see what Mother wants.

[*She rushes out. Mrs. Buchanan touches the minister's arm.*]

MRS. BUCHANAN:
Oh, such a tragedy, such a terrible cross for you to bear! Little John, I think we had better go, now, the reindeers must be getting restless.

[*John sneezes. She throws her hands up in terror.*]

I knew it, I knew it, I *knew* it! You *have* caught cold!

JOHN:
Oh, for God's sake!

MRS. BUCHANAN:
John!

[*John sneezes again.*]

That settles it, you're going straight home to bed!

[*Mrs. Winemiller rushes into the parlor. Alma follows her.*]

ALMA:
Father, Mother *insists* on remaining downstairs. She says that she wasn't ready to go to bed.

MRS. WINEMILLER [*excitedly*]:
I have found my letter with the address on it. It's Seven Pearl Street in New Orleans. That's where Albertine is with Mr. Schwarzkopf and the Musée Mécanique. Oh, such a lot of news in it!

REV. WINEMILLER:
Yes, I am sure. But let's not discuss the news now.

41

MRS. WINEMILLER [to Mrs. Buchanan]:
Have *you* ever been to the Musée Mécanique?

MRS. BUCHANAN:
Long ago, Grace, long ago I—had that pleasure. . . . [*She touches her lips nervously with her lorgnon.*]

MRS. WINEMILLER:
Then you know what it is? It's a collection of mechanical marvels, invented and operated by my sister's—husband!—Mr. Otto Schwarzkopf! Mechanical marvels, all of them, but, then, you know, when everything's run by mechanics it takes a mechanical genius to keep them in good condition all of the time and sometimes poor Mr. Schwarzkopf is not in condition to keep them all—in—condition. . . .

MRS. BUCHANAN:
Well, this is a mechanical age we live in. . . .

ALMA:
Mother, Mrs. Buchanan has brought her son with her and we are so eager to hear about his work and his—studies at—Johns Hopkins!

JOHN:
Oh, let's hear about the Museum, Miss Alma.

MRS. WINEMILLER:
Yes! That's what I'm telling you about, the Museum!—of mechanical marvels. Do you know what they are? Well, let me tell you. There's the mechanical man that plays the flute. There's the mechanical drummer—oh, such a sweet little boy all made out of tin that shines like a brand new dollar! Boom, boom, boom, beats the drum. Toot, toot, toot, goes the flute. And the mechanical soldier waves his flag, waves it, waves it, and waves it! Ha ha ha!—And oh!

42

Oh!—the loveliest thing of all—the mechanical bird-girl! Yes, the mechanical bird-girl is almost the biggest mechanical triumph since the Eiffel Tower, according to people who know. She's made of sterling silver! Every three minutes, right on the dot, a little mechanical bird pops out of her mouth and sings three beautiful notes, as clear as—a bell!

REV. WINEMILLER:

Grace, Mrs. Buchanan remembers all of that.

MRS. WINEMILLER:

The young man *doesn't!* I don't believe he's seen the Musée Mécanique.

JOHN:

No, I've never. It sounds very exciting!

MRS. WINEMILLER:

Well, lately, I personally think they have made a mistake. I think it was a mistake to buy the *big snake!*

JOHN:

A mechanical snake?

MRS. WINEMILLER:

Oh no, a real one, a live one, a boa constrictor. Some meddlesome maddie told them "Big snakes pay good."—So Mr. Schwarzkopf, who is not a practical man, a genius without any business sense whatsoever—mortgaged the whole Museum to pay for this great big snake!—So far, so good!— But! The snake was used to living in a warm climate. It was winter. New Orleans *can* be cold!—The snake seemed chilly, it became *very stupid,* and so they gave it a *blanket!* —Well!—Now in this letter I've just received today—Albertine tells me a *terrible* thing has happened!

JOHN:
What did the big snake do?

MRS. WINEMILLER:
Nothing!—JUST *swallowed* his *blanket*!

JOHN:
I thought you were going to say it swallowed Mr. Schwarz-kopf.

MRS. BUCHANAN:
Oh, now, Little John, *hush,* you bad boy, you! [*She touches her lips with the lorgnon.*]

MRS. WINEMILLER:
Swallowed its blanket!

JOHN:
Did the blanket disagree with it?

MRS. WINEMILLER:
Disagree with it? I should say it did! What can a stomach, even the stomach of a boa constrictor, do with a heavy blanket?

JOHN:
What did they do about the—situation?

MRS. WINEMILLER:
Everything they could think of—which wasn't *much* . . . Veterinarians, experts from the—zoo!—Nobody could suggest anything to . . . Finally they sent a telegram to the man who had sold them the snake. "The big snake has swallowed his blanket! What shall we do?"—He'd told them big snakes pay good, but *dead* snakes—what do they pay?—They pay what the little boy shot at!—Well!—Do you know what the man that sold the snake to them wired back?—"All you can do is get on your knees and pray!" That's what he replied.

44

MRS. BUCHANAN:
Oh, now, really! How cruel!

JOHN:
Ha ha ha!

ALMA [*desperately*]:
Mother, I think you—

JOHN:
And did they pray for the snake?

MRS. WINEMILLER:
They prayed for the big investment!—They should have stuck to mechanics in the—Museum—but somebody told them that big snakes pay good. . . .

ALMA:
Mother, it's past your bedtime. You go up to bed and I will bring you a slice of delicious fruitcake. Won't that be nice?

MRS. WINEMILLER:
Yes!—if you really bring it. [*She starts hurriedly off, then turns and waves to the company.*] Merry Christmas!

REV. WINEMILLER:
She is—well, as you see . . . she's . . .

MRS. BUCHANAN:
Yes! A little disturbed right now. All the excitement of the holiday season. Little John, we must be running along, don't you think? Big John's waiting for us.

JOHN:
I've just persuaded Miss Alma to sing us something.

MRS. BUCHANAN:
Oh! [*insincerely*] How nice!

[*Alma is at the piano.*]

ALMA:
Would you care for something profane or sacred?

JOHN:
Oh, something profane, by all means!

REV. WINEMILLER [*weakly*]:
I think I will try a little of this eggnog. . . .

[*Miss Alma sings. It is not necessary for the actress to have a very good voice. If she has no singing voice at all, the song can be dubbed, the piano placed so her back or her profile will be to the audience.*]

ALMA [*singing*]:

> From the land of the sky-blue water,
> They brought a captive maid,
> Her eyes are lit with lightning,
> Her heart is not afraid!

> I stole to her tent at dawning.
> I wooed her with my flute!
> She is sick for the sky-blue water.
> The captive maid is mute. . . .

MRS. BUCHANAN [*interrupting the song*]:
Oh, how lovely, how lovely, one of my favorite pieces, and such a beautiful voice!—Before I forget it, Mrs. Santie Claus has some gifts to put under your tree. . . . —Where *is* your Christmas tree?

ALMA:
Oh, this year we put it up in Father's study!

[*Rev. Winemiller leads Mrs. Buchanan offstage. Alma and John remain by the piano.*]

ALMA:
My hands are so stiff from the cold I could hardly touch the right keys. . . .

46

JOHN:

Shall we sit by the fire?

ALMA:

Oh, yes, that's a good suggestion . . . an excellent suggestion!

JOHN:

You sing very well, Miss Alma.

ALMA:

Thank you—thank you . . . [*Pause. She clears her throat.*]

JOHN:

Don't they call you "the Nightingale of the Delta"?

ALMA:

Sarcastically, perhaps!

[*She has drawn up a hassock to the imagined fireplace. He sits on the floor with his palms extended toward the flickering red glow.*]

I have a lyric soprano. Not strong enough to make a career of singing but just about right for the church and for social occasions and I—teach singing!—But let's—let's talk about you—your—your—life and your—plans! Such a wonderful profession, being a doctor! Most of us lead such empty, useless lives! But a doctor!—Oh!—With his wonderful ability to relieve—human suffering, of which there is always —so—much! [*Her tongue runs away with her.*] I don't think it's just a profession, it's a *vocation*! I think it's something to which some people are just—*appointed by God*! [*She claps her hands together and rolls her eyes.*] Yes, just divinely appointed!—Some of us have no choice but to lead a useless existence—endure for the sake of endurance—but a young doctor, you!—with *surgeon's fingers*!

[*She has sprung up to fill his cup with eggnog. The silver ladle slips from her fingers. She utters a startled cry.*]

47

Ouuu!—Oh, look what I've done! I've dropped the spoon in the bowl and it is completely submerged! What can I fish it out with, oh, what can I fish it out with?

JOHN:
Do you mind if I use my surgeon's fingers?

ALMA:
Ohhhhh—pleeeeeeeease!—do—ha ha ha! [*She gasps.*]

JOHN:
Well!—that was not such a delicate operation. . . .

ALMA:
Now you must have a napkin to wipe those fingers!

JOHN:
My handkerchief will do!

ALMA:
No, no, no, no, no, not that beautiful handkerchief with your monogram on it!—probably given you by someone who loves you for—Christmas. . . .

[*She picks up a napkin, grabs his hand, and wipes his fingers with tremulous care.*]

I guess you're totally "booked up," as they say, for the short time you'll be home from your laboratory?

JOHN [*gently*]:
Just about all.

ALMA:
There's a group of young people with interests in common meeting here at the Rectory Monday. Monday evening. I know you'd like them *so* much!—Wouldn't you be able to—drop over? For just a *while*?

48

JOHN:

What sort of interests do they have in common?

ALMA:

Oh!—vaguely—*cultural,* I guess. . . . We write things, we read things aloud, we—criticize and—discuss!

JOHN:

At what time does it start, this—meeting?

ALMA:

Oh, *early*—at eight!

JOHN:

I'll—try to make it.

ALMA:

Don't say *try* as if it required some Herculean effort. All you have to do is cross the yard.—We serve refreshments, both liquid and solid!

JOHN:

Reserve me a seat by the punch bowl.

ALMA [*her voice nearly failing with emotion*]:

That gives me a splendid idea. I *will* serve punch. Fruit punch with claret in it.—Do you like claret?

JOHN:

Oh yes. I'm crazy about it.

ALMA:

We *start* so early. We *finish* early, too! You'll have time for something exciting later. Your evenings are long ones, I know that!—I'll tell you *how* I know!—Your *room* is—opposite *mine.* . . .

JOHN:

How do you know?

ALMA:
Your light—shines in my *window*! ha ha ha!

JOHN:
At two or three in the morning?

ALMA:
Or *three* or *four*!—in the morning! ha ha!

JOHN:
It—wakes you up? [*He smiles warmly. She glances away.*]

ALMA:
Ha ha—yes . . .

JOHN:
You should have let me know, you should have—complained about it.

ALMA:
Complained?—Goodness, no—why *should* I?

JOHN:
Well, if it . . .

ALMA:
Oh, it . . .

JOHN:
It doesn't?

ALMA [*very flustered*]:
What?

JOHN:
Wake you up? Disturb your sleep?

ALMA:
Oh, no, I'm—awake, already. . . .

JOHN:

You must not sleep very well, or maybe you're getting home from late parties, too!

ALMA:

The first supposition, I'm afraid, is the right one.

JOHN:

I'll give you a prescription for sleeping tablets.

ALMA:

Oh no. You misunderstood me. I *finally* sleep, I, I, I— wasn't complaining.

[*He suddenly takes her hand.*]

JOHN:

What is the matter?

ALMA:

What is the matter? I don't understand that question.

JOHN:

Yes, you do. What is the matter, Miss Alma?

[*Mrs. Winemiller has appeared at the edge of the lighted area in her nightgown. She suddenly announces—*]

MRS. WINEMILLER:

Alma has fallen in love with that tall boy!

ALMA [*springing up*]:

Mother! What do you want downstairs?

MRS. WINEMILLER:

That piece of fruitcake you said you would bring up to me.

ALMA:

Go back to your bedroom. I will bring it up.

51

MRS. WINEMILLER:
Now?

ALMA:
Yes. Yes, now. Right now!

[*She steals a frightened glance at John, touches her throat as the stage dims out and the returning voices of Mrs. Buchanan and Rev. Winemiller fade in.*]

[*Fade out.*]

ACT TWO

THE TENDERNESS
OF A MOTHER

SCENE ONE

The Buchanans's. We see John in pajamas seated on the floor, smoking before the fireplace; nothing else.

His mother, Mrs. Buchanan, enters the lighted area in her lace negligee.

MRS. BUCHANAN:
Son?

JOHN:
Yes, Mother?

MRS. BUCHANAN:
You mustn't misunderstand me about Miss Alma. Naturally I feel sorry for her, too. But, precious, precious! In every Southern town there's a girl or two like that. People feel sorry for them, they're kind to them, but, darling, they keep at a distance, they don't get involved with them. Especially not in a sentimental way.

JOHN:
I don't know what you mean about Miss Alma. She's a little bit—quaint, she's very excitable, but—there's nothing *wrong* with her.

MRS. BUCHANAN:
Precious, can't you see? Miss Alma is an *eccentric*!

JOHN:
You mean she isn't like all the other girls in Glorious Hill?

MRS. BUCHANAN:
There's always at least one like her in every Southern town, sometimes, like Miss Alma, rather sweet, sometimes even

gifted, and I think that Miss Alma *does* have a rather appealing voice when she doesn't become too carried away by her singing. Sometimes, but not often, pretty. I have seen Miss Alma when she was almost pretty. But never, never *quite*.

JOHN:
There are moments when she has beauty.

MRS. BUCHANAN:
Those moments haven't occurred when *I* looked at her! Such a wide mouth she has, like the mouth of a clown! And she distorts her face with all those false expressions. However, Miss Alma's looks are beside the point.

JOHN:
Her, her eyes are fascinating!

MRS. BUCHANAN:
Goodness, yes, disturbing!

JOHN:
No, quite lovely, I think. They're never the same for two seconds. The light keeps changing in them like, like—a running stream of clear water. . . .

MRS. BUCHANAN:
They have a demented look!

JOHN:
She's not demented, Mother.

MRS. BUCHANAN:
Ha! You should see her in the Square when she feeds the birds.

[*John laughs a little.*]

Talks to them, calls them! "Here, birds, here, birds, here, birdies!" Holding out her hand with some scraps of bread! —huh!—Son, your hair is still damp. It's lucky that Mother peeped in. Now let me rub those curls dry.—My boy's such a handsome boy, and I'm so proud of him! I can see his future so clearly, such a wonderful future! I can see the girl that he will marry! A girl with every advantage, nothing less will do!

JOHN:
A girl with money?

MRS. BUCHANAN:
Everything, everything! Intelligence, beauty, charm, background—yes! Wealth, wealth, too! It's not to be sneezed at, money, especially in the wife of a young doctor. It takes a while for a doctor to get established, and I want you to take your time and not make any mistakes and go a long, long, long, long way!—further, much further than your dear father, although he hasn't done badly. . . . Yes, Mother can see her future daughter-in-law!—Healthy! Normal! Pretty!

JOHN:
A girl like all the others?

MRS. BUCHANAN:
Superior to the others!

JOHN:
And sort of smug about it?

MRS. BUCHANAN:
Oh, people have to be slightly smug sometimes. A little bit snobbish, even. People who have a position have to hold it, and my future daughter-in-law, my coming daugh-

57

ter—she'll have the sort of poise that only comes with the very best of breeding and all the advantages that the best background can give her.

JOHN:
She won't be tiresome, will she?

MRS. BUCHANAN:
Heavens, no! How could she?

JOHN:
I've met some debutantes in Baltimore that found, somehow, a way of being tiresome....

MRS. BUCHANAN:
Just wait till you meet the right one! I have already met her, in my dreams! Oh, son, how she will adore you!

JOHN:
More than she does herself?

MRS. BUCHANAN:
She'll worship the ground you walk on.

JOHN:
And her babies, how will they be?

MRS. BUCHANAN:
Healthy! Normal!

JOHN:
Not little pink and white pigs? With ribbons around their tails?

MRS. BUCHANAN:
Ho-ho-ho-ho-ho! Your babies, my son's babies, pigs?! Oh, precious! I see them, I know them, I feel their dear little bodies in my arms! My adorable little grandchildren. Little

pink things for the girl. Little blue things for the boy. A nursery full of their funny little toys. Mother Goose illustrations on the wallpaper, and their own wee little table where they sit with their bibs and their silver spoons, just so high, yes, and their own little chairs, their tiny straight-back chairs and their wee little rockers, ho, ho, ho!—And on the lawn, on the enormous, grassy, shady lawn of the— Georgian, yes, *Georgian* mansion, not Greek revival, I'm tired of Greek revival!—will be their swing, their shallow pool for goldfish, their miniature train, their pony—oh, no, not a pony, no, no, not a pony!—I knew a little girl, once, that fell off a pony and landed on her head! *Goodness, she grew up to be almost as odd as Miss Alma!*

[*At this point a dim spot of light appears on Miss Alma standing raptly before a window frame at the other side of the stage. A strain of music is heard.*]

JOHN:
Miss Alma has asked me over next Monday night!

MRS. BUCHANAN:
Oh, I knew it, trying to rope you in!

JOHN:
She says there's to be a club meeting at the Rectory. A little group of young people with interests in common.

MRS. BUCHANAN:
Oh, yes, I know, I know what they have in common, the freaks of the town! Every Southern town has them and probably every Northern town has them, too. A certain little group that don't fit in with the others, sort of outcast people that have, or imagine they have, little talents for this thing or that thing or the other—over which they make a

big fuss among themselves in order to bolster up their poor little, hurt little egos! They band together, they meet at each other's houses once a week, and make believe they're disliked and not wanted at other places because they're special, superior—gifted! . . . Now your curls are all dry! But let me feel your footsies, I want to make sure the footsies are dry, too, I bet anything they're not, I bet they're damp! Let Mother feel them! [*He extends his bare feet.*] Ho, ho, ho, ho! What enormous little footsies!

JOHN [*as she rubs them with towel*]:
You know, Mama, I never dreamed that you could be such an old tiger. Tigress, I mean.

MRS. BUCHANAN:
Every mother's a tiger when her son's future happiness is threatened.

JOHN:
I'm not in love with Miss Alma, if that's what you're scared of. I just *respect* her. . . .

MRS. BUCHANAN:
For what?

JOHN:
I'm not quite sure what it is, but it's something she has, a sort of—*gallantry,* maybe. . . .

MRS. BUCHANAN:
Admire her for her good qualities and I am sure she must have some, but *do not get involved*! Don't go to the little club meeting. Make an excuse and don't go. Write a sweet little note explaining that you had forgotten another engagement. Or let Mother do it. Mother can do it sweetly. There won't be any hurt feelings. . . . Now give me that

cigarette. I won't leave you to smoke it in bed. That's how fires start. I don't want us all burned up like the Musée Mécanique!

JOHN:
Oh, did the Museum burn?

MRS. BUCHANAN:
Heavens, yes, that's a story, but it's too long for bedtime. [*She bends to kiss him fondly, with a lingering caress.*] Good night, my precious! Sleep tight!

[*She turns out the light as she leaves. The dim spot remains on Miss Alma a moment longer. . . .*]

ALMA:
Oh, my love, my love, your light is out, now—I can sleep!

SCENE TWO

The following Monday evening. The little group is meeting in the Rectory parlor. An animated discussion is in progress.

VERNON:

I think it's a question of whether or not we have a serious purpose. I was under the impression that we *had* a serious purpose, but of course, if we *don't* have a serious purpose—

ALMA:

Of course we *do* have a serious purpose, but I don't see why that means we have to publish a—manifesto about it!

ROGER:

What's wrong with a manifesto?

VERNON:

Even if nobody reads the manifesto, it—*crystallizes!*—our purpose, in our own minds.

ALMA:

Oh, but to say that we—have such lofty ambitions.

ROGER:

But, Miss Alma, *you* are the one who said we were going to make Glorious Hill the *Athens of the Delta!*

ALMA:

Yes, but in the manifesto it says the Athens of the whole *South,* and besides an ambition, a hope of that kind, doesn't have to be—published! In a way to publish it—destroys it! —a little. . . .

MRS. BASSETT:

The manifesto is beautiful, *perfectly* beautiful, it made me *cry!*

VERNON [*who composed it*]:
Thank you, Nancy.

ROGER:
Boys and girls, the meeting is called to order. Miss Alma will read us the minutes of the last meeting.

MRS. BASSETT:
Oh, let's skip the minutes! Who cares what happened last time? Let's concentrate on the present and the future! That's a widow's philosophy!

[*The doorbell rings. Alma drops her papers.*]

Butter fingers!

ALMA [*breathlessly*]:
Did I—hear the bell—ring?

[*The bell rings again.*]

Yes!—it did! [*She starts to pick up the papers; they slip again.*]

MRS. BASSETT:
Miss Alma, I don't think I've ever seen you quite so nervous!

ALMA:
I forgot to mention it!—I . . . invited a . . . guest!—someone just home for the holidays—young Doctor Buchanan, the old doctor's son, you know!—he—lives next door!—and he . . .

VERNON:
I thought we had all agreed not to have outsiders unless we took a vote on them beforehand!

ALMA:
It was presumptuous of me, but I'm sure you'll forgive me when you meet him!

[*She flies out. They all exchange excited looks and whispers as she is heard offstage admitting John to the hall.*]

ROSEMARY:
I don't care who he is, if a group *is* a group there must be something a *little* exclusive about it!—otherwise it . . .

MRS. BASSETT:
Listen! Why, she is *hysterical* about him!

[*Miss Alma's excited voice is heard and her breathless laughter offstage racing.*]

ALMA:
Well, well, well, our guest of honor has finally made his appearance!

JOHN:
Sorry I'm late.

ALMA:
Oh, you're not *very* late.

JOHN:
Dad's laid up. I have to call on his patients.

ALMA:
Oh, is your father *not well*?

JOHN:
Just a slight touch of grippe.

ALMA:
There's so much going around.

JOHN:
These Delta houses aren't built for cold weather.

ALMA:
Indeed they aren't! The Rectory's made out of paper, I believe.

[*All of this is said offstage, in the hall.*]

ROSEMARY:
Her voice has gone up *two octaves*!

MRS. BASSETT:
Obviously *infatuated* with him!

ROSEMARY:
Oh, my *stars*!

MRS. BASSETT:
The last time I was here—the lunatic mother made a sudden entrance!

VERNON:
Shhhh!—girls!

[*Alma enters with John. He is embarrassed by the curious intensity of her manner and the greedily curious glances of the group.*]

ALMA:
Everybody!—this is Doctor John Buchanan, *Junior*!

JOHN:
Hello, everybody. I'm sorry if I interrupted the meeting.

MRS. BASSETT:
Nothing was interrupted. We'd decided to skip the minutes.

ALMA:
Mrs. Bassett says it's a widow's philosophy to skip the minutes. And so we are skipping the minutes—ha, ha, ha! I hope everybody is comfortable?

ROSEMARY:
I'm just as cold as Greenland's icy mountains!

ALMA:

Rosemary, you always are chilly, even in warm weather. I think you must be thin-blooded!—Here. Take this shawl!

ROSEMARY:

No thank you, not a shawl!—at least not a gray woolen shawl, I'm not *that* old yet, that I have to be wrapped in a gray shawl.

ALMA:

Excuse me, *do forgive* me!—John, I'll put you on this love seat, next to me.—Well, now we are completely assembled!

MRS. BASSETT:

Vernon has his verse play with him tonight!

ALMA [*uneasily*]:

Is that right, Vernon?

[*He has a huge manuscript in his lap which he solemnly elevates.*]

Oh, I *see* that you have.

ROSEMARY:

I thought that I was supposed to read my paper on William Blake at the meeting.

ALMA:

Well, obviously we can't have both at once. That would be an embarrassment of riches!—Now why don't we save the verse play, which appears to be rather long, till some more comfortable evening. I think it's too important to hear under any but ideal circumstances, in warmer weather, with—with *music!*—planned to go with it. . . .

ROGER:

Yes, let's hear Rosemary's paper on William Blake!

MRS. BASSETT:

No, no, no, those dead poets can keep!—Vernon's alive and he's got his verse play with him; he's brought it three times! And each time been disappointed.

VERNON:

I am not disappointed not to read my verse play, *that* isn't the point at all, *but—*

ALMA:

Shall we take a standing vote on the question?

ROGER:

Yes, let's do.

ALMA:

Good, good, perfect, let's do! A standing vote. All in favor of postponing the verse play till the next meeting, stand up!

[*Rosemary is late in rising.*]

ROSEMARY:

Is this a vote?

[*As she starts to rise Mrs. Bassett jerks her arm.*]

ROGER:

Now, Mrs. Bassett, no rough tactics, please!

ALMA:

So we'll save the verse play and begin the New Year with it!

[*Rosemary puts on her glasses and rises portentously.*]

ROSEMARY:

The poet—William Blake!

MRS. BASSETT:

Insane, insane, that man was a mad fanatic!

67

[*She squints her eyes tight shut and thrusts her thumbs into her ears. The reactions range from indignant to conciliatory.*]

ROGER:
Now, Mrs. Bassett!

MRS. BASSETT:
This is a free country. I can speak my opinion. And I have *read up* on him. Go on, Rosemary. I wasn't criticizing your paper.

[*But Rosemary sits down, hurt.*]

ALMA:
Mrs. Bassett is only joking, Rosemary.

ROSEMARY:
No, I don't want to read it if she feels that strongly about it.

MRS. BASSETT:
Not a bit, don't be silly! I just don't see why we should encourage the writings of people like that who have already gone into a drunkard's grave!

VARIOUS VOICES [*exclaiming*]:
Did he? I never heard that about him. Is that true?

ALMA:
Mrs. Bassett is mistaken about that. Mrs. Bassett, you have confused Blake with someone else.

MRS. BASSETT [*positively*]:
Oh, no, don't tell me. I've read up on him and know what I'm talking about. He traveled around with that Frenchman who took a shot at him and landed them both in jail! Brussels, Brussels!

68

ROGER [*gaily*]:
Brussels sprouts!

MRS. BASSETT:
That's where it happened, fired a gun at him in a drunken
stupor, and later one of them died of t.b. in the gutter!
All right. I'm finished. I won't say anything more. Go on
with your˙ paper, Rosemary. There's nothing like contact
with culture!

[*Alma gets up.*]

ALMA:
Before Rosemary reads her paper on Blake, I think it
would be a good idea, since some of us aren't acquainted
with his work, to preface the critical and biographical comments with a reading of one of his loveliest lyric poems.

ROSEMARY:
I'm not going to read anything at all! Not I!

ALMA:
Then let me read it then. [*She takes a paper from Rosemary.*] . . . This is called "Love's Secret."

[*She clears her throat and waits for a hush to settle.
Rosemary looks stonily at the carpet. Mrs. Bassett looks
at the ceiling. John coughs.*]

> Never seek to tell thy love,
> Love that never told can be;
> For the gentle wind doth move
> Silently, invisibly.
>
> I told my love, I told my love,
> I told him all my heart.
> Trembling, cold, in ghastly fear
> Did my love depart.

69

No sooner had he gone from me
Than a stranger passing by,
Silently, invisibly,
Took him with a sigh!

[*There are various effusions and enthusiastic applause.*]

MRS. BASSETT:

Honey, you're right. That isn't the man I meant. I was thinking about the one who wrote about the "bought red lips." Who was it that wrote about the "bought red lips"?

ALMA:

You're thinking about a poem by Ernest Dowson.

[*The bell rings.*]

MRS. BASSETT:

Ohhhhh, the doorbell *again*!

MRS. WINEMILLER [*above*]:

Alma, Alma!

[*Alma crosses the stage and goes out.*]

ROSEMARY:

Aren't you all cold? I'm just freezing to death! I've never been in a house as cold as this!

ALMA [*in the hall*]:

Why, Mrs. Buchanan! How sweet of you to—drop over....

MRS. BUCHANAN:

I can't stay, Alma. I just came to fetch my Little John home:

ALMA:

Fetch—John!?

MRS. BUCHANAN:

His father's just received an urgent call from old Mrs. Arbuckle's house. The poor woman is in a dreadful pain.

70

John? John, darling? I hate to drag you away but your
father can't budge from the house!

ALMA:

Mrs. Buchanan, do you know everybody?

MRS. BUCHANAN:

Why, yes, I think so. —John? Come, dear! I'm so sorry . . .

[*It is obvious that she is delivering a cool snub to the
gathering. There are various embarrassed murmurs as
John makes his departure. Miss Alma appears quite
stricken.*]

ALMA [*after the departure*]:

Shall we go on with the reading?

ROSEMARY:

"The Poet, William Blake, was born in the year of our
Lord, 1757. . . ."

[*Mrs. Winemiller cries out and bursts into the room half
in and out of her clothes.*]

MRS. WINEMILLER:

Alma, Alma, I've got to go to New Orleans right away,
immediately, Alma, by the midnight train. They've closed
the Museum, confiscated the marvels! Mr. Schwarzkopf is
almost out of his mind. He's going to burn the place up,
he's going to set it on fire—before the auction—Monday!

ALMA:

Oh, Mother! [*She makes a helpless gesture; then bursts
into tears and runs out of the room, followed by Mrs.
Winemiller.*]

MRS. BASSETT:

I think we'd all better go—poor Miss Alma!

ROGER:

I move that the meeting adjourn.

VERNON:
I second the motion!

MRS. BASSETT:
Poor Miss Alma! But I knew it was a mistake to have us meet here. [*Sotto voce*] *Nobody* comes to the Rectory any more!—this *always* happens . . . the *mother!*—invariably makes a scene of some kind. . . .

[*They trail off.*]

ROSEMARY [*slowly, wonderingly, as she follows them off*]: I don't understand!—What happened?

[*Fade out.*]

SCENE THREE

Later that night.

The interior of the doctor's office is suggested by a chart of anatomy, a black leather divan and an oak desk and chair behind it.

A buzzer sounds in the dark.

VOICES MURMUR ABOVE:

—John?

—Hannh?

—The bell's ringing in the office. You'd better answer it or it will wake up your father.

—All right, Mama.

[*A panicky knocking begins. John enters in pajamas and robe, carrying a book. There are sounds of releasing a lock. Lights go up as Miss Alma enters. She has thrown on a coat over a nightgown, her hair is in disorder, and her appearance very distracted. She is having "an attack."*]

JOHN:
Why, it's you, Miss Alma!

ALMA [*panting*]:
Your father, please.

JOHN:
Is something the matter?

ALMA:
I have to see your father.

JOHN:

Won't I do?

ALMA:

No, I think not. Please call your father.

JOHN:

Big John's asleep, he's not well.

ALMA:

I'm having an attack, I've got to see him!

JOHN:

It's after two, Miss Alma.

ALMA:

I know the time, I know what time it is! Do you think I'd run over here at two in the morning if I weren't terribly ill?

JOHN:

I don't think you would be able to run over here at two in the morning if you *were* terribly ill. Now sit down here. [*He leads her to the divan.*] And stop swallowing air.

ALMA:

Swallowing what?

JOHN:

Air. You swallow air when you get overexcited. It presses against your heart and starts it pounding. That frightens you more. You swallow more air and get more palpitations and before you know it you're in a state of panic like this. Now you lean back. No, no, lean all the way back and just breathe slowly and deeply. You're not going to suffocate and your heart's going to keep on beating. Look at your fingers, shame on you! You've got them clenched like you're getting ready to hit me. Are you going to hit me? Let those fingers loosen up, now.

ALMA:
I can't, I can't, I'm too . . .

JOHN:
You couldn't sleep?

ALMA:
I couldn't sleep.

JOHN:
You felt walled in, the room started getting smaller?

ALMA:
I felt—walled in—suffocated!

JOHN:
You started hearing your heart as if somebody had stuffed it in the pillow?

ALMA:
Yes, like a drum in the pillow.

JOHN:
A natural thing. But it scared you. [*He hands her a small glass of brandy.*] Toss this down.

[*He places a hand behind her, raising her shoulders from the divan.*]

ALMA:
What is it?

JOHN:
Shot of brandy.

ALMA:
Oh, that's a stimulant, I need something to calm me.

JOHN:
This will calm you.

ALMA:
Your father gives me—

JOHN:
Let's try this to begin with.

ALMA:
He gives me some little white tablets dissolved in—

JOHN:
Get this down.

[*She sips and chokes.*]

ALMA:
Oh!

JOHN:
Went down the wrong way?

ALMA:
The muscles of my throat are paralyzed!

JOHN:
Undo those fists, undo them, loosen those fingers. [*He presses her hands between his.*]

ALMA:
I'm sorry I—woke you up. . . .

JOHN:
I was reading in bed. A physicist named Albert Einstein. I'm going to turn this light out.

ALMA:
Oh, no!

JOHN:
Why not? Are you afraid of the dark?

ALMA:
Yes . . .

JOHN:

It won't be very dark. I'm going to open these shutters
and you can look at the stars while I tell you what I was
reading.

[*He turns off the lamp on the desk. Crossing to the
window frame, he makes a motion of opening shutters.
A dim blue radiance floods the stage.*]

I was reading that time is one side of the four-dimensional
continuum that we exist in. I was reading that space is
curved. It turns back on itself instead of going on indefinitely like we used to believe, and it's hanging adrift in
something that's even less than space; it's hanging like a
soap bubble in something less than space. . . .

ALMA:

Where is the . . .?

JOHN:

Brandy? Right here . . . Throat muscles still paralyzed?

ALMA:

No, I—think I can—get it down, now. . . .

JOHN:

There's nothing wrong with your heart but a little functional disturbance, but I'll check it for you. Unbutton your
gown.

ALMA:

Unbutton? . . .

JOHN:

Just the top of your gown.

ALMA:

Hadn't I better come back in the morning when your
father is . . .?

JOHN:
Sure. If you'd rather.

ALMA:
I—my fingers are . . .

JOHN:
Fingers won't work?

ALMA:
They are just as if frozen!

JOHN [*kneeling beside her*]:
Let me. [*He leans over her, unbuttoning the gown.*] Little
pearl buttons . . . [*Stethoscope to her chest*] Breathe.—Now
out . . . Breathe . . . Now out . . . [*Finally he rises.*] Um-
hmmmm.

ALMA:
What do you hear in my heart?

JOHN:
Just a little voice saying, "Miss Alma is lonesome."

[*She springs up angrily.*]

ALMA:
If your idea of helping a patient is to ridicule and insult—

JOHN:
My idea of helping you is to tell you the truth.

ALMA [*snatching up her cloak*]:
Oh, how wise and superior you are! John Buchanan, Junior,
graduate of Johns Hopkins, *magna cum laude!*—Brilliant,
yes, as the branches after the ice storm, and just as cold
and inhuman! Oh, you put us in our place tonight, my,
my little collection of—eccentrics, my club of—fellow misfits! You sat among us like a lord of the earth, the only

handsome one there, the one superior one! And oh, how we all devoured you with our eyes, you were like holy bread being broken among us.—But snatched away! Fetched home by your mother with that lame excuse, that invention about Mrs. Arbuckle's turn for the worse. I called the Arbuckles.—Better, much better, they told me, no doctor was called! Oh I suppose you're right to despise us, my little company of the faded and frightened and different and odd and lonely. You don't belong to that club but I hold an office in it! [*She laughs harshly.*]

JOHN:

Hush, Miss Alma, you'll wake up the house!

ALMA:

Wake up my wealthy neighbors? Oh, no, I mustn't. Everything in this house is *comme il faut.*

[*A clock strikes offstage.*]

Even the clock makes music when it strikes, a dainty little music. Hear it, hear it? It sounds like the voice of your mother, saying, "John? John, darling? We must go home now!" [*She laughs convulsively, then chokes, and seizes the brandy glass.*] And when you marry, you'll marry some Northern beauty. She will have no eccentricities but the eccentricity of beauty and perfect calm. Her hands will have such repose, such perfect repose when she speaks. They won't fly about her like wild birds, oh, no, she'll hold them together, press the little pink tips of her fingers together, making a—steeple—or fold them sweetly and gravely in her lap! She'll only move them when she lifts a teacup—they won't reach above her when she cries out in the night! Suddenly, desperately—fly up, fly up in the night!—reaching for something—nothing!—clutching at—space. . . .

JOHN:
Please! Miss Alma! You are—exhausting yourself. . . .

ALMA:
No, the bride will have beauty! [*Her voice is now a shrill whisper; she leans far toward him across the desk.*] The bride will have beauty, beauty! Admirable family background, no lunacy in it, no skeletons in the closet—no Aunt Albertine and Mr. Otto Schwarzkopf, no Musée Mécanique with a shady past!—No, no, nothing morbid, nothing peculiar, nothing eccentric! No—deviations!—But everything perfect and regular as the—tick of that—clock!

MRS. BUCHANAN'S VOICE [*above*]:
John! John, darling! What on earth is the matter down there?

JOHN [*at the door*]:
Nothing. Go to sleep, Mother.

MRS. BUCHANAN'S VOICE:
Is someone badly hurt?

JOHN:
Yes, Mother. Hurt. But not badly. Go back to sleep.

[*He closes the door.*]

Now. You see? You are gasping for breath again. Lie down, lie down. . . .

ALMA:
I am not afraid any more and I don't care to lie down.

JOHN:
Perhaps, after all, that outburst did you some good.

ALMA:
Yes—Yes—[*Then suddenly*] *I'm so ashamed of myself!*

80

JOHN:
You should be proud of yourself. You know, you know, it's surprising how few people there are that dare in this world to say what is in their hearts.

ALMA:
I had no right—to talk to you like that. . . .

JOHN:
I was—stupid, I—hurt you. . . .

ALMA:
No. I hurt myself! I exposed myself. Father is frightened of me and he's right. On the surface I'm still the Episcopal minister's daughter but there's something else that's—

JOHN:
Yes, something else! What is it?

ALMA [*slowly shaking her head*]:
Something—else that's—frantic!

JOHN:
A *Doppelgänger?*

ALMA [*nodding slowly*]:
A—*Doppelgänger!*

JOHN:
Fighting for its life in the prison of a little conventional world full of walls and . . .

ALMA:
What was it you said about space when you turned the light out?

JOHN:
Space, I said, is curved.

81

ALMA:
Then even space is a prison!—not—infinite. . . .

JOHN:
A very large prison, even large enough for you to feel free in, Miss Alma. [*He takes her hand and blows his breath on her fingers.*] Are your fingers still frozen?

[*She leans against the desk, turning her face to the audience, closing her eyes.*]

ALMA:
Your breath!—is . . . *warm.* . . .

JOHN:
Yours, too. Your breath is warm.

ALMA:
All human breath is warm—so pitifully! So pitifully warm and soft as children's fingers. . . . [*She turns her face to him and takes his face between the fingers of both her hands.*] The brandy worked very quickly. You know what I feel like now. I feel like a water lily on a—Chinese lagoon. . . . I will sleep, perhaps. But—I won't see you—again. . . .

JOHN:
I'm leaving next Monday.

ALMA:
Monday . . .

JOHN:
Aren't there any more meetings we could—go to?

ALMA:
You don't like meetings.

JOHN:
The only meetings I like are between two people.

ALMA:

We are two people, we've met—did you like our meeting?

[*John nods, smiling.*]

Then meet me again!

JOHN:

I'll take you to see Mary Pickford at the Delta Brilliant tomorrow.

[*Alma throws back her head with a gasping laugh, checks it quickly. She retreats with a slight gasp as Mrs. Buchanan enters in a lace negligee.*]

MRS. BUCHANAN [*with acid sweetness*]:
Oh, the patient's Miss *Alma!*

ALMA:

Yes. Miss Alma's the patient. Forgive me for disturbing you. Good night. [*She turns quickly but with a fleeting glance at John, who grins by the door.*] Au revoir! [*She goes out.*]

MRS. BUCHANAN:
And what was the matter with *her?!*

JOHN:
Palpitations, Mother. [*He turns out the office light.*] *Haven't* you ever had them?

MRS. BUCHANAN:
Had them? *Yes!*—But *controlled* them!

[*He laughs gaily on the stairs. She follows with an outraged "Huh!"*]

[*Dim out.*]·

SCENE FOUR

The next night, New Year's Eve. Roger and Miss Alma are in the Rectory parlor with a magic lantern.

ROGER:
Is it in focus, Miss Alma?

ALMA [*absently*]:
Yes.

[*The image is completely blurred.*]

ROGER:
Are you sure it's in focus?

ALMA [*in a sad whisper*]:
Yes, perfectly in focus.

ROGER [*rising from behind the lantern*]:
What is it a picture of?

ALMA [*faintly*]:
What, Roger?

ROGER:
I said, "What is it a picture of?"

ALMA:
Why, I can't tell, it seems to be out of focus. . . .

ROGER:
You just now said that it was in perfect focus.

ALMA:
Excuse me, Roger. My wits are woolgathering.

ROGER:

I will turn off the lantern and put the slides away. [*He does so.*] Now let's turn the sofa to face the window so we won't have to twist our necks to gaze at the house next door.—You were expecting him tonight?

ALMA:

He'd asked me to go to the movies.

ROGER:

Then why did you ask me to bring my magic lantern?

ALMA:

Some people called for him at seven. He left the house. I think he'd forgotten he asked me to go to the movies. I just couldn't sit here alone waiting to see if he had, or if he'd remember. I just couldn't bear it!

ROGER:

How late is he now?

ALMA:

Twenty, no, twenty-five minutes!

ROGER:

I think I would go and give him up then.

ALMA:

I have, almost. I almost wish I was dead!

ROGER:

People who bark up wrong trees . . .

ALMA:

Sometimes the only tree you want to bark up is the wrong one. . . . Don't you know that?

ROGER:

Miss Alma, we're fond of each other. We get along well together. We have interests in common. Companionship is something.

ALMA:

Something, but not enough. I want more than that.—*I see him!*—No . . . No, that isn't him. . . . You and I, we have no desire for each other. They intimated to you at the bank that you'd be advanced more rapidly if you were married. But, Roger, I want more than that. . . . Even if all I get in the end is a button—like Aunt Albertine. . . .

ROGER:

A button?

ALMA:

You've heard her story?

ROGER:

I've heard your mother make some allusions to it, but nothing very—coherent. . . .

ALMA:

She grew up, like me, in the shadow of the church. Until one Sunday a strange man came to the service and dropped a ten-dollar bill in the collection plate! —Of course he was immediately invited to dinner at the Rectory. . . . At dinner he sat next to my Aunt Albertine—the next day she bought a plumed hat and the following Wednesday he took her away from the Rectory forever. . . . He'd been married twice already, without a divorce, but bigamy was the least of his delinquencies, and obviously Aunt Albertine found living in sin preferable to life in the Rectory.—Mr. Schwarz-kopf was a mechanical genius. They traveled about the

South with a sort of show called the Musée Mécanique.
I'm sure you've heard Mother speak of it—a collection of
mechanical marvels that Mr. Schwarzkopf had created.
Among them was a mechanical bird-girl. She was his mas-
terpiece. Every five minutes a tin bird flew out of her
mouth and whistled three times, clear as a bell, and flew
back in again. She smiled and nodded, lifted her arms as
if to embrace a lover. Mr. Schwarzkopf was enchanted by
his bird-girl. Everything else was neglected. . . . He'd suddenly get out of bed in the night and go downstairs to wind
her up and sit in front of her, drinking, until she seemed
alive to him. . . . Then one winter they made a dreadful
mistake. They mortgaged the whole Museum to buy a boa
constrictor because somebody had told them "Big snakes
pay good"—well, this one didn't, it swallowed a blanket
and died. . . . You may have heard Mother speak of it. But
not of the fire. She refuses to believe in the fire.

ROGER:
There was a fire?

ALMA:

Oh, yes. Creditors took the Museum and locked Mr.
Schwarzkopf out. There was to be an auction of the me-
chanical marvels but the night before the auction Mr.
Schwarzkopf broke into the Museum and set it on fire.
Albertine rushed into the burning building and caught
Mr. Schwarzkopf by the sleeve of his coat but he broke
away from her. When they dragged her out, she was dying,
but still holding onto a button she'd torn from his sleeve.
"Some people," she said, "don't even die empty-handed!"

ROGER:
What did she mean by that?

ALMA:

The button, of course . . . all that was left of her darling
Mr. Schwarzkopf!

[*The bell rings. She seems paralyzed for a moment, then
gasps and rushes out of the lighted area. A moment later
her voice is heard.*]

I'd almost given you up!

[*Dim out.*]

ACT THREE

A CAVALIER'S PLUME

SCENE ONE

*That night, after the movies, before the angel of the foun-
tain.*

ALMA:
May we stop here for a moment?

JOHN:
You're not cold?

ALMA:
No.

[*A silence.*]

JOHN:
You've been very quiet, Miss Alma.

ALMA:
I always say too much or say too little. The few young men
I've gone out with have found me . . . I've only gone out
with three at all seriously—and with each one there was a
desert between us.

JOHN:
What do you mean by a desert?

ALMA:
Oh, wide, wide stretches of uninhabitable ground. I'd try
to talk, he'd try to talk. Oh, we'd talk quite a lot—but then
it would be—exhausted—the talk, the effort. I'd twist the
ring on my finger, so hard sometimes it would cut my
finger. He'd look at his watch as if he had never seen a
watch before. . . . And we would both know that the use-

less undertaking had come to a close. At the door— [*She turns slowly to the fountain.*] At the door he would say, "I'll call you." "I'll call you" meant goodbye! [*She laughs a little.*]

JOHN [*gently*]:
Would you care much?

ALMA:
Not—not about them. . . .

JOHN:
Then about what would you care?

[*From far away comes nonrealistic baying of a hound. "Valse des Regrets" by Brahms fades in softly.*]

ALMA:
They only mattered as shadows of some failure that would come later.

JOHN:
What failure?

ALMA:
A failure such as—tonight. . . .

JOHN:
Tonight is a failure?

ALMA:
I think it will be a failure. Look. My ring has cut my finger. No! I shall have to be honest! I can't play any kind of a game! Do you remember what Mother said when she burst into the room? "Alma has fallen in love with that tall boy!" It's true. I had. But longer ago than that. I remember

92

the long afternoons of our childhood when I had to stay indoors and practice my music. I heard your playmates calling you, "Johnny, Johnny!" Oh, how it used to go through me just to hear your name called. I ran to the window to watch you jump the porch railing, stood at a distance halfway down the block only to keep in sight of your torn red sweater racing about the vacant lot you played in. "Johnny, Johnny!"—It had begun that early, this affliction of love, and it's never let go of me since, but kept on growing and growing. I've lived next door to you all the days of my life, a weak and divided person, lived in your shadow, no, I mean in your brightness which made a shadow I lived in, but lived in adoring awe of your radiance, your strength . . . your singleness. Now Father tells me that I am becoming known as an eccentric. People think me affected, laugh at me, imitate me at parties! I'm marked to be different, it's stamped on me in big letters so people can read from a distance: "This Person Is Strange." . . . Well, I may be eccentric but not so eccentric that I don't have the ordinary human need for love. I have that need, and I must satisfy it, in whatever way my good or bad fortune will make possible for me. . . . One time in the movies I sat next to a strange man. I didn't look at his face, but after a while I felt the pressure of his knee against mine. I thought it might be accidental. I moved aside. But then it began again. I didn't look at him. I sprang from my seat. I rushed out of the theater. I wonder sometimes. If I had dared to look at his face in the queer flickering white light that comes from the screen, and it had been like yours, at *all* like yours, even the *faintest resemblance*—Would I have sprung from my seat, or would I have *stayed*?

JOHN:
A dangerous speculation for a minister's daughter!

ALMA:

Very dangerous indeed! But not as dangerous as what I did tonight. Didn't you feel it? Didn't you feel the pressure of my—knee? —Tonight? —In the movies?

[*The audience may laugh at this question. Take a count of ten. Perhaps John crosses slowly to drink at the fountain.*]

I have embarrassed you.

JOHN [*gently*]:
Yes.

ALMA:

I told you I had to be honest. Now you take me home. You may take me back to the house between your house and the Episcopal church, you may take me back there, now, un-less—unless . . .

JOHN:
Unless what, Miss Alma?

ALMA:

Unless, unless—by the most unlikely chance in the world you wanted to take me somewhere else!

JOHN:
Where is—"somewhere else"?

ALMA:
Anywhere that two people could be alone.

JOHN:
Oh . . .

ALMA:
I told you I had to be honest.

JOHN:

We are alone in the Square.

ALMA:

I was thinking of—

JOHN:

A room?

ALMA:

A—little room with—a fireplace ...

JOHN:

One of those rooms that people engage for an hour? A bottle of wine in a bucket of ice—brrr! No!—No ice—No, one of those red wines in straw-covered bottles from Italy. I think they call it—Chianti. ...

ALMA:

Just—four walls and a—fireplace ...

JOHN:

I'm glad you include a fireplace. That might be necessary to take the chill off, Miss Alma.

ALMA:

Are there—are there such places?

JOHN:

Yes. There have been such places since the beginning of time. Little rooms that seem empty even when you are in them but have sad little tokens of people that occupied them before you, a sprinkle of light pink powder on the dresser, a hairpin on the carpet—a few withered rose petals —in the wastebasket of course an empty pint bottle of some inexpensive whisky. Yes. There is such a place in Glorious Hill—even ...

ALMA:

Do you—know where to find it?

JOHN:

I could find it blindfolded.

ALMA:

You've been to it often?

JOHN:

I grew up in this town. Yes. I remember the place. It wasn't attractive, Miss Alma, you wouldn't like it.

ALMA:

I would like it with you.

JOHN:

You might think that you would until you got there and then discover you didn't. The first time I went there was with one of those anonymous young ladies who get off the Cannonball Express at midnight and stand aimlessly around the entrance to the waiting room at the depot with one small suitcase like a small dog close to their slippers—that first time I went there because *she* knew of the place. . . . I made an excuse to slip away from the room, and I ran like a rabbit, ha ha, I ran like a rabbit! —I left a white linen jacket over a chair with a wallet containing eight dollars. Later, much later, I believe a year later, yes, the following summer—I went back there again, and the grinning old colored porter handed me the white jacket. "A young lady left it for you, Mistuh Johnny, one time last summer," he told me. The wallet was still in the pocket, and in the wallet was a note from the lady. "Baby, I took five dollars to get me to Memphis."—Ha ha ha—signed "Alice" . . .

ALMA:

Alice . . .

JOHN:

Yes. Alice. She had a small nose with freckles which is probably still leading her into trouble as straight as a good bird dog will point at a partridge! Ha ha ha!—No, Miss Alma, you wouldn't care for the place, and besides it's New Year's Eve and it will be crowded, there, and after all, you're not unknown in this town, you're the Nightingale of the Delta! Oh, they wouldn't be people you'd run into at church, but . . .

ALMA:

John, I want to go there. I want to be in a small room with you at midnight when the bells ring!

JOHN:

You're quite sure that you want to?

ALMA:

Do you see any shadow of doubt in my eyes?

JOHN:

No—No, not in your eyes—but of course you know that it might turn out badly.

[*She nods her head slowly and gravely. He grips her gloved hands.*]

It would be an experiment that might fail so miserably that it would have been much better not to have tried it. Be-cause—well—"propinquity," as you call it—just propinquity —sometimes isn't enough. Oh, I wouldn't run out of the room like a rabbit and leave my jacket over the back of the chair! I'm a *big* boy, now! But you know, Miss Alma —or *do* you know?—that regardless of how it was, whether or not the experiment went well or very badly—you must know that I couldn't—couldn't—

97

ALMA:
Go on with it? Yes. I know that.

JOHN:
There are many practical reasons.

ALMA:
And many impractical reasons. I know all of that!

JOHN:
The most important one is the one I'd rather not say, but I guess you know what it is.

ALMA:
I know that you don't love me.

JOHN:
No. No, I'm not in love with you.

ALMA:
I wasn't counting on that tonight or ever.

JOHN:
God. Yes, God. You talk as straight as a man and you look right into my eyes and say you're expecting *nothing*?!

ALMA:
I'm looking into your eyes but I'm not saying that. I expect a great deal. But for tonight only. Afterward, nothing, nothing! Nothing at all.

JOHN:
Afterward would come quickly in a room that you rent for an hour.

ALMA:
An hour is the lifetime of some creatures.

JOHN:

Generations of some creatures can be fitted into an hour, the sort of creatures I see through my microscope. But you're not one of those creatures. You're a complex being. You have that mysterious something, as thin as smoke, that makes the difference between the human and all other beings! An hour isn't a lifetime for you, Miss Alma.

ALMA:

Give me the hour, and I'll make a lifetime of it.

JOHN [*smiling a little*]:

For you, Miss Alma, the name of the stone angel is barely long enough and nothing less than that *could* be!

ALMA:

What is the answer, John?

JOHN:

Excuse me a minute. I will find a taxi.

ALMA:

Leave something with me to guarantee your return!

[*Her laughter rings out high and clear, not like a woman's: more like the cry of a bird. He half turns as if startled; then grins wryly, raises an arm, and shouts: "Taxi!"*]

[*The scene dims out.*]

[*A soprano sings: "I Love You" by Grieg, during the change of scene.*]

SCENE TWO

A short while later that night. The skeletal set is a bedroom in a small hotel of the sort that is called, sometimes, a "house of convenience": a place where rooms are let out for periods as brief as an hour. Next door is a night resort. We hear a mechanical piano playing ragtime.

A Negro porter enters and prepares the room for occupants waiting outside. He sets whisky and two glasses on a small round table by the bed. The long shadows of the waiting couple, still outside, are thrown across the lighted area, until the porter withdraws. Then John and Alma enter the lighted area; they stand silent on the edge of it for a moment like timid bathers at the edge of cold water.

JOHN:
The room is cold.

ALMA:
Will—will—will the fire light?

JOHN:
That remains to be seen. . . .

ALMA:
Try it, try to light it!

[*He still pauses.*]

What are you waiting for, John?

JOHN:
For you to think . . .

ALMA:
Think about what?

JOHN:
If you really want to go on with this—adventure. . . .

ALMA:
My answer is yes! What's yours?

[*Another long pause.*]

JOHN [*finally*]:
This room reminds me of a hospital room. Even a folding white screen of the sort they put around patients about to expire.

ALMA:
Rooms of this kind, are they always like this?

JOHN:
You think I've had a vast experience with them?

ALMA:
I'm sure you must have had some.

JOHN:
Actually, probably not much more than *you've* had.

[*She crosses to the table by the bed.*]

ALMA:
Oh, look, I've found a withered rose petal and a sprinkle of powder!

JOHN:
That takes the curse off a little.

ALMA:
Turn out the light. Let's see how it looks with the light out.

[*He switches off the bare bulb.*]

JOHN:

You know what it looks like now? It looks like a cave in Capri that's called the Blue Grotto!

ALMA:

Put a match to the fire.

JOHN [*crouching before the fireplace*]:
The logs are damp.

ALMA:

There's paper underneath them.

JOHN:

It's damp, too.

ALMA:

But try!

JOHN:

I shall try, Miss Alma. —But you know I told you this could turn out badly.

ALMA:

Yes, I know. You warned me.

[*He strikes a match. A flickering red glow falls upon their figures as he draws the match back from the fire.*]

There, there now, it's burning!

JOHN:

Temporarily . . .

ALMA:

Let's pray it will keep! . . . Put paper on it, put more paper on.

JOHN:

I have none!

ALMA:

There must be some. Quick, quick, it's expiring! Ring for the boy, ring for the boy! We must have a fire to take the chill off the room!

JOHN:

Are you sure that a fire would take the chill off the room?

[*She suddenly seizes her hat and tears off the plume, starts to cast the plume into the fireplace. He seizes her hand.*]

Miss Alma!

ALMA:

This plume will burn!

JOHN:

Don't!

ALMA:

This plume will burn! Something has to be sacrificed to a fire.

JOHN [*still gripping her hand that holds the.plume*]:

Miss Alma. Miss Alma. The fire has gone out and nothing will revive it. Take my word for it, nothing!

[*Music is heard very faintly.*]

It never was much of a fire, it never really got started, and now it's out. . . . Sometimes things say things for people. Things that people find too painful or too embarrassing to say, a thing will say it, a thing will say it for them so they don't have to say it. . . . The fire is out, it's gone out, and you feel how the room is now, it's deathly chill. There's no use in staying in it.

[*She turns on the light, walks a few steps from him, twisting her ring. There is a pause.*]

You are twisting your ring. [*He catches hold of her hand again and holds it still.*]

ALMA:

How gently a failure can happen! The way that some people die, lightly, unconsciously, losing themselves with their breath. . . .

JOHN:

Why—why call it a failure?

ALMA:

Why call a spade a spade? I have to be honest. If I had had beauty and desirability and the grace of a woman, it would not have been necessary for me to be honest. My eccentricities—made it necessary. . . .

JOHN:

I think your honesty is the plume on your hat. And you ought to wear it proudly.

ALMA:

Proudly or not proudly, I shall wear it. Now I must put it back on. Where is my hat?—Oh.—Here—the plume is restored to its place!

[*Downstairs a hoarse whisky contralto starts singing "Hello, my honey, hello, my baby, hello, my ragtime doll!"*]

Who is—what is . . . Oh!—a party—downstairs . . .

JOHN:

This is—a honky-tonk.

ALMA:

Yes! Perhaps I shall get to know it a great deal better!

JOHN:

The plume on your hat is lovely, it almost sweeps the ceiling!

ALMA:

You *flatterer!* [*She smiles at him with harshness, almost mockery.*]

JOHN:

Don't!—we have to still like each other!—Don't be *harsh.*

ALMA:

If I wore a tall hat in a sunny room,
I would sweep the ceiling with a cavalier's plume—
If I wore a frock coat on a polished stair,
I would charm a grande dame with my gallant air.
If I wore a . . .

I don't remember the rest of it. Do you?

JOHN:

If I wore a gold sword on a white verandah,
I would shock a simple heart with my heartless candor!

ALMA:

Yes, that's how it goes. . . .

[*The music dies out. All over town the church bells begin to ring in various tones, some urgent, some melancholy, some tender, and horns are blown and things exploded or rattled.*]

There. There it is, the New Year! I hope it will be all that you want it to be! [*She says this with a sudden warm sincerity, smiling directly into his face.*] What a strange way we've spent New Year's Eve! Going to a Mary Pickford picture at the Delta Brilliant, having a long conversation in a cold square, and coming to a strange and bare little

105

room like a hospital room where a fire wouldn't burn, in spite of our invocations!—But now—it's another year. . . . Another stretch of time to be discovered and entered and explored, and who knows what we'll find in it? Perhaps the coming true of our most improbable dreams!—I'm not ashamed of tonight! I think that you and I have been honest together, even though we failed!

[*Something changes between them. He reaches above him, turns out the light bulb. Almost invisibly at first a flickering red glow comes from the fireplace. She has lowered the veil attached to her plumed hat. He turns it gently back from her face.*]

ALMA:
What are you doing that for?

JOHN:
So that I won't get your veil in my mouth when I kiss you. [*He does.*]

[*Alma turns her face to the audience. The stage has darkened but a flickering red glow now falls across their figures. The fire has miraculously revived itself, a phoenix.*]

ALMA:
I don't dare to believe it, but look, oh, look, look, John! [*She points at the fireplace from which the glow springs.*] Where did the fire come from?

JOHN:
No one has ever been able to answer that question!

[*The red glow brightens.*]

[*The scene dims gradually out.*]

EPILOGUE

The Square, before the stone angel. A Fourth of July night an indefinite time later. Another soprano is singing.

A young traveling salesman approaches the bench on which Alma is seated. Band music is heard.

ALMA:
How did you like her voice?

SALESMAN:
She sang all right.

ALMA:
Her face was blank. She didn't seem to know what to do with her hands. And I didn't think she sang with any emotion. A singer's face and her hands and even her heart are part of her equipment and ought to be used expressively when she sings. That girl is one of my former vocal pupils— I used to teach singing here—and so I feel that I have a right to be critical. I used to sing at public occasions like this. I don't any more.

SALESMAN:
Why don't you any more?

ALMA:
I'm not asked any more.

SALESMAN:
Why's that?

[*Alma shrugs slightly and unfolds her fan. The salesman coughs a little.*]

ALMA:
You're a stranger in town?

SALESMAN:
I'm a traveling salesman.

ALMA:
Ahhhh. A salesman who travels. You're younger than most of them are, and not so fat.

SALESMAN:
I'm—uh—just starting out. . . .

ALMA:
Oh.—The pyrotechnical display is late in starting.

SALESMAN:
What—what did you say?

ALMA:
The fireworks, I said. I said they ought to be starting.—I don't suppose you're familiar with this town. This town is Glorious Hill, Mississippi, population five thousand souls and an equal number of bodies.

SALESMAN:
Ha ha! An equal number of bodies, that's good, ha ha!

ALMA:
Isn't it? My name is Alma. Alma is Spanish for soul. Usted habla Español, señor?

SALESMAN:
Un poquito. Usted habla Español, señorita?

ALMA:
Tambien! Un poquito.

SALESMAN:

Sometimes un poquito is plenty!

ALMA:

Yes, indeed, and we have to be grateful for it. Sit down and I'll point out a few of our historical landmarks to you. Directly across the Square is the county courthouse: slaves were sold on the steps before the abolition of slavery in the South; now gray old men with nothing better to do sit on them all day. Over there is the Roman Catholic Church, a small unimpressive building, this being a Protestant town. And there—

[*She points in another direction.*]

—There is the Episcopal church. My father was rector of it before his death. It has an unusual steeple.

[*Her voice is rising in volume and tempo. One or two indistinct figures pause behind the stone bench, whispering, laughing at her. She turns about abruptly, imitating the laughter with a rather frightening boldness: the figures withdraw. She continues.*]

Yes, instead of a cross on top of the steeple, it has an enormous gilded hand with its index finger pointing straight up, accusingly, at—heaven. . . . [*She holds her hand up to demonstrate.*]

[*The young salesman laughs uneasily and glances back of him as other figures appear in silhouette behind them.*]

Are you looking at the angel of the fountain? It's the loveliest thing in Glorious Hill. The angel's name is Eternity. The name is carved in the stone block at the base of the statue, but it's not visible in this light, you'd have to read

109

it with your fingers as if you were blind. . . . Straight ahead but not visible, either, is another part of town: it's concealed by the respectable front of the Square: it's called Tiger Town, it's the part of town that a traveling salesman might be interested in. Are you interested in it?

SALESMAN:
What's it got to offer?

ALMA:
Saloons, penny arcades, and rooms that can be rented for one hour, which is a short space of time for human beings, but there are living—organisms—only visible through a microscope—that live and die and are succeeded by several generations in an hour, or less than an hour, even. . . . Oh! —There goes the first skyrocket! Look at it burst into a million stars!

[*A long-drawn "Ahhh" from the unseen crowd in the Square as a rocket explodes above it and casts a dim gold radiance on Alma's upturned face. She closes her eyes very tightly for a moment, then rises, smiling down at the young salesman.*]

Now would you like to go to Tiger Town? The part of town back of the courthouse?

SALESMAN [*rising, nervously grinning*]:
Sure, why not, let's go!

ALMA:
Good, go ahead, get a taxi, it's better if I follow a little behind you. . . .

SALESMAN:
Don't get lost, don't lose me!

[*The salesman starts off jauntily as the band strikes up "The Santiago Waltz."*]

ALMA:

Oh, no, I'm not going to lose you before I've lost you!

[*He is out of the lighted area.*]

[*Another rocket explodes, much lower and brighter: The angel, Eternity, is clearly revealed for a moment or two. Alma gives it a little parting salute as she follows after the young salesman, touching the plume on her hat as if to see if it were still there.*]

[*The radiance of the skyrocket fades out; the scene is dimmed out with it.*]

THE END

SUMMER AND SMOKE

Who, if I were to cry out, would hear me among the angelic orders?
RILKE

FOR CARSON MCCULLERS

CHARACTERS

ALMA as a child

JOHN as a child

———

ALMA WINEMILLER

THE REVEREND WINEMILLER, her father

MRS. WINEMILLER, her mother

JOHN BUCHANAN, JR.

DR. BUCHANAN, his father

ROSA GONZALES

PAPA GONZALES, her father

NELLIE EWELL

MRS. BASSETT

ROGER DOREMUS

MR. KRAMER

ROSEMARY

VERNON

DUSTY

SCENES

The entire action of the play takes place in Glorious Hill, Mississippi. The time is the turn of the century through 1916.

AUTHOR'S PRODUCTION NOTES

As the concept of a design grows out of reading a play I will not do more than indicate what I think are the most essential points.

First of all—*The Sky*.

There must be a great expanse of sky so that the entire action of the play takes place against it. This is true of interior as well as exterior scenes. But in fact there are no really interior scenes, for the walls are omitted or just barely suggested by certain necessary fragments such as might be needed to hang a picture or to contain a doorframe.

During the day scenes the sky should be a pure and intense blue (like the sky of Italy as it is so faithfully represented in the religious paintings of the Renaissance) and costumes should be selected to form dramatic color contrasts to this intense blue which the figures stand against. (Color harmonies and other visual effects are tremendously important.)

In the night scenes, the more familiar constellations, such as Orion and the Great Bear and the Pleiades, are clearly projected on the night sky, and above them, splashed across the top of the cyclorama, is the nebulous radiance of the Milky Way. Fleecy cloud forms may also be projected on this cyclorama and made to drift across it.

So much for *The Sky*.

Now we descend to the so-called interior sets of the play. There are two of these "interior" sets, one being the parlor of an Episcopal Rectory and the other the home of a doctor next door to the Rectory. The architecture of these houses is barely suggested but is of an American Gothic design of the Victorian era. There are no actual doors or windows or walls. Doors and windows are represented by delicate frameworks of Gothic design. These frames have strings of ivy clinging to them, the leaves of emerald and amber. Sections of wall are used only where they are functionally required. There should be a fragment of wall in back of the Rectory sofa, supporting a romantic landscape in a gilt frame. In the doctor's house there should be a section of wall to support the chart of anatomy. Chirico has used fragmentary walls and interiors in a very evocative way in his painting called "Conversation among the Ruins." We will deal more specifically with these interiors as we come to them in the course of the play.

Now we come to the main exterior set which is a promontory in a park or public square in the town of Glorious Hill. Situated on this promontory is a fountain in the form of a stone angel, in a gracefully crouching position with wings lifted and her hands held together to form a cup from which water flows, a public drinking fountain. The stone angel of the fountain should probably be elevated so that it appears in the background of the interior scenes as a symbolic figure (Eternity) brooding over the course of the play. *This entire exterior set may be on an upper level, above that of the two fragmentary interiors.* I would like all three units to form an harmonious whole like one complete picture rather than three separate ones. An imaginative designer may solve these plastic problems in a variety of ways and should not feel bound by any of my specific suggestions.

120

There is one more set, a very small exterior representing an arbor, which we will describe when we reach it.

Everything possible should be done to give an unbroken fluid quality to the sequence of scenes.

There should be no curtain except for the intermission. The other divisions of the play should be accomplished by changes of lighting.

Finally, the matter of music. One basic theme should recur and the points of recurrence have been indicated here and there in the stage directions.

Rome, March, 1948.

Summer and Smoke was first produced by Margo Jones at her theater in Dallas, Texas. It was later produced and directed by Miss Jones in New York, opening at the Music Box Theater, October 6, 1948, with Margaret Phillips and Tod Andrews in the two leading roles; incidental music by Paul Bowles and setting by Jo Mielziner.

CAST OF THE NEW YORK PRODUCTION

ALMA as a child	ARLENE MCQUADE
JOHN as a child	DONALD HASTINGS
REV. WINEMILLER	RAYMOND VAN SICKLE
MRS. WINEMILLER	MARGA ANN DEIGHTON
ALMA WINEMILLER	MARGARET PHILLIPS
JOHN BUCHANAN, Jr.	TOD ANDREWS
DR. BUCHANAN	RALPH THEADORE
ROSA GONZALES	MONICA BOYAR
PAPA GONZALES	SID CASSEL
NELLIE EWELL	ANNE JACKSON
MRS. BASSETT	BETTY GREENE LITTLE
ROGER DOREMUS	EARL MONTGOMERY
MR. KRAMER	RAY WALSTON
ROSEMARY	ELLEN JAMES
VERNON	SPENCER JAMES
DUSTY	WILLIAM LAYTON
A GIRL	HILDY PARKS

A SUMMER

PROLOGUE

In the park near the angle of the fountain. At dusk of an evening in May, in the first few years of this century.

Alma, as a child of ten, comes into the scene. She wears a middy blouse and has ribboned braids. She already has the dignity of an adult; there is a quality of extraordinary delicacy and tenderness or spirituality in her, which must set her distinctly apart from other children. She has a habit of holding her hands, one cupped under the other in a way similar to that of receiving the wafer at Holy Communion. This is a habit that will remain with her as an adult. She stands like that in front of the stone angel for a few moments; then bends to drink at the fountain.

While she is bent at the fountain, John, as a child, enters. He shoots a peashooter at Alma's bent-over back. She utters a startled cry and whirls about. He laughs.

JOHN:
Hi, Preacher's daughter. [*He advances toward her.*] I been looking for you.

ALMA [*hopefully*]:
You have?

JOHN:
Was it you that put them handkerchiefs on my desk? [*Alma smiles uncertainly.*] Answer up!

ALMA:
I put a box of handkerchiefs on your desk.

JOHN:
I figured it was you. What was the idea, Miss Priss?

ALMA:
You needed them.

JOHN:

Trying to make a fool of me?

ALMA:

Oh, no!

JOHN:

Then what was the idea?

ALMA:

You have a bad cold and your nose has been running all week. It spoils your appearance.

JOHN:

You don't have to look at me if you don't like my appearance.

ALMA:

I like your appearance.

JOHN [*coming closer*]:

Is that why you look at me all the time?

ALMA:

I—don't!

JOHN:

Oh, yeh, you do. You been keeping your eyes on me all the time. Every time I look around I see them cat eyes of yours looking at me. That was the trouble today when Miss Blanchard asked you where the river Amazon was. She asked you twice and you still didn't answer because you w' lookin' at me. What's the idea? What've y' got on y' mind anyhow? Answer up!

ALMA:

I was only thinking how handsome you'd be if your face wasn't dirty. You know why your face is dirty? Because you don't use a handkerchief and you wipe your nose on the sleeve of that dirty old sweater.

JOHN [*indignantly*]:
Hah!

ALMA:
That's why I put the handkerchiefs on your desk and I wrapped them up so nobody would know what they were. It isn't my fault that you opened the box in front of everybody!

JOHN:
What did you think I'd do with a strange box on my desk? Just leave it there till it exploded or something? Sure I opened it up. I didn't expect to find no—*handkerchiefs!*—in it . . .

ALMA [*in a shy trembling voice*]:
I'm sorry that you were embarrassed. I honestly am awfully sorry that you were embarrassed. Because I wouldn't embarrass you for the world!

JOHN:
Don't flatter yourself that I was embarrassed. I don't embarrass that easy.

ALMA:
It was stupid and cruel of those girls to laugh.

JOHN:
Hah!

ALMA:
They should all realize that you don't have a mother to take care of such things for you. It was a pleasure to me to be able to do something for you, only I didn't want you to know it was me who did it.

JOHN:
Hee-haw! Ho-hum! Take 'em back! [*He snatches out the box and thrusts it toward her.*]

127

ALMA:
Please keep them.

JOHN:
What do I want with them?

[*She stares at him helplessly. He tosses the box to the ground and goes up to the fountain and drinks. Something in her face mollifies him and he sits down at the base of the fountain with a manner that does not preclude a more friendly relation. The dusk gathers deeper.*]

ALMA:
Do you know the name of the angel?

JOHN:
Does she have a name?

ALMA:
Yes, I found out she does. It's carved in the base, but it's all worn away so you can't make it out with your eyes.

JOHN:
Then how do you know it?

ALMA:
You have to read it with your fingers. I did and it gave me cold shivers! *You* read it and see if it doesn't give *you* cold shivers! Go on! Read it with your fingers!

JOHN:
Why don't you tell me and save me the trouble?

ALMA:
I'm not going to tell you.

[*John grins indulgently and turns to the pediment, crouching before it and running his fingers along the worn inscription.*]

JOHN:
E?

ALMA:
Yes, E is the first letter!

JOHN:
T?

ALMA:
Yes!

JOHN:
E?

ALMA:
E!

JOHN:
K?

ALMA:
No, no, not K!—R! [*He slowly straightens up.*]

JOHN:
Eternity?

ALMA:
Eternity!—Didn't it give you the cold shivers?

JOHN:
Nahh.

ALMA:
Well, it did me!

JOHN:
Because you're a preacher's daughter. Eternity. What is eternity?

ALMA [*in a hushed wondering voice*]:
It's something that goes on and on when life and death and time and everything else is all through with.

JOHN:

There's no such thing.

ALMA:

There is. It's what people's souls live in when they have left their bodies. My name is Alma and Alma is Spanish for soul. Did you know that?

JOHN:

Hee-haw! Ho-hum! Have you ever seen a dead person?

ALMA:

No.

JOHN:

I have. They made me go in the room when my mother was dying and she caught hold of my hand and wouldn't let me go—and so I screamed and hit her.

ALMA:

Oh, you didn't do that.

JOHN [*somberly*]:

Uh-huh. She didn't look like my mother. Her face was all ugly and yellow and—terrible—bad-smelling! And so I hit her to make her let go of my hand. They told me that I was a devil!

ALMA:

You didn't know what you were doing.

JOHN:

My dad is a doctor.

ALMA:

I know.

JOHN:

He wants to send me to college to study to be a doctor but I wouldn't be a doctor for the world. And have to go in a room and watch people dying! . . . Jesus!

ALMA:

You'll change your mind about that.

JOHN:

Oh, no, I won't. I'd rather *be* a devil, like they called me and go to South America on a boat! . . . Give me one of them handkerchiefs. [*She brings them eagerly and humbly to the fountain. He takes one out and wets it at the fountain and scrubs his face with it.*] Is my face clean enough to suit you now?

ALMA:

Yes!—Beautiful!

JOHN:

What!

ALMA:

I said "Beautiful"!

JOHN:

Well—let's—kiss each other.

[*Alma turns away.*]

JOHN:

Come on, let's just try it!

[*He seizes her shoulders and gives her a quick rough kiss. She stands amazed with one hand cupping the other.*

[*The voice of a child in the distance calls "Johnny! Johnny!"*

[*He suddenly snatches at her hair-ribbon, jerks it loose and then runs off with a mocking laugh.*

[*Hurt and bewildered, Alma turns back to the stone angel, for comfort. She crouches at the pediment and touches the inscription with her fingers. The scene dims out with music.*]

131

SCENE ONE

*Before the curtain rises a band is heard playing a patriotic
anthem, punctuated with the crackle of fireworks.*

*The scene is the same as for the Prologue. It is the evening
of July 4th in a year shortly before the First World War.
There is a band concert and a display of fireworks in the
park. During the scene the light changes from faded sunlight to dusk. Sections of roof, steeples, weather vanes, should
have a metallic surface that catches the mellow light on the
backdrop; when dusk has fallen the stars should be visible.*

*As the curtain rises, the Rev. and Mrs. Winemiller come in
and sit on the bench near the fountain. Mrs. Winemiller was
a spoiled and selfish girl who evaded the responsibilities of
later life by slipping into a state of perverse childishness. She
is known as Mr. Winemiller's "Cross."*

MR. WINEMILLER [*suddenly rising*]:
There is Alma, getting on the bandstand! [*Mrs. Winemiller
is dreamily munching popcorn.*]

AN ANNOUNCER'S VOICE [*at a distance*]:
The Glorious Hill Orchestra brings you Miss Alma Winemiller, The Nightingale of the Delta, singing . . . "La Golondrina."

MR. WINEMILLER [*sitting back down again*]:
This is going to provoke a lot of criticism.

[*The song commences. The voice is not particularly
strong, but it has great purity and emotion. John Buchanan
comes along. He is now a Promethean figure, brilliantly
and restlessly alive in a stagnant society. The excess of his
power has not yet found a channel. If it remains without
one, it will burn him up. At present he is unmarked by the
dissipations in which he relieves his demoniac unrest; he*

*has the fresh and shining look of an epic hero. He walks
leisurely before the Winemillers' bench, negligently touching the crown of his hat but not glancing at them; climbs
the steps to the base of the fountain, then turns and looks
in the direction of the singer. A look of interest touched
with irony appears on his face. A couple, strolling in the
park, pass behind the fountain.*]

THE GIRL:
Look who's by the fountain!

THE MAN:
Bright as a new silver dollar!

JOHN:
Hi, Dusty! Hi, Pearl!

THE MAN:
How'd you make out in that floating crap game?

JOHN:
I floated with it as far as Vicksburg, then sank.

THE GIRL:
Everybody's been calling: "Johnny, Johnny—where's Johnny?"

[*John's father, Dr. Buchanan, comes on from the right, as
Rev. and Mrs. Winemiller move off the scene to the left,
toward the band music. Dr. Buchanan is an elderly man
whose age shows in his slow and stiff movements. He
walks with a cane. John sees him coming, but pretends
not to and starts to walk off.*]

DR. BUCHANAN:
John!

JOHN [*slowly turning around, as the couple move off*]:
Oh! Hi, Dad. . . . [*They exchange a long look.*] I—uh—
meant to wire you but I must've forgot. I got tied up in

133

Vicksburg Friday night and just now got back to town. Haven't been to the house yet. Is everything . . . going okay? [*He takes a drink of water at the fountain.*]

DR. BUCHANAN [*slowly, in a voice hoarse with emotion*]: There isn't any room in the medical profession for wasters, drunkards and lechers. And there isn't any room in my house for wasters—drunkards—lechers! [*A child is heard calling "I sp-yyyyyy!" in the distance.*] I married late in life. I brought over five hundred children into this world before I had one of my own. And by God it looks like I've given myself the rottenest one of the lot. . . . [*John laughs uncertainly.*] You will find your things at the Alhambra Hotel.

JOHN:
Okay. If that's how you want it.

[*There is a pause. The singing comes through on the music. John tips his hat diffidently and starts away from the fountain. He goes a few feet and his father suddenly calls after him.*]

DR. BUCHANAN:
John! [*John pauses and looks back.*] Come here.

JOHN:
Yes, Sir? [*He walks back to his father and stands before him.*]

DR. BUCHANAN [*hoarsely*]:
Go to the Alhambra Hotel and pick up your things and—bring them back to the house.

JOHN [*gently*]:
Yes, Sir. If that's how you want it. [*He diffidently extends a hand to touch his father's shoulder.*]

DR. BUCHANAN [*brushing the hand roughly off*]:
You! . . . You infernal *whelp*, you!

134

[*Dr. Buchanan turns and goes hurriedly away. John looks after him with a faint, affectionate smile, then sits down on the steps with an air of relief, handkerchief to forehead, and a whistle of relief. Just then the singing at the bandstand ends and there is the sound of applause. Mrs. Winemiller comes in from the left, followed by her husband.*]

MRS. WINEMILLER:
Where is the ice cream man?

MR. WINEMILLER:
Mother, hush! [*He sees his daughter approaching.*] Here we are, Alma!

[*The song ends. There is applause. Then the band strikes up the "Santiago Waltz."*

[*Alma Winemiller enters. Alma had an adult quality as a child and now, in her middle twenties, there is something prematurely spinsterish about her. An excessive propriety and self-consciousness is apparent in her nervous laughter; her voice and gestures belong to years of church entertainments, to the position of hostess in a rectory. People her own age regard her as rather quaintly and humorously affected. She has grown up mostly in the company of her elders. Her true nature is still hidden even from herself. She is dressed in pale yellow and carries a yellow silk parasol.*

[*As Alma passes in front of the fountain, John slaps his hands resoundingly together a few times. She catches her breath in a slight laughing sound, makes as if to retreat, with a startled "Oh!", but then goes quickly to her parents. The applause from the crowd continues.*]

MR. WINEMILLER:
They seem to want to hear you sing again, Alma.

135

[*She turns nervously about, touching her throat and her chest. John grins, applauding by the fountain. When the applause dies out, Alma sinks faintly on the bench.*]

ALMA:

Open my bag, Father. My fingers have frozen stiff! [*She draws a deep labored breath.*] I don't know what came over me—absolute panic! Never, never again, it isn't worth it—the tortures that I go through!

MR. WINEMILLER [*anxiously*]:

You're having one of your nervous attacks?

ALMA:

My heart's beating so! It seemed to be in my *throat* the whole time I was singing! [*John laughs audibly from the fountain.*] Was it noticeable, Father?

MR. WINEMILLER:

You sang extremely well, Alma. But you know how I feel about this, it was contrary to my wishes and I cannot imagine why you wanted to do it, especially since it seemed to upset you so.

ALMA:

I don't see how anyone could object to my singing at a patriotic occasion. If I had just sung well! But I barely got through it. At one point I thought that I wouldn't. The words flew out of my mind. Did you notice the pause? Blind panic! They really never came back, but I went on singing —I think I must have been improvising the lyric! Whew! Is there a handkerchief in it?

MRS. WINEMILLER [*suddenly*]:

Where is the ice cream man?

ALMA [*rubbing her fingers together*]:

Circulation is slowly coming back . . .

MR. WINEMILLER:

Sit back quietly and take a deep breath, Alma.

ALMA:

Yes, my handkerchief—now . . .

MRS. WINEMILLER:

Where is the ice cream man?

MR. WINEMILLER:

Mother, there isn't any ice cream man.

ALMA:

No, there isn't any ice cream man, Mother. But on the way home Mr. Doremus and I will stop by the drugstore and pick up a pint of ice cream.

MR. WINEMILLER:

Are you intending to stay here?

ALMA:

Until the concert is over. I promised Roger I'd wait for him.

MR. WINEMILLER:

I suppose you have noticed who is by the fountain?

ALMA:

Shhh!

MR. WINEMILLER:

Hadn't you better wait on a different bench?

ALMA:

This is where Roger will meet me.

MR. WINEMILLER:

Well, Mother, we'll run along now. [*Mrs. Winemiller has started vaguely toward the fountain, Mr. Winemiller firmly restraining her.*] This way, this way, Mother! [*He takes her arm and leads her off.*]

MRS. WINEMILLER [*calling back, in a high, childish voice*]:

137

Strawberry, Alma. Chocolate, chocolate and strawberry mixed! Not vanilla!

ALMA [*faintly*]:
Yes, yes, Mother—vanilla . . .

MRS. WINEMILLER [*furiously*]:
I said *not* vanilla. [*shouting*] Strawberry!

MR. WINEMILLER [*fiercely*]:
Mother! We're attracting attention. [*He propels her forcibly away.*]

[*John laughs by the fountain. Alma moves her parasol so that it shields her face from him. She leans back closing her eyes. John notices a firecracker by the fountain. He leans over negligently to pick it up. He grins and lights it and tosses it toward Alma's bench. When it goes off she springs up with a shocked cry, letting the parasol drop.*]

JOHN [*jumping up as if outraged*]:
Hey! Hey, you! [*He looks off to the right. Alma sinks back weakly on the bench. John solicitously advances.*] Are you all right?.

ALMA:
I can't seem to—catch my breath! Who threw it?

JOHN:
Some little rascal.

ALMA:
Where?

JOHN:
He ran away quick when I hollered!

ALMA:
There ought to be an ordinance passed in this town forbidding firecrackers.

JOHN:

Dad and I treated fifteen kids for burns the last couple of days. I think you need a little restorative, don't you? [*He takes out a flask.*] Here!

ALMA:

What is it?

JOHN:

Applejack brandy.

ALMA:

No thank you.

JOHN:

Liquid dynamite.

ALMA:

I'm sure.

[*John laughs and returns it to his pocket. He remains looking down at her with one foot on the end of her bench. His steady, smiling look into her face is disconcerting her.*

[*In Alma's voice and manner there is a delicacy and elegance, a kind of "airiness," which is really natural to her as it is, in a less marked degree, to many Southern girls. Her gestures and mannerisms are a bit exaggerated but in a graceful way. It is understandable that she might be accused of "putting on airs" and of being "affected" by the other young people of the town. She seems to belong to a more elegant age, such as the Eighteenth Century in France. Out of nervousness and self-consciousness she has a habit of prefacing and concluding her remarks with a little breathless laugh. This will be indicated at points, but should be used more freely than indicated; however, the characterization must never be stressed to the point of*

139

*making her at all ludicrous in a less than sympathetic
way.*]

ALMA:

You're—home for the summer? [*John gives an affirmative
grunt.*] Summer is not the pleasantest time of year to renew
an acquaintance with Glorious Hill—is it? [*John gives an
indefinite grunt. Alma laughs airily.*] The Gulf wind has
failed us this year, disappointed us dreadfully this summer.
We used to be able to rely on the Gulf wind to cool the
nights off for us, but this summer has been an exceptional
season. [*He continues to grin disconcertingly down at her;
she shows her discomfiture in flurried gestures.*]

JOHN [*slowly*]:

Are you—disturbed about something?

ALMA:

That firecracker was a shock.

JOHN:

You should be over that shock by now.

ALMA:

I don't get over shocks quickly.

JOHN:

I see you don't.

ALMA:

You're planning to stay here and take over some of your
father's medical practice?

JOHN:

I haven't made up my mind about anything yet.

ALMA:

I hope so, we all hope so. Your father was telling me that
you have succeeded in isolating the germ of that fever epidemic that's broken out at Lyon.

140

JOHN:

Finding something to kill it is more of a trick.

ALMA:

You'll do that! He's so positive that you will. He says that you made a special study of bacter—bacter . . .

JOHN:

Bacteriology!

ALMA:

Yes! At Johns Hopkins! That's in Boston, isn't it?

JOHN:

No. Baltimore.

ALMA:

Oh, Baltimore. Baltimore, Maryland. Such a beautiful combination of names. And bacteriology—isn't that something you do with a microscope?

JOHN:

Well—partly. . . .

ALMA:

I've looked through a telescope, but never a microscope. What . . . what do you—see?

JOHN:

A—universe, Miss Alma.

ALMA:

What kind of a universe?

JOHN:

Pretty much the same kind that you saw through the lens of a telescope—a mysterious one. . . .

ALMA:

Oh, yes. . . .

JOHN:

Part anarchy—and part order!

ALMA:
The footprints of God!

JOHN:
But not God.

ALMA [*ecstatically*]:
To be a doctor! And deal with these mysteries under the microscope lens . . . I think it is more religious than being a priest! There is so much suffering in the world it actually makes one sick to think about it, and most of us are so helpless to relieve it. . . . But a physician! Oh, my! With his magnificent gifts and training what a joy it must be to know that he is equipped and appointed to bring relief to all of this fearful suffering—and fear! And it's an expanding profession, it's a profession that is continually widening its horizons. So many diseases have already come under scientific control but the commencement is just—beginning! I mean there is so much more that is yet to be done, such as mental afflictions to be brought under control. . . . And with your father's example to inspire you! Oh, my!

JOHN:
I didn't know you had so many ideas about the medical profession.

ALMA:
Well, I am a great admirer of your father, as well as a patient. It's such a comfort knowing that he's right next door, within arm's reach as it were!

JOHN:
Why? Do you have fits? . . .

ALMA:
Fits? [*She throws back her head with a peal of gay laughter.*] Why no, but I do have attacks!—of nervous heart

142

trouble. Which can be so alarming that I run straight to your father!

JOHN:
At two or three in the morning?

ALMA:
Yes, as late as that, even . . . occasionally. He's very patient with me.

JOHN:
But does you no good?

ALMA:
He always reassures me.

JOHN:
Temporarily?

ALMA:
Yes . . .

JOHN:
Don't you want more than that?

ALMA:
What?

JOHN:
It's none of my business.

ALMA:
What were you going to say?

JOHN:
You're Dad's patient. But I have an idea . . .

ALMA:
Please go on! [*John laughs a little.*] Now you have to go on! You can't leave me up in the air! What were you going to tell me?

143

JOHN:

Only that I suspect you need something more than a little temporary reassurance.

ALMA:

Why? Why? You think it's more serious than . . . ?

JOHN:

You're swallowing air.

ALMA:

I'm what?

JOHN:

You're swallowing air, Miss Alma.

ALMA:

I'm swallowing air?

JOHN:

Yes, you swallow air when you laugh or talk. It's a little trick that hysterical women get into.

ALMA [*uncertainly*]:

Ha-ha . . . !

JOHN:

You swallow air and it presses on your heart and gives you palpitations. That isn't serious in itself but it's a symptom of something that is. Shall I tell you frankly?

ALMA:

Yes!

JOHN:

Well, what I think you have is a *Doppelgänger!* You have a *Doppelgänger* and the *Doppelgänger* is badly irritated.

ALMA:

Oh, my goodness! I have an irritated *Doppelgänger!* [*She tries to laugh, but is definitely uneasy.*] How awful that sounds! What exactly *is* it?

144

JOHN:

It's none of *my* business. You are not *my* patient.

ALMA:

But that's downright wicked of you! To tell me I have something awful-sounding as that, and then refuse to let me know what it is! [*She tries to laugh again, unsuccessfully.*]

JOHN:

I shouldn't have said anything! I'm not your doctor. . . .

ALMA:

Just how did you arrive at this—diagnosis of my case? [*She laughs.*] But of course you're teasing me. Aren't you? . . . There, the Gulf wind is stirring! He's actually moving the leaves of the palmetto! And listen to them complaining. . . .

[*As if brought in by this courier from the tropics, Rosa Gonzales enters and crosses to the fountain. Her indolent walk produces a sound and an atmosphere like the Gulf wind on the palmettos, a whispering of silk and a slight rattle of metallic ornaments. She is dressed in an almost outrageous finery, with lustrous feathers on her hat, greenish blue, a cascade of them, also diamond and emerald earrings.*]

JOHN [*sharply*]:
Who is that?

ALMA:

I'm surprised that you don't know.

JOHN:

I've been away quite a while.

ALMA:

That's the Gonzales girl. . . . Her father's the owner of the gambling casino on Moon Lake. [*Rosa drinks at the foun-*

145

tain and wanders leisurely off.] She smiled at you, didn't she?

JOHN:
I thought she did.

ALMA:
I hope that you have a strong character. [*He places a foot on the end of the bench.*]

JOHN:
Solid rock.

ALMA [*nervously*]:
The pyrotechnical display is going to be brilliant.

JOHN:
The what?

ALMA:
The fireworks.

JOHN:
Aw!

ALMA:
I suppose you've lost touch with most of your *old* friends here.

JOHN [*laconically*]:
Yeah.

ALMA:
You must make some *new* ones! I belong to a little group that meets every ten days. I think you'd enjoy them, too. They're young people with—intellectual and artistic interests. . . .

JOHN [*sadly*]:
Aw, I see . . . intellectual. . . .

ALMA:

You must come!—sometime—I'm going to remind you of
it. . . .

JOHN:

Thanks. Do you mind if I sit down?

ALMA:

Why, certainly not, there's room enough for two! Neither
of us are—terribly large in diameter! [*She laughs shrilly.*]

[*A girl's voice is heard calling: "Goodbye, Nellie!" and
another answers: "Goodbye!" Nellie Ewell enters—a girl
of sixteen with a radiantly fresh healthy quality.*]

ALMA:

Here comes someone much nicer! One of my adorable little
vocal pupils, the youngest and prettiest one with the least
gift for music.

JOHN:

I know that one.

ALMA:

Hello, there, Nellie dear!

NELLIE:

Oh, Miss Alma, your singing was so beautiful it made me
cry.

ALMA:

It's sweet of you to fib so. I sang terribly.

NELLIE:

You're just being modest, Miss Alma. Hello, Dr. John! Dr.
John?

JOHN:

Yeah?

NELLIE:

That book you gave me is too full of long words.

147

JOHN:

Look 'em up in the dictionary, Nellie.

NELLIE:

I did, but you know how dictionaries are. You look up one long word and it gives you another and you look up that one and it gives you the long word you looked up in the first place. [*John laughs.*] I'm coming over tomorrow for you to explain it all to me. [*She laughs and goes off.*]

ALMA:

What book is she talking about?

JOHN:

A book I gave her about the facts of nature. She came over to the office and told me her mother wouldn't tell her anything and she had to know because she'd fallen in love.

ALMA:

Why the precocious little—imp! [*She laughs.*]

JOHN:

What sort of a mother has she?

ALMA:

Mrs. Ewell's the merry widow of Glorious Hill. They say that she goes to the depot to meet every train in order to make the acquaintance of traveling salesmen. Of course she is ostracized by all but a few of her own type of women in town, which is terribly hard for Nellie. It isn't fair to the child. Father didn't want me to take her as a pupil because of her mother's reputation, but I feel that one has a duty to perform toward children in such—circumstances. . . . And I always say that life is such a mysteriously complicated thing that no one should really presume to judge and condemn the behavior of anyone else!

[*There is a faraway "puff" and a burst of golden light over their heads. Both look up. There is a long-drawn*

"Ahhh . . ." from the invisible crowd. This is an effect that will be repeated at intervals during the scene.]

There goes the first skyrocket! Oh, look at it burst into a million stars!

[*John leans way back to look up and allows his knees to spread wide apart so that one of them is in contact with Alma's. The effect upon her is curiously disturbing.*]

JOHN [*after a moment*]:
Do you have a chill?

ALMA:
Why, no!—no. Why?

JOHN:
You're shaking.

ALMA:
Am I?

JOHN:
Don't you feel it?

ALMA:
I have a touch of malaria lingering on.

JOHN:
You have malaria?

ALMA:
Never severely, never really severely. I just have touches of it that come and go. [*She laughs airily.*]

JOHN [*with a gentle grin*]:
Why do you laugh that way?

ALMA:
What way?

[*John imitates her laugh. Alma laughs again in embarrassment.*]

149

JOHN:
Yeah. That way.

ALMA:
I do declare, you haven't changed in the slightest. It used to delight you to embarrass me and it still does!

JOHN:
I guess I shouldn't tell you this, but I heard an imitation of you at a party.

ALMA:
Imitation? Of what?

JOHN:
You.

ALMA:
I?—I? Why, *what* did they imitate?

JOHN:
You singing at a wedding.

ALMA:
My voice?

JOHN:
Your gestures and facial expression!

ALMA:
How mystifying!

JOHN:
No, I shouldn't have told you. You're upset about it.

ALMA:
I'm not in the least upset, I am just mystified.

JOHN:
Don't you know that you have a reputation for putting on airs a little—for gilding the lily a bit?

ALMA:
I have no idea what you are talking about.

JOHN:

Well, some people seem to have gotten the idea that you are just a little bit—affected!

ALMA:

Well, well, well, well. [*She tries to conceal her hurt.*] That may be so, it may seem so to some people. But since I am innocent of any attempt at affectation, I really don't know what I can do about it.

JOHN:

You have a rather fancy way of talking.

ALMA:

Have I?

JOHN:

Pyrotechnical display instead of fireworks, and that sort of thing.

ALMA:

So?

JOHN:

And how about that accent?

ALMA:

Accent? This leaves me quite speechless! I have sometimes been accused of having a put-on accent by people who disapprove of good diction. My father was a Rhodes scholar at Oxford, and while over there he fell into the natural habit of using the long A where it is correct to use it. I suppose I must have picked it up from him, but it's entirely unconscious. Who gave this imitation at this party you spoke of?

JOHN [*grinning*]:

I don't think she'd want that told.

ALMA:

Oh, it was a *she* then?

151

JOHN:

You don't think a man could do it?

ALMA:

No, and I don't think a lady would do it either!

JOHN:

I didn't think it would have made you so mad, or I wouldn't have brought it up.

ALMA:

Oh, I'm not mad. I'm just mystified and amazed as I always am by unprovoked malice in people. I don't understand it when it's directed at me and I don't understand it when it is directed at anybody else. I just don't understand it, and perhaps it is better not to understand it. These people who call me affected and give these unkind imitations of me—I wonder if they stop to think that I have had certain difficulties and disadvantages to cope with—which may be partly the cause of these peculiarities of mine—which they find so offensive!

JOHN:

Now, Miss Alma, you're making a mountain out of a molehill!

ALMA:

I wonder if they stop to think that my circumstances are somewhat different from theirs? My father and I have a certain—cross—to bear!

JOHN:

What cross?

ALMA:

Living next door to us, you should know what cross.

JOHN:

Mrs. Winemiller?

ALMA:

She had her breakdown while I was still in high school. And from that time on I have had to manage the Rectory and take over the social and household duties that would ordinarily belong to a minister's wife, not his daughter. And that may have made me seem strange to some of my more critical contemporaries. In a way it may have—deprived me of—my youth. . . .

[*Another rocket goes up. Another "Ahhh . . ." from the crowd.*]

JOHN:

You ought to go out with young people.

ALMA:

I am not a recluse. I don't fly around here and there giving imitations of other people at parties. But I am not a recluse by any manner of means. Being a minister's daughter I have to be more selective than most girls about the—society I keep. But I do go out now and then. . . .

JOHN:

I have seen you in the public library and the park, but only two or three times have I seen you out with a boy and it was always someone like this Roger Doremus.

ALMA:

I'm afraid that you and I move in different circles. If I wished to be as outspoken as you are, which is sometimes just an excuse for being rude—I might say that I've yet to see you in the company of a—well, a—reputable young woman. You've heard unfavorable talk about me in your circle of acquaintances and I've heard equally unpleasant things about you in mine. And the pity of it is that you are preparing to be a doctor. You're intending to practice your father's profession here in Glorious Hill. [*She catches*

153

her breath in a sob.] Most of us have no choice but to lead useless lives! But you have a gift for scientific research! You have a chance to serve humanity. Not just to go on enduring for the sake of endurance, but to serve a noble, humanitarian cause, to relieve human suffering. And what do you do about it? Everything that you can to alienate the confidence of nice people who love and respect your father. While he is devoting himself to the fever at Lyon you drive your automobile at a reckless pace from one disorderly roadhouse to another! You say you have seen two things through the microscope, anarchy and order? Well, obviously *order* is not the thing that impressed you . . . conducting yourself like some overgrown schoolboy who wants to be known as the wildest fellow in town! And you—a gifted young doctor—*magna cum laude!* [*She turns aside, touching her eyelids with a handkerchief.*] You know what I call it? I call it a *desecration!* [*She sobs uncontrollably. Then she springs up from the bench. John catches her hand.*]

JOHN:
You're not going to run off, are you?

ALMA:
Singing in public always—always upsets me!—Let go of my hand. [*He holds on to it, grinning up at her in the deepening dusk. The stars are coming out in the cyclorama with its leisurely floating cloud-forms. In the distance the band is playing "La Golondrina."*] Please let go of my hand.

JOHN:
Don't run off mad.

ALMA:
Let's not make a spectacle of ourselves.

JOHN:
Then sit back down.

[A skyrocket goes up. The crowd "Ahhh .. s."]

ALMA:

You threw that firecracker and started a conversation just in order to tease me as you did as a child. You came to this bench in order to embarrass me and to hurt my feelings with the report of that vicious—imitation! No, let go of my hand so I can leave, now. You've succeeded in your purpose. I *was* hurt, I *did* make a fool of myself as you intended! So let me go now!

JOHN:

You're attracting attention! Don't you know that I really *like* you, Miss Alma?

ALMA:

No, you don't.

[Another skyrocket.]

JOHN:

Sure I do. A lot. Sometimes when I come home late at night I look over at the Rectory. I see something white at the window. Could that be you, Miss Alma? Or, is it your *Doppelgänger,* looking out of the window that faces my way?

ALMA:

Enough about *Doppelgänger*—whatever that is!

JOHN:

There goes a nice one, Roman candle they call it!

[This time the explosion is in back of them. A Roman candle shoots up puffs of rainbow-colored light in back of the stone angel of the fountain. They turn in profile to watch it.]

155

JOHN [*counting the puffs of light*]:
Four—five—six—that's all? No—seven! [*There is a pause.
Alma sits down slowly.*]

ALMA [*vaguely*]:
Dear me . . . [*She fans herself.*]

JOHN:
How about going riding?

ALMA [*too eagerly*]:
When . . . now?

[*Rosa Gonzales has wandered up to the fountain again.
John's attention drifts steadily toward her and away from
Alma.*]

JOHN [*too carelessly*]:
Oh . . . some afternoon.

ALMA:
Would you observe the speed limit?

JOHN:
Strictly with you, Miss Alma.

ALMA:
Why then, I'd be glad to—John.

[*John has risen from the bench and crosses to the fountain.*]

JOHN:
And wear a hat with a plume!

ALMA:
I don't have a hat with a plume!

JOHN:
Get one!

[*Another skyrocket goes up, and there is another long
"Ahhh . . ." from the crowd. John saunters up to the*

*fountain. Rosa has lingered beside it. As he passes her
he whispers something. She laughs and moves leisurely
off. John takes a quick drink at the fountain, then follows
Rosa, calling back "Good night" to Alma. There is a
sound of laughter in the distance. Alma sits motionless
for a moment, then touches a small white handkerchief to
her lips and nostrils. Mr. Doremus comes in, carrying a
French horn case. He is a small man, somewhat like a
sparrow.*]

ROGER:

Whew! Golly! Moses! —Well, how did it go, Miss Alma?

ALMA:

How did—what—go?

ROGER [*annoyed*]:

My solo on the French horn.

ALMA [*slowly, without thinking*]:

I paid no attention to it. [*She rises slowly and takes his arm.*]
I'll have to hang on your arm—I'm feeling so dizzy!

[*The scene dims out. There is a final skyrocket and a last
"Ahhh . . ." from the crowd in the distance. Music is
heard, and there is light on the angel.*]

SCENE TWO

Inside the Rectory, which is lighted. Mrs. Winemiller comes in and makes her way stealthily to the love seat, where she seats herself. Opening her parasol, she takes out a fancy white-plumed hat which she had concealed there. Rising, she turns to the mirror on the wall over the love seat and tries on the hat. She draws a long, ecstatic breath as she places it squarely on her head. At that moment the telephone rings. Startled, she snatches off the hat, hides it behind the center table and quickly resumes her seat. The telephone goes on ringing. Alma comes in to answer it.

ALMA:

Hello. . . . Yes, Mr. Gillam. . . . She did? . . . Are you sure? . . . How shocking! . . . [*Mrs. Winemiller now retrieves the hat, seats herself in front of Alma and puts the hat on.*] Thank you, Mr. Gillam . . . the hat is here.

[*Mr. Winemiller comes in. He is distracted.*]

MR. WINEMILLER:

Alma! Alma, your mother . . . !

ALMA [*coming in*]:

I know, Father, Mr. Gillam just phoned. He told me she picked up a white plumed hat and he pretended not to notice in order to save you the embarrassment, so I—I told him to just charge it to us.

MR. WINEMILLER:

That hat looks much too expensive.

ALMA:

It's fourteen dollars. You pay six of it, Father, and I'll pay eight. [*She gives him the parasol.*]

MR. WINEMILLER:

What an insufferable cross we have to bear. [*He retires despairingly from the room.*]

[*Alma goes over to her mother and seats her in a chair at the table.*]

ALMA:

I have a thousand and one things to do before my club meeting tonight, so you work quietly on your picture puzzle or I shall take the hat back, plume and all.

MRS. WINEMILLER [*throwing a piece of the puzzle on the floor*]:

The pieces don't fit! [*Alma picks up the piece and puts it on the table.*] The pieces don't fit!

[*Alma stands for a moment in indecision. She reaches for the phone, then puts it down. Then she takes it up again, and gives a number. The telephone across the way in the doctor's office rings and that part of the scene lights up. John comes in.*]

JOHN [*answering the phone*]:
Hello?

ALMA:

John! [*She fans herself rapidly with a palm leaf clutched in her free hand and puts on a brilliant, strained smile as if she were actually in his presence.*]

JOHN:
Miss Alma?

ALMA:
You recognized my voice?

JOHN:
I recognized your laugh.

159

ALMA:

Ha-ha! How are you, you stranger you?

JOHN:

I'm pretty well, Miss Alma. How're you doing?

ALMA:

Surviving, just surviving! Isn't it fearful?

JOHN:

Uh-huh.

ALMA:

You seem unusually laconic. Or perhaps I should say more than usually laconic.

JOHN:

I had a big night and I'm just recovering from it.

ALMA:

Well, sir, I have a bone to pick with you!

JOHN:

What's that, Miss Alma? [*He drains a glass of Bromo.*]

ALMA:

The time of our last conversation on the Fourth of July, you said you were going to take me riding in your automobile.

JOHN:

Aw. Did I say that?

ALMA:

Yes indeed you did, sir! And all these hot afternoons I've been breathlessly waiting and hoping that you would remember that promise. But now I know how insincere you are. Ha-ha! Time and again the four-wheeled phenomenon flashes by the Rectory and I have yet to put my—my quaking foot in it!

[*Mrs. Winemiller begins to mock Alma's speech and laughter.*]

JOHN:

What was that, Miss Alma? I didn't understand you.

ALMA:

I was just reprimanding you, sir! Castigating you verbally! Ha-ha!

MRS. WINEMILLER [*grimacing*]:

Ha-ha.

JOHN:

What about, Miss Alma? [*He leans back and puts his feet on table.*]

ALMA:

Never mind. I know how busy you are! [*She whispers.*] Mother, *hush!*

JOHN:

I'm afraid we have a bad connection.

ALMA:

I hate telephones. I don't know why but they always make me laugh as if someone were poking me in the ribs! I swear to goodness they do!

JOHN:

Why don't you just go to your window and I'll go to mine and we can holler across?

ALMA:

The yard's so wide I'm afraid it would crack my voice! And I've got to sing at somebody's wedding tomorrow.

JOHN:

You're going to sing at a wedding?

ALMA:

Yes. "The Voice That Breathed O'er Eden!" And I'm

161

as hoarse as a frog! [*Another gale of laughter almost shakes her off her feet.*]

JOHN:
Better come over and let me give you a gargle.

ALMA:
Nasty gargles—I hate them!

MRS. WINEMILLER [*mockingly*]:
Nasty gargles—I hate them!

ALMA:
Mother, shhh!—please! As you no doubt have gathered, there is some interference at this end of the line! What I wanted to say is—you remember my mentioning that little club I belong to?

JOHN:
Aw! Aw, yes! Those intellectual meetings!

ALMA:
Oh, now, don't call it that. It's just a little informal gathering every Wednesday and we talk about the new books and read things out loud to each other!

JOHN:
Serve any refreshments?

ALMA:
Yes, we serve refreshments!

JOHN:
Any liquid refreshments?

ALMA:
Both liquid and solid refreshments.

JOHN:
Is this an invitation?

ALMA:
Didn't I promise I'd ask you? It's going to be tonight!—at

162

eight at my house, at the Rectory, so all you'll have to do is
cross the yard!

JOHN:
I'll try to make it, Miss Alma.

ALMA:
Don't say try as if it required some Herculean effort! All
you have to do is . . .

JOHN:
Cross the yard! Uh-huh—reserve me a seat by the punch
bowl.

ALMA:
That gives me an idea! We *will* have punch, fruit punch,
with claret in it. Do you like claret?

JOHN:
I just dote on claret.

ALMA:
Now you're being sarcastic! Ha-ha-ha!

JOHN:
Excuse me, Miss Alma, but Dad's got to use this phone.

ALMA:
I won't hang up till you've said you'll come without fail!

JOHN:
I'll be there, Miss Alma. You can count on it.

ALMA:
Au revoir, then! Until eight.

JOHN:
G'bye, Miss Alma.

[*John hangs up with an incredulous grin. Alma remains
holding the phone with a dazed smile until the office
interior has dimmed slowly out.*]

163

MRS. WINEMILLER:

Alma's in love—in love. [*She waltzes mockingly.*]

ALMA [*sharply*]:

Mother, you are wearing out my patience! Now I am expecting another music pupil and I have to make preparations for the club meeting so I suggest that you . . . [*Nellie rings the bell.*] Will you go up to your room? [*Then she calls sweetly.*] Yes, Nellie, coming, Nellie. All right, stay down here then. But keep your attention on your picture puzzle or there will be no ice cream for you after supper!

[*She admits Nellie, who is wildly excited over something. This scene should be played lightly and quickly.*]

NELLIE:

Oh, Miss Alma!

[*She rushes past Alma in a distracted manner, throws herself on the sofa and hugs herself with excited glee.*]

ALMA:

What is it, Nellie? Has something happened at home? [*Nellie continues her exhilaration.*] Oh, now, Nellie, stop that! Whatever it is, it can't be *that* important!

NELLIE [*blurting out suddenly*]:

Miss Alma, haven't you ever had—*crushes?*

ALMA:

What?

NELLIE:

Crushes?

ALMA:

Yes—I suppose I have. [*She sits down.*]

NELLIE:

Did you know that I used to have a crush on *you*, Miss Alma?

164

ALMA:
No, Nellie.

NELLIE:
Why do you think that I took singing lessons?

ALMA:
I supposed it was because you wished to develop your voice.

NELLIE [*cutting in*]:
Oh, you know, and I know, I never had any voice. I had a crush on you though. Those were the days when I had crushes on girls. Those days are all over, and now I have crushes on boys. Oh, Miss Alma, you know about Mother, how I was brought up so nobody nice except you would have anything to do with us—Mother meeting the trains to pick up the traveling salesmen and bringing them home to drink and play poker—all of them acting like pigs, pigs, pigs!

MRS. WINEMILLER [*mimicking*]:
Pigs, pigs, pigs!

NELLIE:
Well, I thought I'd always hate men. Loathe and despise them. But last night— Oh!

ALMA:
Hadn't we better run over some scales until you are feeling calmer?

NELLIE [*cutting in*]:
I'd heard them downstairs for hours but didn't know who it was—I'd fallen asleep—when all of a sudden my door banged open. He'd thought it was the bathroom!

ALMA [*nervously*]:
Nellie, I'm not sure I want to hear any more of this story.

165

NELLIE [*interrupting*]:
Guess who it was?

ALMA:
I couldn't possibly guess.

NELLIE:
Someone you know. Someone I've seen you with.

ALMA:
Who?

NELLIE:
The wonderfullest person in all the big wide world! When he saw it was me he came and sat down on the bed and held my hand and we talked and talked until Mother came up to see what had happened to him. You should have heard him bawl her out. Oh, he laid the law down! He said she ought to send me off to a girl's school because she wasn't fit to bring up a daughter! Then she started to bawl him out. You're a fine one to talk, she said, you're not fit to call yourself a doctor. [*Alma rises abruptly.*]

ALMA:
John Buchanan?

NELLIE:
Yes, of course, Dr. Johnny.

ALMA:
Was—with—your—mother?

NELLIE:
Oh, he wasn't her beau! He had a girl with him, and Mother had somebody else!

ALMA:
Who—did—he—have?

NELLIE:
Oh, some loud tacky thing with a Z in her name!

ALMA:

Gonzales? Rosa Gonzales?

NELLIE:

Yes, that was it! [*Alma sits slowly back down.*] But him!
Oh, Miss Alma! He's the *wonderfullest* person that I . . .

ALMA [*interrupting*]:

Your mother was right! He isn't fit to call himself a doctor!
I hate to disillusion you, but this wonderfullest person is
pitiably weak.

[*Someone calls "Johnny" outside.*]

NELLIE [*in hushed excitement*]:

Someone is calling him now!

ALMA:

Yes, these people who shout his name in front of his house
are of such a character that the old doctor cannot permit
them to come inside the door. And when they have brought
him home at night, left him sprawling on the front steps,
sometimes at daybreak—it takes two people, his father and
the old cook, one pushing and one pulling, to get him upstairs. [*She sits down.*] All the gifts of the gods were showered on him. . . . [*The call of "Johnny" is repeated.*] But all
he cares about is indulging his senses! [*Another call of
"Johnny."*]

NELLIE:

Here he comes down the steps! [*Alma crosses toward the
window.*] Look at him jump!

ALMA:

Oh.

NELLIE:

Over the banisters. Ha-ha!

167

ALMA:

Nellie, don't lean out the window and have us caught spying.

MRS. WINEMILLER [*suddenly*]:

Show Nellie how *you* spy on him! Oh, she's a good one at spying. She stands behind the curtain and *peeks* around it, and . . .

ALMA [*frantically*]:
Mother!

MRS. WINEMILLER:

She spies on him. Whenever he comes in at night she rushes downstairs to watch him out of this window!

ALMA [*interrupting her*]:
Be still!

MRS. WINEMILLER [*going right on*]:

She called him just now and had a fit on the telephone! [*The old lady cackles derisively. Alma snatches her cigarette from her and crushes it under her foot.*] Alma's in love! Alma's in love!

ALMA [*interrupting*]:
Nellie, Nellie, please go.

NELLIE [*with a startled giggle*]:

All right, Miss Alma, I'm going. [*She crosses quickly to the door, looking back once with a grin.*] Good night, Mrs. Winemiller!

[*Nellie goes out gaily, leaving the door slightly open. Alma rushes to it and slams it shut. She returns swiftly to Mrs. Winemiller, her hands clenched with anger.*]

ALMA:

If ever I hear you say such a thing again, if ever you dare to repeat such a thing in my presence or anybody else's—

then it will be the last straw! You understand me? Yes, you understand me! You act like a child, but you have the devil in you. And God will punish you—yes! I'll punish you too. I'll take your cigarettes from you and give you no more. I'll give you no ice cream either. Because I'm tired of your malice. Yes, I'm tired of your malice and your self-indulgence. People wonder why I'm tied down here! They pity me—think of me as an old maid already! In spite of I'm young. Still young! It's you—it's you, you've taken my youth away from me! I wouldn't say that—I'd try not even to think it—if you were just kind, just simple! But I could spread my life out like a rug for you to step on and you'd step on it, and not even say "Thank you, Alma!" Which is what you've done always—and now you dare to tell a disgusting lie about me—in front of that girl!

MRS. WINEMILLER:

Don't you think I hear you go to the window at night to watch him come in and . . .

ALMA:

Give me that plumed hat, Mother! It goes back now, it goes back!

MRS. WINEMILLER:
Fight! Fight!

[*Alma snatches at the plumed hat. Mrs. Winemiller snatches too. The hat is torn between them. Mrs. Winemiller retains the hat. The plume comes loose in Alma's hand. She stares at it a moment with a shocked expression.*]

ALMA [*sincerely*]:
Heaven have mercy upon us!

SCENE THREE

Inside the Rectory.

The meeting is in progress, having just opened with the reading of the minutes by Alma. She stands before the green plush sofa and the others. This group includes Mr. Doremus, Vernon, a willowy younger man with an open collar and Byronic locks, the Widow Bassett, and a wistful older girl with a long neck and thick-lensed glasses.

ALMA [*reading*]:
Our last meeting which fell on July fourteenth . . .

MRS. BASSETT:
Bastille Day!

ALMA:
Pardon me?

MRS. BASSETT:
It fell on Bastille Day! But, honey, that was the meeting before last.

ALMA:
You're perfectly right. I seem to be on the wrong page. . . . [*She drops the papers.*]

MRS. BASSETT:
Butterfingers!

ALMA:
Here we are! July twenty-fifth! Correct?

MRS. BASSETT:
Correct! [*A little ripple of laughter goes about the circle.*]

ALMA [*continuing*]:
It was debated whether or not we ought to suspend opera-

tions for the remainder of the summer as the departure of several members engaged in the teaching profession for their summer vacations . . .

MRS. BASSETT:
Lucky people!

ALMA:
. . . had substantially contracted our little circle.

MRS. BASSETT:
Decimated our ranks! [*There is another ripple of laughter.*]

[*John appears outside the doorframe and rings the bell.*]

ALMA [*with agitation*]:
Is that—is that—the doorbell?

MRS. BASSETT:
It sure did sound like it to me.

ALMA:
Excuse me a moment. I think it may be . . .

[*She crosses to the doorframe and makes the gesture of opening the door. John steps in, immaculately groomed and shining, his white linen coat over his arm and a white Panama hat in his hand. He is a startling contrast to the other male company, who seem to be outcasts of a state in which he is a prominent citizen.*]

ALMA [*shrilly*]:
Yes, it is—our guest of honor! Everybody, this is Dr. John Buchanan, Jr.

JOHN [*easily glancing about the assemblage*]:
Hello, everybody.

MRS. BASSETT:
I never thought he'd show up. Congratulations, Miss Alma.

171

JOHN:
Did I miss much?

ALMA:
Not a thing! Just the minutes—I'll put you on the sofa. Next to me. [*She laughs breathlessly and makes an uncertain gesture. He settles gingerly on the sofa. They all stare at him with a curious sort of greediness.*] Well, now! we are completely assembled!

MRS. BASSETT [*eagerly*]:
Vernon has his verse play with him tonight!

ALMA [*uneasily*]:
Is that right, Vernon? [*Obviously, it is. Vernon has a pile of papers eight inches thick on his knees. He raises them timidly with downcast eyes.*]

ROGER [*quickly*]:
We decided to put that off till cooler weather. Miss Rosemary is supposed to read us a paper tonight on William Blake.

MRS. BASSETT:
Those dead poets can keep!

[*John laughs.*]

ALMA [*excitedly jumping up*]:
Mrs. Bassett, everybody! This is the way I feel about the verse play. It's too important a thing to read under any but ideal circumstances. Not only atmospheric—on some cool evening with music planned to go with it!—but everyone present so that nobody will miss it! Why don't we . . .

ROGER:
Why don't we take a standing vote on the matter?

ALMA:
Good, good, perfect!

172

ROGER:

All in favor of putting the verse play off till cooler weather, stand up!

[*Everybody rises but Rosemary and Mrs. Bassett. Rosemary starts vaguely to rise, but Mrs. Bassett jerks her arm.*]

ROSEMARY:

Was this a vote?

ROGER:

Now, Mrs. Bassett, no rough tactics, please!

ALMA:

Has everybody got fans? John, you haven't got one!

[*She looks about for a fan for him. Not seeing one, she takes Roger's out of his hand and gives it to John. Roger is nonplused. Rosemary gets up with her paper.*]

ROSEMARY:

The poet—William Blake.

MRS. BASSETT:

Insane, insane, that man was a mad fanatic! [*She squints her eyes tight shut and thrusts her thumbs into her ears. The reactions range from indignant to conciliatory.*]

ROGER:

Now, Mrs. Bassett!

MRS. BASSETT:

This is a free country. I can speak my opinion. And I have *read up* on him. Go on, Rosemary. I wasn't criticizing your paper. [*But Rosemary sits down, hurt.*]

ALMA:

Mrs. Bassett is only joking, Rosemary.

ROSEMARY:

No, I don't want to read it if she feels that strongly about it.

MRS. BASSETT:

Not a bit, don't be silly! I just don't see why we should encourage the writings of people like that who have already gone into a drunkard's grave!

VARIOUS VOICES [*exclaiming*]:

Did he? I never heard that about him. Is that true?

ALMA:

Mrs. Bassett is mistaken about that. Mrs. Bassett, you have confused Blake with someone else.

MRS. BASSETT [*positively*]:

Oh, no, don't tell me. I've read up on him and know what I'm talking about. He traveled around with that Frenchman who took a shot at him and landed them both in jail! Brussels, Brussels!

ROGER [*gaily*]:

Brussels sprouts!

MRS. BASSETT:

That's where it happened, fired a gun at him in a drunken stupor, and later one of them died of t.b. in the gutter! All right. I'm finished. I won't say anything more. Go on with your paper, Rosemary. There's nothing like contact with culture!

[*Alma gets up.*]

ALMA:

Before Rosemary reads her paper on Blake, I think it would be a good idea, since some of us aren't acquainted with his work, to preface the critical and biographical comments with a reading of one of his loveliest lyric poems.

ROSEMARY:

I'm not going to read anything at all! Not I!

174

ALMA:

Then let me read it then. [*She takes a paper from Rose-mary.*] ... This is called "Love's Secret."

[*She clears her throat and waits for a hush to settle. Rose-mary looks stonily at the carpet. Mrs. Bassett looks at the ceiling. John coughs.*]

> Never seek to tell thy love,
> Love that never told can be,
> For the gentle wind doth move
> Silently, invisibly.
>
> I told my love, I told my love,
> I told him all my heart.
> Trembling, cold in ghastly fear
> Did my love depart.
>
> No sooner had he gone from me
> Than a stranger passing by,
> Silently, invisibly,
> Took him with a sigh!

[*There are various effusions and enthusiastic applause.*]

MRS. BASSETT:

Honey, you're right. That isn't the man I meant. I was thinking about the one who wrote about "the bought red lips." Who was it that wrote about the "bought red lips"?

[*John has risen abruptly. He signals to Alma and points to his watch. He starts to leave.*]

ALMA [*springing up*]:
John!

JOHN [*calling back*]:
I have to call on a patient!

ALMA:
Oh, John!

[*She calls after him so sharply that the group is startled into silence.*]

ROSEMARY [*interpreting this as a cue to read her paper*]:
"The poet, William Blake, was born in 1757 . . ."

[*Alma suddenly rushes to the door and goes out after John.*]

ROGER:
Of poor but honest parents.

MRS. BASSETT:
No supercilious comments out of you, sir. Go on Rosemary. [*She speaks loudly.*] She has such a beautiful *voice!*

[*Alma returns inside, looking stunned.*]

ALMA:
Please excuse the interruption, Rosemary. Dr. Buchanan had to call on a patient.

MRS. BASSETT [*archly*]:
I bet I know who the patient was. Ha-ha! That Gonzales girl whose father owns Moon Lake Casino and goes everywhere with two pistols strapped on his belt. Johnny Buchanan will get himself shot in that crowd!

ALMA:
Why, Mrs. Bassett, what gave you such an idea? I don't think that John even knows that Gonzales girl!

MRS. BASSETT:
He knows her, all right. In the Biblical sense of the word, if you'll excuse me!

176

ALMA:

No, I will not excuse you! A thing like that is inexcusable!

MRS. BASSETT:

Have you fallen for him, Miss Alma? Miss Alma has fallen
for the young doctor! They tell me he has lots of new lady
patients!

ALMA:

Stop it! [*She stamps her foot furiously and crushes the palm
leaf fan between her clenched hands.*] I won't have malicious talk here! You drove him away from the meeting
after I'd bragged so much about how bright and interesting
you all were! You put your worst foot forward and simpered
and chattered and carried on like idiots, idiots! What am I
saying? I—I—please excuse me!

[*She rushes out the inner door.*]

ROGER:

I move that the meeting adjourn.

MRS. BASSETT:

I second the motion.

ROSEMARY:

I don't understand. What happened?

MRS. BASSETT:

Poor Miss Alma!

ROGER:

She hasn't been herself lately. . . .

[*They all go out. After a moment Alma reenters with a
tray of refreshments, looks about the deserted interior and
bursts into hysterical laughter. The light dims out.*]

SCENE FOUR

In the doctor's office.

John has a wound on his arm which he is bandaging with Rosa's assistance.

JOHN:
Hold that end. Wrap it around. Pull it tight.

[*There is a knock at the door. They look up silently. The knock is repeated.*]

I better answer before they wake up the old man.

[*He goes out. A few moments later he returns followed by Alma. He is rolling down his sleeve to conceal the bandage. Alma stops short at the sight of Rosa.*]

Wait outside, Rosa. In the hall. But be quiet!

[*Rosa gives Alma a challenging look as she withdraws from the lighted area. John explains about Rosa.*]

A little emergency case.

ALMA:
The patient you had to call on. [*John grins.*] I want to see your father.

JOHN:
He's asleep. Anything I can do?

ALMA:
No, I think not. I have to see your father.

JOHN:
It's 2 A.M., Miss Alma.

ALMA:

I know, I'm afraid I'll have to see him.

JOHN:

What's the trouble?

[*The voice of John's father is heard, calling from above.*]

DR. BUCHANAN:

John! What's going on down there?

JOHN [*at the door*]:

Nothing much, Dad. Somebody got cut in a fight.

DR. BUCHANAN:

I'm coming down.

JOHN:

No. Don't! Stay in bed! [*He rolls up his sleeve to show Alma the bandaged wound. She gasps and touches her lips.*] I've patched him up, Dad. You sleep!

[*John executes the gesture of closing a door quietly on the hall.*]

ALMA:

You've been in a brawl with that—woman! [*John nods and rolls the sleeve back down. Alma sinks faintly into a chair.*]

JOHN:

Is your *Doppelgänger* cutting up again?

ALMA:

It's your father I want to talk to.

JOHN:

Be reasonable, Miss Alma. You're not that sick.

ALMA:

Do you suppose I would come here at two o'clock in the morning if I were not seriously ill?

JOHN:

It's no telling what you would do in a state of hysteria. [*He puts some powders in a glass of water.*] Toss that down, Miss Alma.

ALMA:

What is it?

JOHN:

A couple of little white tablets dissolved in water.

ALMA:

What kind of tablets?

JOHN:

You don't trust me?

ALMA:

You are not in any condition to inspire much confidence. [*John laughs softly. She looks at him helplessly for a moment, then bursts into tears. He draws up a chair beside hers and puts his arm gently about her shoulders.*] I seem to be all to pieces.

JOHN:

The intellectual meeting wore you out.

ALMA:

You made a quick escape from it.

JOHN:

I don't like meetings. The only meetings I like are between two people.

ALMA:

Such as between yourself and the lady outside?

JOHN:

Or between you and me.

ALMA [*nervously*]:

Where is the . . . ?

JOHN:

Oh. You've decided to take it?

ALMA:

Yes, if you . . .

[*She sips and chokes. He gives her his handkerchief. She touches her lips with it.*]

JOHN:

Bitter?

ALMA:

Awfully bitter.

JOHN:

It'll make you sleepy.

ALMA:

I do hope so. I wasn't able to sleep.

JOHN:

And you felt panicky?

ALMA:

Yes. I felt walled in.

JOHN:

You started hearing your heart?

ALMA:

Yes, like a drum!

JOHN:

It scared you?

ALMA:

It always does.

JOHN:

Sure. I know.

ALMA:

I don't think I will be able to get through the summer.

181

JOHN:
You'll get through it, Miss Alma.

ALMA:
How?

JOHN:
One day will come after another and one night will come after another till sooner or later the summer will be all through with and then it will be fall, and you will be saying, I don't see how I'm going to get through the fall.

ALMA:
Oh . . .

JOHN:
That's right. Draw a deep breath!

ALMA:
Ah . . .

JOHN:
Good. Now draw another!

ALMA:
Ah . . .

JOHN:
Better? Better?

ALMA:
A little.

JOHN:
Soon you'll be much better. [*He takes out a big silver watch and holds her wrist.*] Did y' know that time is one side of the four-dimensional continuum we're caught in?

ALMA:
What?

JOHN:
Did you know space is curved, that it turns back onto itself

182

like a soap bubble, adrift in something that's even less than space. [*He laughs a little as he replaces the watch.*]

ROSA [*faintly from outside*]:
Johnny!

JOHN [*looking up as if the cry came from there*]:
Did you know that the Magellanic clouds are a hundred thousand light years away from the earth? No? [*Alma shakes her head slightly.*] That's something to think about when you worry over your heart, that little red fist that's got to keep knocking, knocking against the big black door.

ROSA [*more distinctly*]:
Johnny!

[*She opens the door a crack.*]

JOHN:
Calla de la boca! [*The door closes and he speaks to Alma.*] There's nothing wrong with your heart but a little functional disturbance, like I told you before. You want me to check it? [*Alma nods mutely. John picks up his stethoscope.*]

ALMA:
The lady outside, I hate to keep her waiting.

JOHN:
Rosa doesn't mind waiting. Unbutton your blouse.

ALMA:
Unbutton . . .?

JOHN:
The blouse.

ALMA:
Hadn't I better—better come back in the morning, when your father will be able to . . . ?

183

JOHN:

Just as you please, Miss Alma. [*She hesitates. Then begins to unbutton her blouse. Her fingers fumble.*] Fingers won't work?

ALMA [*breathlessly*]:

They are just as if frozen!

JOHN [*smiling*]:

Let me. [*He leans over her.*] Little pearl buttons . . .

ALMA:

If your father discovered that woman in the house . . .

JOHN:

He won't discover it.

ALMA:

It would distress him terribly.

JOHN:

Are you going to tell him?

ALMA:

Certainly not! [*He laughs and applies the stethoscope to her chest.*]

JOHN:

Breathe! . . . Out! . . . Breathe! . . . Out! ·

ALMA:

Ah . . .

JOHN:

Um-hmmm . . .

ALMA:

What do you hear?

JOHN:

Just a little voice saying—"Miss Alma is lonesome!" [*She rises and turns her back to him.*]

ALMA:

If your idea of helping a patient is to ridicule and insult . . .

JOHN:

My idea of helping you is to tell you the truth. [*Alma looks up at him. He lifts her hand from the chair arm.*] What is this stone?

ALMA:

A topaz.

JOHN:

Beautiful stone. . . . Fingers still frozen?

ALMA:

A little. [*He lifts her hand to his mouth and blows his breath on her fingers.*]

JOHN:

I'm a poor excuse for a doctor, I'm much too selfish. But let's try to think about you.

ALMA:

Why should you bother about me? [*She sits down.*]

JOHN:

You know I like you and I think you're worth a lot of consideration.

ALMA:

Why?

JOHN:

Because you have a lot of feeling in your heart, and that's a rare thing. It makes you too easily hurt. Did I hurt you tonight?

ALMA:

You hurt me when you sprang up from the sofa and rushed from the Rectory in such—in such mad haste that you left your coat behind you!

185

JOHN:

I'll pick up the coat sometime.

ALMA:

The time of our last conversation you said you would take me riding in your automobile sometime, but you forgot to.

JOHN:

I didn't forget. Many's the time I've looked across at the Rectory and wondered if it would be worth trying, you and me. . . .

ALMA:

You decided it wasn't?

JOHN:

I went there tonight, but it wasn't you and me. . . . Fingers warm now?

ALMA:

Those tablets work quickly. I'm already feeling drowsy. [*She leans back with her eyes nearly shut.*] I'm beginning to feel almost like a water lily. A water lily on a Chinese lagoon.

[*A heavy iron bell strikes three.*]

ROSA:

Johnny?

[*Alma starts to rise.*]

ALMA:

I *must* go.

JOHN:

I will call for you Saturday night at eight o'clock.

ALMA:

What?

JOHN:

I'll give you this box of tablets but watch how you take them. Never more than one or two at a time.

ALMA:

Didn't you say something else a moment ago?

JOHN:

I said I would call for you at the Rectory Saturday night.

ALMA:

Oh . . .

JOHN:

Is that all right? [*Alma nods speechlessly. She remains with the box resting in the palm of her hand as if not knowing it was there. John gently closes her fingers on the box.*]

ALMA:

Oh! [*She laughs faintly.*]

ROSA [*outside*]:
Johnny!

JOHN:

Do you think you can find your way home, Miss Alma?

[*Rosa steps back into the office with a challenging look. Alma catches her breath sharply and goes out the side door.*

[*John reaches above him and turns out the light. He crosses to Rosa by the anatomy chart and takes her roughly in his arms. The light lingers on the chart as the interior dims out.*]

187

SCENE FIVE

In the Rectory.

Before the light comes up a soprano voice is heard singing "From the Land of the Sky Blue Waters."

As the curtain rises, Alma gets up from the piano. Mr. and Mrs. Winemiller, also, are in the lighted room.

ALMA:
What time is it, Father? [*He goes on writing. She raises her voice.*] What time is it, Father?

MR. WINEMILLER:
Five of eight. I'm working on my sermon.

ALMA:
Why don't you work in the study?

MR. WINEMILLER:.
The study is suffocating. So don't disturb me.

ALMA:
Would there be any chance of getting Mother upstairs if someone should call?

MR. WINEMILLER:
Are you expecting a caller?

ALMA:
Not expecting. There is just a chance of it.

MR. WINEMILLER:
Whom are you expecting?

ALMA:
I said I wasn't expecting anyone, that there was just a possibility . . .

MR. WINEMILLER:

Mr. Doremus? I thought that this was his evening with his mother?

ALMA:

Yes, it is his evening with his mother.

MR. WINEMILLER:

Then who is coming here, Alma?

ALMA:

Probably no one. Probably no one at all.

MR. WINEMILLER:

This is all very mysterious.

MRS. WINEMILLER:

That tall boy next door is coming to see her, that's who's coming to see her.

ALMA:

If you will go upstairs, Mother, I'll call the drug store and ask them to deliver a pint of fresh peach ice cream.

MRS. WINEMILLER:

I'll go upstairs when I'm ready—good and ready, and you can put that in your pipe and smoke it, Miss Winemiller!

[*She lights a cigarette. Mr. Winemiller turns slowly away with a profound sigh.*]

ALMA:

I may as well tell you who might call, so that if he calls there will not be any unpleasantness about it. Young Dr. John Buchanan said he might call.

MRS. WINEMILLER:

See!

MR. WINEMILLER:

You can't be serious.

MRS. WINEMILLER:

Didn't I tell you?

ALMA:

Well, I am.

MR. WINEMILLER:

That young man might come here?

ALMA:

He asked me if he might and I said, yes, if he wished to. But it is now after eight so it doesn't look like he's coming.

MR. WINEMILLER:

If he does come you will go upstairs to your room and I will receive him.

ALMA:

If he does come I'll do no such thing, Father.

MR. WINEMILLER:

You must be out of your mind.

ALMA:

I'll receive him myself. You may retire to your study and Mother upstairs. But if he comes I'll receive him. I don't judge people by the tongues of gossips. I happen to know that he has been grossly misjudged and misrepresented by old busybodies who're envious of his youth and brilliance and charm!

MR. WINEMILLER:

If you're not out of your senses, then I'm out of mine.

ALMA:

I daresay we're all a bit peculiar, Father. . . .

MR. WINEMILLER:

Well, I have had one almost insufferable cross to bear and perhaps I can bear another. But if you think I'm retiring into my study when this young man comes, probably with

190

a whiskey bottle in one hand and a pair of dice in the other,
you have another think coming. I'll sit right here and look
at him until he leaves. [*He turns back to his sermon.*]

[*A whistle is heard outside the open door.*]

ALMA [*speaking quickly*]:
As a matter of fact I think I'll walk down to the drugstore
and call for the ice cream myself. [*She crosses to the door,
snatching up her hat, gloves and veil.*]

MRS. WINEMILLER:
There she goes to him! Ha-ha! [*Alma rushes out.*]

MR. WINEMILLER [*looking up*]:
Alma! Alma!

MRS. WINEMILLER:
Ha-ha-haaaaa!

MR. WINEMILLER:
Where is Alma?—Alma! [*He rushes through the door.*]
Alma!

MRS. WINEMILLER:
Ha-ha! Who got fooled? Who got fooled! Ha-haaaa! Insufferable cross yourself, you old—windbag. . . .

[*The curtain comes down.*]

SCENE SIX

A delicately suggested arbor, enclosing a table and two chairs. Over the table is suspended a torn paper lantern. This tiny set may be placed way downstage in front of the two interiors, which should be darkened out, as in the fountain scenes. In the background, as it is throughout the play, the angel of the fountain is dimly visible.

Music from the nearby pavilion of the Casino can be used when suitable for background.

John's voice is audible before he and Alma enter.

JOHN [*from the darkness*]:
I don't understand why we can't go in the casino.

ALMA:
You do understand. You're just pretending not to.

JOHN:
Give me one reason.

ALMA [*coming into the arbor*]:
I am a minister's daughter.

JOHN:
That's no reason. [*He follows her in. He wears a white linen suit, carrying the coat over his arm.*]

ALMA:
You're a doctor. That's a better reason. You can't any more afford to be seen in such places than I can—less!

JOHN [*bellowing*]:
Dusty!

DUSTY [*from the darkness*]:
Coming!

JOHN:
What are you fishing in that pocketbook for?

ALMA:
Nothing.

JOHN:
What have you got there?

ALMA:
Let go!

JOHN:
Those sleeping tablets I gave you?

ALMA:
Yes.

JOHN:
What for?

ALMA:
I need one.

JOHN:
Now?

ALMA:
Yes.

JOHN:
Why?

ALMA:
Why? Because I nearly died of heart failure in your automobile. What possessed you to drive like that? A demon?

[*Dusty enters.*]

JOHN:
A bottle of vino rosso.

DUSTY:
Sure. [*He withdraws.*]

193

JOHN:

Hey! Tell Shorty I want to hear the "Yellow Dog Blues."

ALMA:

Please give me back my tablets.

JOHN:

You want to turn into a dope fiend taking this stuff? I said take one when you need one.

ALMA:

I need one now.

JOHN:

Sit down and stop swallowing air. [*Dusty returns with a tall wine bottle and two thin-stemmed glasses.*] When does the cock-fight start?

DUSTY:

'Bout ten o'clock, Dr. Johnny.

ALMA:

When does *what start?*

JOHN:

They have a cockfight here every Saturday night. Ever seen one?

ALMA:

Perhaps in some earlier incarnation of mine.

JOHN:

When you wore a brass ring in your nose?

ALMA:

Then maybe I went to exhibitions like that.

JOHN:

You're going to see one tonight.

ALMA:

Oh, no, I'm not.

JOHN:

That's what we came here for.

ALMA:

I didn't think such exhibitions were legal.

JOHN:

This is Moon Lake Casino where anything goes.

ALMA:

And you're a frequent patron?

JOHN:

I'd say constant.

ALMA:

Then I'm afraid you must be serious about giving up your medical career.

JOHN:

You bet I am! A doctor's life is walled in by sickness and misery and death.

ALMA:

May I be so presumptuous as to inquire what you'll do when you quit?

JOHN:

You may be so presumptuous as to inquire.

ALMA:

But you won't tell me?

JOHN:

I haven't made up my mind, but I've been thinking of South America lately.

ALMA [*sadly*]:

Oh . . .

JOHN:

I've heard that cantinas are lots more fun than saloons, and senoritas are caviar among females.

195

ALMA:

Dorothy Sykes' brother went to South America and was never heard of again. It takes a strong character to survive in the tropics. Otherwise it's a quagmire.

JOHN:

You think my character's weak?

ALMA:

I think you're confused, just awfully, awfully confused, as confused as I am—but in a different way. . . .

JOHN [*stretching out his legs*]:

Hee-haw, ho-hum.

ALMA:

You used to say that as a child—to signify your disgust!

JOHN [*grinning*]:

Did I?

ALMA [*sharply*]:

Don't sit like that!

JOHN:

Why not?

ALMA:

You look so indolent and worthless.

JOHN:

Maybe I am.

ALMA:

If you must go somewhere, why don't you choose a place with a bracing climate?

JOHN:

Parts of South America are as cool as a cucumber.

ALMA:

I never knew that.

JOHN:

Well, now you do.

ALMA:

Those Latins all dream in the sun—and indulge their senses.

JOHN:

Well, it's yet to be proven that anyone on this earth is crowned with so much glory as the one that uses his senses to get all he can in the way of—satisfaction.

ALMA:

Self-satisfaction?

JOHN:

What other kind is there?

ALMA:

I will answer that question by asking you one. Have you ever seen, or looked at a picture, of a Gothic cathedral?

JOHN:

Gothic cathedrals? What about them?

ALMA:

How everything reaches up, how everything seems to be straining for something out of the reach of stone—or human —fingers? . . . The immense stained windows, the great arched doors that are five or six times the height of the tallest man—the vaulted ceiling and all the delicate spires— all reaching up to something beyond attainment! To me— well, that is the secret, the principle back of existence—the everlasting struggle and aspiration for more than our human limits have placed in our reach. . . . Who was that said that—oh, so beautiful thing!—"All of us are in the gutter, but some of us are looking at the stars!"

JOHN:

Mr. Oscar Wilde.

ALMA [*somewhat taken aback*]:
Well, regardless of who said it, it's still true. Some of us are looking at the stars! [*She looks up raptly and places her hand over his.*]

JOHN:
It's no fun holding hands with gloves on, Miss Alma.

ALMA:
That's easily remedied. I'll just take the gloves off. [*Music is heard.*]

JOHN:
Christ! [*He rises abruptly and lights a cigarette.*] Rosa Gonzales is dancing in the casino.

ALMA:
You *are* unhappy. You hate me for depriving you of the company inside. Well, you'll escape by and by. You'll drive me home and come back out by yourself. . . . I've only gone out with three young men at all seriously, and with each one there was a desert between us.

JOHN:
What do you mean by a desert?

ALMA:
Oh—wide, wide stretches of uninhabitable ground.

JOHN:
Maybe you made it that way by being standoffish.

ALMA:
I made quite an effort with one or two of them.

JOHN:
What kind of an effort?

ALMA:
Oh, I—tried to entertain them the first few times. I would play and sing for them in the Rectory parlor.

JOHN:

With your father in the next room and the door half open?

ALMA:

I don't think that was the trouble.

JOHN:

What was the trouble?

ALMA:

I—I didn't have my heart in it. [*She laughs uncertainly.*]
A silence would fall between us. You know, a silence?

JOHN:

Yes, I know a silence.

ALMA:

I'd try to talk and he'd try to talk and neither would make
a go of it.

JOHN:

The silence would fall?

ALMA:

Yes, the enormous silence.

JOHN:

Then you'd go back to the piano?

ALMA:

I'd twist my ring. Sometimes I twisted it so hard that the
band cut my finger! He'd glance at his watch and we'd
both know that the useless undertaking had come to a
close. . . .

JOHN:

You'd call it quits?

ALMA:

Quits is—what we'd call it. . . . One or two times I was
rather sorry about it.

199

JOHN:

But you didn't have your heart in it?

ALMA:

None of them really engaged my serious feelings.

JOHN:

You do have serious feelings—of that kind?

ALMA:

Doesn't everyone—sometimes?

JOHN:

Some women are cold. Some women are what is called frigid.

ALMA:

Do I give that impression?

JOHN:

Under the surface you have a lot of excitement, a great deal more than any other woman I have met. So much that you have to carry these sleeping pills with you. The question is why? [*He leans over and lifts her veil.*]

ALMA:

What are you doing that for?

JOHN:

So that I won't get your veil in my mouth when I kiss you.

ALMA [*faintly*]:

Do you want to do that?

JOHN [*gently*]:

Miss Alma. [*He takes her arms and draws her to her feet.*] Oh, Miss Alma, Miss Alma! [*He kisses her.*]

ALMA [*in a low, shaken voice*]:

Not "Miss" any more. Just Alma.

JOHN [*grinning gently*]:

"Miss" suits you better, Miss Alma. [*He kisses her again. She hesitantly touches his shoulders, but not quite to push him away. John speaks softly to her.*] Is it so hard to forget you're a preacher's daughter?

ALMA:

There is no reason for me to forget that I am a minister's daughter. A minister's daughter's no different from any other young lady who tries to remember that she *is* a lady.

JOHN:

This lady stuff, is that so important?

ALMA:

Not to the sort of girls that you may be used to bringing to Moon Lake Casino. But suppose that some day . . . [*She crosses out of the arbor and faces away from him.*] suppose that some day you—*married. . . .* The woman that you selected to be your wife, and not only your wife but—the mother of your children! [*She catches her breath at the thought.*] Wouldn't you want that woman to be a lady? Wouldn't you want her to be somebody that you, as her husband, and they as her precious children—could look up to with very deep respect? [*There is a pause.*]

JOHN:

There's other things between a man and a woman besides respect. Did you know that, Miss Alma?

ALMA:

Yes. . . .

JOHN:

There's such a thing as intimate relations.

ALMA:

Thank you for telling me that. So plainly.

JOHN:

It may strike you as unpleasant. But it does have a good

201

deal to do with—connubial felicity, as you'd call it. There are some women that just give in to a man as a sort of obligation imposed on them by the—cruelty of nature! [*He finishes his glass and pours another.*] And there you are.

ALMA:
There *I* am?

JOHN:
I'm speaking generally.

ALMA:
Oh.

[*Hoarse shouts go up from the casino.*]

JOHN:
The cockfight has started!

ALMA:
Since you have spoken so plainly, I'll speak plainly, too. There are some women who turn a possibly beautiful thing into something no better than the coupling of beasts!—but love is what you bring to it.

JOHN:
You're right about that.

ALMA:
Some people bring just their bodies. But there are some people, there are some women, John—who can bring their hearts to it, also—who can bring their souls to it!

JOHN [*derisively*]:
Souls again, huh?—those Gothic cathedrals you dream of!

[*There is another hoarse prolonged shout from the casino.*]

Your name is Alma and Alma is Spanish for soul. Sometime I'd like to show you a chart of the human anatomy that I have in the office. It shows what our insides are like, and maybe you can show me where the beautiful soul is located on the chart. [*He drains the wine bottle.*] Let's go watch the cockfight.

ALMA:

No! [*There is a pause.*]

JOHN:

I know something else we could do. There are rooms above the casino . . .

ALMA [*her back stiffening*]:

I'd heard that you made suggestions like that to girls that you go out with, but I refused to believe such stories were true. What made you think I might be amenable to such a suggestion?

JOHN:

I counted your pulse in the office the night you ran out because you weren't able to sleep.

ALMA:

The night I was ill and went to your father for help.

JOHN:

It was me you went to.

ALMA:

It was your father, and you wouldn't call your father.

JOHN:

Fingers frozen stiff when I . . .

ALMA [*rising*]:

Oh! I want to go home. But I won't go with you. I will go in a taxi! [*She wheels about hysterically.*] Boy! Boy! Call a taxi!

JOHN:

I'll call one for you, Miss Alma.—Taxi! [*He goes out of the arbor.*]

ALMA [*wildly*]:
You're not a gentleman!

JOHN [*from the darkness*]:
Taxi!

ALMA:
You're not a gentleman!

[*As he disappears she makes a sound in her throat like a hurt animal. The light fades out of the arbor and comes up more distinctly on the stone angel of the fountain.*]

PART TWO

A WINTER

SCENE SEVEN

*The sky and the southern constellations, almost impercep-
tibly moving with the earth's motion, appear on the great
cyclorama.*

*The Rectory interior is lighted first, disclosing Alma and
Roger Doremus seated on the green plush sofa under the
romantic landscape in its heavy gilt frame. On a tiny table
beside them is a cut-glass pitcher of lemonade with cherries
and orange slices in it, like a little aquarium of tropical fish.
Roger is entertaining Alma with a collection of photographs
and post cards, mementos of his mother's trip to the Orient.
He is enthusiastic about them and describes them in phrases
his mother must have assimilated from a sedulous study of
literature provided by Cook's Tours. Alma is less enthusiastic; she is preoccupied with the sounds of a wild party
going on next door at the doctor's home. At present there is
Mexican music with shouts and stamping.*

*Only the immediate area of the sofa is clearly lighted; the
fountain is faintly etched in light and the night sky walls
the interior.*

ROGER:
And this is Ceylon, The Pearl of the Orient!

ALMA:
And who is this fat young lady?

ROGER:
That is Mother in a hunting costume.

ALMA:
The hunting costume makes her figure seem bulky. What
was your mother hunting?

ROGER [*gaily*]:

Heaven knows what she was hunting! But she found Papa.

ALMA:

Oh, she met your father on this Oriental tour?

ROGER:

Ha-ha!—yes. . . . He was returning from India with dysentery and they met on the boat.

ALMA [*distastefully*]:

Oh . . .

ROGER:

And here she is on top of a ruined temple!

ALMA:

How did she get up there?

ROGER:

Climbed up, I suppose.

ALMA:

What an active woman.

ROGER:

Oh, yes, active—is no word for it! Here she is on an elephant's back in Burma.

ALMA:

Ah!

ROGER:

You're looking at it upside down, Miss Alma!

ALMA:

Deliberately—to tease you. [*The doorbell rings.*] Perhaps that's your mother coming to fetch you home.

ROGER:

It's only ten-fifteen. I never leave till ten-thirty.

[*Mrs. Bassett comes in.*]

ALMA:

Mrs. Bassett!

MRS. BASSETT:

I was just wondering who I could turn to when I saw the Rectory light and I thought to myself, Grace Bassett, you trot yourself right over there and talk to Mr. Winemiller!

ALMA:

Father has retired.

MRS. BASSETT:

Oh, what a pity. [*She sees Roger.*] Hello, Roger! . . . I saw that fall your mother took this morning. I saw her come skipping out of the Delta Planters' Bank and I thought to myself, now isn't that remarkable, a woman of her age and weight so light on her feet? And just at that very moment— *down she went!* I swear to goodness I thought she had broken her hip! Was she bruised much?

ROGER:

Just shaken up, Mrs. Bassett.

MRS. BASSETT:

Oh, how lucky! She certainly must be made out of India rubber! [*She turns to Alma.*] Alma—Alma, if it is not too late for human intervention, your father's the one right person to call up old Dr. Buchanan at the fever clinic at Lyon and let him know!

ALMA:

About—what?

MRS. BASSETT:

You must be stone-deaf if you haven't noticed what's been going on next door since the old doctor left to fight the epidemic. One continual orgy! Well, not five minutes ago a friend of mine who works at the County Courthouse called

209

to inform me that young Dr. John and Rosa Gonzales have taken a license out and are going to be married tomorrow!

ALMA:

Are you—quite certain?

MRS. BASSETT:

Certain? I'm always certain before I speak!

ALMA:

Why would he—do such a thing?

MRS. BASSETT:

August madness! They say it has something to do with the falling stars. Of course it might also have something to do with the fact that he lost two or three thousand dollars at the casino which he can't pay except by giving himself to Gonzales' daughter. [*She turns to Alma.*] Alma, what are you doing with that picture puzzle?

ALMA [*with a faint, hysterical laugh*]:

The pieces don't fit!

MRS. BASSETT [*to Roger*]:

I shouldn't have opened my mouth.

ALMA:

Will both of you please go!

[*Roger goes out.*]

MRS. BASSETT:

I knew this was going to upset you. Good night, Alma. [*She leaves. Alma suddenly springs up and seizes the telephone.*]

ALMA:

Long distance. . . . Please get me the fever clinic at Lyon, . . . I want to speak to Dr. Buchanan.

[*The light in the Rectory dims out and light comes on in the doctor's office. Rosa's voice is heard calling.*]

210

ROSA:

Johnny!

[*The offstage calling of John's name is used throughout the play as a cue for theme music.*]

[*John enters the office interior. He is dressed, as always, in a white linen suit. His face has a look of satiety and confusion. He throws himself down in a swivel chair at the desk.*]

[*Rosa Gonzales comes in. She is dressed in a Flamenco costume and has been dancing. She crosses and stands before the anatomy chart and clicks her castanets to catch his attention, but he remains looking up at the roofless dark. She approaches him.*]

ROSA:

You have blood on your face!

JOHN:

You bit my ear.

ROSA:

Ohhh . . . [*She approaches him with exaggerated concern.*]

JOHN:

You never make love without scratching or biting or something. Whenever I leave you I have a little blood on me. Why is that?

ROSA:

Because I know I can't hold you.

JOHN:

I think you're doing a pretty good job of it. Better than anyone else. Tomorrow we leave here together and Father or somebody else can tell old Mrs. Arbuckle her eighty-five years are enough and she's got to go now on the wings of carcinoma. Dance, Rosa! [*Accordion music is heard. She*

211

performs a slow and joyless dance around his chair. John continues while she dances.] Tomorrow we leave here together. We sail out of Galveston, don't we?

ROSA:
You say it but I don't believe it.

JOHN:
I have the tickets.

ROSA:
Two pieces of paper that you can tear in two.

JOHN:
We'll go all right, and live on fat remittances from your Papa! Ha-ha!

ROSA:
Ha-ha-ha!

JOHN:
Not long ago the idea would have disgusted me, but not now. [*He catches her by the wrist.*] Rosa! Rosa Gonzales! Did anyone ever slide downhill as fast as I have this summer? Ha-ha! Like a greased pig. And yet every evening I put on a clean white suit. I have a dozen. Six in the closet and six in the wash. And there isn't a sign of depravity in my face. And yet all summer I've sat around here like *this,* remembering last night, anticipating the next one! The trouble with me is, I should have been *castrated!* [*He flings his wineglass at the anatomy chart. She stops dancing.*] Dance, Rosa! Why don't you dance? [*Rosa shakes her head dumbly.*] What is the matter, Rosa? Why don't you go on dancing? [*The accordion continues; he thrusts her arm savagely over her head in the Flamenco position.*]

ROSA [*suddenly weeping*]:
I can't dance any more! [*She throws herself to the floor,*

212

*pressing her weeping face to his knees. The voice of her
father is heard, bellowing, in the next room.*]

GONZALES:
The sky is the limit!

[*John is sobered.*]

JOHN:
Why does your father want me for a son-in-law?

ROSA [*sobbing*]:
I want you—I, I want you!

JOHN [*raising her from the floor*]:
Why do you?

ROSA [*clinging to him*]:
Maybe because—I was born in Piedras Negras, and grew
up in a one-room house with a dirt floor, and all of us had
to sleep in that one room, five Mexicans and three geese
and a little gamecock named Pepe! Ha-Ha! [*She laughs
hysterically.*] Pepe was a good fighter! That's how Papa
began to make money, winning bets on Pepe! Ha-ha! We
all slept in the one room. And in the night, I would hear
the love-making. Papa would grunt like a pig to show his
passion. I thought to myself, how dirty it was, love-making,
and how dirty it was to be Mexicans and all have to sleep
in one room with a dirt floor and not smell good because
there was not any bathtub! [*The accordion continues.*]

JOHN:
What has that got to do with . . . ?

ROSA:
Me wanting you? You're tall! You smell good! And, oh,
I'm so glad that you never grunt like a pig to show your
passion! [*She embraces him convulsively.*] Ah, but *quien*

sabe! Something might happen tonight, and I'll wind up with some dark little friend of Papa's.

GONZALES [*imperiously*]:
Rosa! Rosa!

ROSA:
Si, si, Papa, aqui estoy!

GONZALES [*entering unsteadily*]:
The gold beads . . . [*He fingers a necklace of gold beads that Rosa is wearing.*] Johnny . . . [*He staggers up to John and catches him in a drunken embrace.*] Listen! When my girl Rosa was little she see a string a gold bead and she want those gold bead so bad that she cry all night for it. I don' have money to buy a string a gold bead so next day I go for a ride up to Eagle Pass and I walk in a dry good store and I say to the man: "Please give me a string a gold bead." He say: "Show me the money," and I say: "Here is the money!" And I reach down to my belt and I pull out—not the money—but this! [*He pulls out a revolver.*] Now—now I have money, but I still have this! [*laughing*] She got the gold bead. Anything that she want I get for her with this [*He pulls out a roll of bills.*] or this! [*He waves the revolver.*]

JOHN [*pushing Gonzales away*]:
Keep your stinking breath out of my face, Gonzales!

ROSA:
Dejalo, dejalo, Papa!

GONZALES [*moving unsteadily to the couch, with Rosa supporting him*]:
Le doy la tierra y si la tierra no basta—le doy el cielo! [*He collapses onto the couch.*] The sky is the limit!

ROSA [*to John*]:
Let him stay there. Come on back to the party.

[*Rosa leaves the room. John goes over to the window facing the Rectory and looks across. The light comes up in the Rectory living room as Alma enters, dressed in a robe. She goes to the window and looks across at the doctor's house. As Alma and John stand at the windows looking toward each other through the darkness music is heard. Slowly, as if drawn by the music, John walks out of his house and crosses over to the Rectory. Alma remains motionless at the window until John enters the room, behind her. The music dies away and there is a murmur of wind. She slowly turns to face John.*]

JOHN:

I took the open door for an invitation. The Gulf wind is blowing tonight . . . cools things off a little. But my head's on fire. . . . [*Alma says nothing. John moves a few steps toward her.*] The silence? [*Alma sinks onto the love seat, closing her eyes.*] Yes, the enormous silence. [*He goes over to her.*] I will go in a minute, but first I want you to put your hands on my face. . . . [*He crouches beside her.*] Eternity and Miss Alma have such cool hands. [*He buries his face in her lap. The attitude suggests a stone Pietà. Alma's eyes remain closed.*]

[*On the other side of the stage Dr. Buchanan enters his house and the light builds a little as he looks around in the door of his office. The love theme music fades out and the Mexican music comes up strongly, with a definitely ominous quality, as Rosa enters the office from the other side.*]

ROSA:

Johnny! [*She catches sight of Dr. Buchanan and checks herself in surprise.*] Oh! I thought you were Johnny! . . . But you are Johnny's father. . . . I'm Rosa Gonzales!

215

DR. BUCHANAN:

I know who you are. What's going on in my house?

ROSA [*nervously*]:

John's giving a party because we're leaving tomorrow. [*defiantly*] Yes! Together! I hope you like the idea, but if you don't, it don't matter, because *we* like the idea and my father likes the idea.

GONZALES [*drunkenly, sitting up on the couch*]:
The sky is the limit!

[*Dr. Buchanan slowly raises his silver-headed cane in a threatening gesture.*]

DR. BUCHANAN:

Get your—swine out of—my house! [*He strikes Gonzales with his cane.*]

GONZALES [*staggering up from the couch in pain and surprise*]:
Aieeeee!

ROSA [*breathlessly, backing against the chart of anatomy*]:
No! No, Papa!

DR. BUCHANAN [*striking at the chest of the bull-like man with his cane*]:
Get your swine out, I said! Get them out of my house!

[*He repeats the blow. The drunken Mexican roars with pain and surprise. He backs up and reaches under his coat.*]

ROSA [*wildly and despairingly*]:
No, no, no, no, no, no!

[*She covers her face against the chart of anatomy. A revolver is fired. There is a burst of light. The cane drops. The music stops short. Everything dims out but a spot of light on Rosa standing against the chart of anatomy with closed eyes and her face twisted like that of a tragic mask.]*

ROSA [*senselessly*]:
Aaaaaahhhhhh . . . Aaaaaahhhhhh . . .

[*The theme music is started faintly and light disappears from everything but the wings of the stone angel.*]

SCENE EIGHT

The doctor's office.

The stone angel is dimly visible above.

John is seated in a hunched position at the table. Alma enters with a coffee tray. The sounds of a prayer come through the inner door.

JOHN:

What is that mumbo jumbo your father is spouting in there?

ALMA:

A prayer.

JOHN:

Tell him to quit. We don't want that worn-out magic.

ALMA:

You may not want it, but it's not a question of what you want any more. I've made you some coffee.

JOHN:

I don't want any.

ALMA:

Lean back and let me wash your face off, John. [*She presses a towel to the red marks on his face.*] It's such a fine face, a fine and sensitive face, a face that has power in it that shouldn't be wasted.

JOHN:

Never mind that. [*He pushes her hand away.*]

ALMA:

You have to go in to see him.

JOHN:

I couldn't. He wouldn't want me.

ALMA:

This happened because of his devotion to you.

JOHN:

It happened because some meddlesome Mattie called him back here tonight. Who was it did that?

ALMA:

I did.

JOHN:

It *was* you then!

ALMA:

I phoned him at the fever clinic in Lyon as soon as I learned what you were planning to do. I wired him to come here and stop it.

JOHN:

You brought him here to be shot.

ALMA:

You can't put the blame on anything but your weakness.

JOHN:

You call me weak?

ALMA:

Sometimes it takes a tragedy like this to make a weak person strong.

JOHN:

You—white-blooded spinster! You so right people, pious pompous mumblers, preachers and preacher's daughter, all muffled up in a lot of worn-out magic! And I was supposed to minister to your neurosis, give you tablets for sleeping and tonics to give you the strength to go on mumbling your worn-out mumbo jumbo!

219

ALMA:
Call me whatever you want, but don't let your father hear your drunken shouting. [*She tries to break away from him.*]

JOHN:
Stay here! I want you to look at something. [*He turns her about.*] This chart of anatomy, look!

ALMA:
I've seen it before. [*She turns away.*]

JOHN:
You've never dared to look at it.

ALMA:
Why should I?

JOHN:
You're scared to.

ALMA:
You must be out of your senses.

JOHN:
You talk about weakness but can't even look at a picture of human insides.

ALMA:
They're not important.

JOHN:
That's your mistake. You think you're stuffed with rose leaves. Turn around and look at it, it may do you good!

ALMA:
How can you behave like this with your father dying and you so . . .

JOHN:
Hold still!

ALMA:

. . . so much to blame for it!

JOHN:

No more than you are!

ALMA:

At least for this little while . . .

JOHN:

Look here!

ALMA:

. . you could feel some shame!

JOHN [*with crazy, grinning intensity*]:

Now listen here to the anatomy lecture! This upper story's the brain which is hungry for something called truth and doesn't get much but keeps on feeling hungry! This middle's the belly which is hungry for food. This part down here is the sex which is hungry for love because it is sometimes lonesome. I've fed all three, as much of all three as I could or as much as I wanted— You've fed none—nothing. Well—maybe your belly a little—watery subsistence— But love or truth, nothing but—nothing but hand-me-down notions!—attitudes!—poses! [*He releases her.*] Now you can go. The anatomy lecture is over.

ALMA:

So that is your high conception of human desires. What you have here is not the anatomy of a beast, but a man. And I —I reject your opinion of where love is, and the kind of truth you believe the brain to be seeking!—There is something not shown on the chart.

JOHN:

You mean the part that Alma is Spanish for, do you?

ALMA:

Yes, that's not shown on the anatomy chart! But it's there,

221

just the same, yes, there! Somewhere, not seen, but there. And it's *that* that I loved you with—that! Not what you mention!—Yes, did love you with, John, did nearly *die* of when you hurt me! [*He turns slowly to her and speaks gently.*]

JOHN:
I wouldn't have made love to you.

ALMA [*uncomprehendingly*]:
What?

JOHN:
The night at the casino—I wouldn't have made love to you. Even if you had consented to go upstairs. I couldn't have made love to you. [*She stares at him as if anticipating some unbearable hurt.*] Yes, yes! Isn't that funny? I'm more afraid of your soul than you're afraid of my body. You'd have been as safe as the angel of the fountain—because I wouldn't feel *decent* enough to touch you. . . .

[*Mr. Winemiller comes in.*]

MR. WINEMILLER:
He's resting more easily now.

ALMA:
Oh . . . [*She nods her head. John reaches for his coffee cup.*] It's cold. I'll heat it.

JOHN:
It's all right.

MR. WINEMILLER:
Alma, Dr. John wants you.

ALMA:
I . . .

MR. WINEMILLER:
He asked if you would sing for him.

ALMA:

I—couldn't—now.

JOHN:

Go in and sing to him, Miss Alma!

[*Mr. Winemiller withdraws through the outer door. Alma looks back at John hunched over the coffee cup. He doesn't return her look. She passes into the blurred orange space beyond the inner door, leaving it slightly open. After a few minutes her voice rises softly within, singing. John suddenly rises. He crosses to the door, shoves it slowly open and enters.*]

JOHN [*softly and with deep tenderness*]:

Father?

[*The light dims out in the house, but lingers on the stone angel.*]

SCENE NINE

The cyclorama is the faint blue of a late afternoon in autumn. There is band music—a Sousa march, in the distance. As it grows somewhat louder, Alma enters the Rectory interior in a dressing gown and with her hair hanging loose. She looks as if she had been through a long illness, the intensity drained, her pale face listless. She crosses to the window frame but the parade is not in sight so she returns weakly to the sofa and sits down closing her eyes with exhaustion.

The Rev. and Mrs. Winemiller enter the outer door frame of the Rectory, a grotesque-looking couple. Mrs. Winemiller has on her plumed hat, at a rakish angle, and a brilliant scarf about her throat. Her face wears a roguish smile that suggests a musical comedy pirate. One hand holds the minister's arm and with the other she is holding an ice cream cone.

MR. WINEMILLER:
Now you may let go of my arm, if you please! She was on her worst behavior. Stopped in front of the White Star Pharmacy on Front Street and stood there like a mule; wouldn't budge till I bought her an ice cream cone. I had it wrapped in tissue paper because she had promised me that she wouldn't eat it until we got home. The moment I gave it to her she tore off the paper and walked home licking it every step of the way!—just—just to humiliate me! [*Mrs. Winemiller offers him the half-eaten cone, saying "Lick?"*]

MR. WINEMILLER:
No, thank you!

ALMA:

Now, now, children.

[*Mr. Winemiller's irritation shifts to Alma.*]

MR. WINEMILLER:

Alma! Why don't you get dressed? It hurts me to see you sitting around like this, day in, day out, like an invalid when there is nothing particularly wrong with you. I can't read your mind. You may have had some kind of disappointment, but you must not make it an excuse for acting as if the world had come to an end.

ALMA:

I have made the beds and washed the breakfast dishes and phoned the market and sent the laundry out and peeled the potatoes and shelled the peas and set the table for lunch. What more do you want?

MR. WINEMILLER [*sharply*]:

I want you to either get dressed or stay in your room. [*Alma rises indifferently, then her father speaks suddenly.*] At night you get dressed. Don't you? Yes, I heard you slipping out of the house at two in the morning. And that was not the first time.

ALMA:

I don't sleep well. Sometimes I have to get up and walk for a while before I am able to sleep.

MR. WINEMILLER:

What am I going to tell people who ask about you?

ALMA:

Tell them I've changed and you're waiting to see in what way.

[*The band music becomes a little louder.*]

MR. WINEMILLER:

Are you going to stay like this indefinitely?

ALMA:

Not indefinitely, but you may wish that I had.

MR. WINEMILLER:

Stop twisting that ring! Whenever I look at you you're twisting that ring. Give me that ring! I'm going to take that ring off your finger! [*He catches her wrist. She breaks roughly away from him.*]

MRS. WINEMILLER [*joyfully*]:

Fight! Fight!

MR. WINEMILLER:

Oh, I give up!

ALMA:

That's better. [*She suddenly crosses to the window as the band music gets louder.*] Is there a parade in town?

MRS. WINEMILLER:

Ha-ha—yes! They met him at the station with a great big silver loving cup!

ALMA:

Who? Who did they . . . ?

MRS. WINEMILLER:

That boy next door, the one you watched all the time!

ALMA:

Is that true, Father?

MR. WINEMILLER [*unfolding his newspaper*]:

Haven't you looked at the papers?

ALMA:

No, not lately.

MR. WINEMILLER [*wiping his eyeglasses*]:

These people are grasshoppers, just as likely to jump one

way as another. He's finished the work his father started, stamped out the fever and gotten all of the glory. Well, that's how it is in this world. Years of devotion and sacrifice are overlooked an' forgotten while someone young an' lucky walks off with the honors!

[*Alma has crossed slowly to the window. The sun brightens and falls in a shaft through the frame.*]

ALMA [*suddenly crying out*]:
There he is! [*She staggers away from the window. There is a roll of drums and then silence. Alma now speaks faintly.*] What . . . happened? Something . . . struck me! [*Mr. Winemiller catches her arm to support her.*]

MR. WINEMILLER:
Alma . . . I'll call a doctor.

ALMA:
No, no, don't. Don't call anybody to help me. I want to die!

[*She collapses on the sofa.*]

[*The band strikes up again and recedes down the street. The Rectory interior dims out. Then the light is brought up in the doctor's office. John enters, with his loving cup. He is sprucely dressed and his whole manner suggests a new-found responsibility. While he is setting the award on the table, removing his coat and starched collar, Nellie Ewell appears in the door behind him. She stands by the anatomy chart and watches him until he discovers her presence. Nellie has abruptly grown up, and wears very adult clothes, but has lost none of her childish impudence and brightness. John gives a startled whistle as he sees her. Nellie giggles.*]

JOHN:
High heels, feathers . . . and paint!

NELLIE:
Not paint!

JOHN:
Natural color?

NELLIE:
Excitement.

JOHN:
Over what?

NELLIE:
Everything! You! You here! Didn't you see me at the depot? I shouted and waved my arm off! I'm home for Thanksgiving.

JOHN:
From where?

NELLIE:
Sophie Newcomb's. [*He remains staring at her, unbelieving. At last she draws a book from under her arm.*] Here is that nasty book you gave me last summer when I was pretending such ignorance of things!

JOHN:
Only pretending?

NELLIE:
Yes. [*He ignores the book. She tosses it on the table.*] ... Well? [*John laughs uneasily and sits on the table.*] Shall I go now, or will you look at my tongue? [*She crosses to him, sticking out her tongue.*]

JOHN:
Red as a berry!

NELLIE:
Peppermint drops! Will you have one? [*She holds out a sack.*]

JOHN:
Thanks. [*Nellie giggles as he takes one.*] What's the joke, Nellie?

NELLIE:
They make your mouth so sweet!

JOHN:
So?

NELLIE:
I always take one when I hope to be kissed.

JOHN [*after a pause*]:
Suppose I took you up on that?

NELLIE:
I'm not scared. Are you?

[*He gives her a quick kiss. She clings to him, raising her hand to press his head against her own. He breaks free after a moment and turns the light back on.*]

JOHN [*considerably impressed*]:
Where did you learn such tricks?

NELLIE:
I've been away to school. But they didn't teach me to love.

JOHN:
Who are you to be using that long word?

NELLIE:
That isn't a long word!

JOHN:
No?[*He turns away from her.*] Run along Nellie before we get into trouble.

NELLIE:
Who's afraid of trouble, you or me?

JOHN:

I am. Run along! Hear me?

NELLIE:

Oh, I'll go. But I'll be back for Christmas!

[*She laughs and runs out. He whistles and wipes his fore-head with a handkerchief.*]

SCENE TEN

An afternoon in December. At the fountain in the park. It is very windy.

Alma enters. She seems to move with an effort against the wind. She sinks down on the bench.

A widow with a flowing black veil passes across the stage and pauses by Alma's bench. It is Mrs. Bassett.

MRS. BASSETT:
Hello Alma.

ALMA:
Good afternoon, Mrs. Bassett.

MRS. BASSETT:
Such wind, such wind!

ALMA:
Yes, it nearly swept me off my feet. I had to sit down to catch my breath for a moment.

MRS. BASSETT:
I wouldn't sit too long if I were you.

ALMA:
No, not long.

MRS. BASSETT:
It's good to see you out again after your illness.

ALMA:
Thank you.

MRS. BASSETT:
Our poor little group broke up after you dropped out.

ALMA [*insincerely*]:
What a pity.

MRS. BASSETT:

You should have come to the last meeting.

ALMA:

Why, what happened?

MRS. BASSETT:

Vernon read his verse play!

ALMA:

Ah, how was it received?

MRS. BASSETT:

Maliciously, spitefully and vindictively torn to pieces, the way children tear the wings off butterflies. I think next spring we might reorganize. [*She throws up her black-gloved hands in a deploring gesture.*]

[*Nellie Ewell appears. She is dressed very fashionably and carrying a fancy basket of Christmas packages.*]

NELLIE:

Miss Alma!

MRS. BASSETT [*rushing off*]:

Goodbye!

NELLIE:

Oh, there you are!

ALMA:

Why Nellie . . . Nellie Ewell!

NELLIE:

I was by the Rectory. Just popped in for a second; the holidays are so short that every minute is precious. They told me you'd gone to the park.

ALMA:

This is the first walk I've taken in quite a while.

NELLIE:

You've been ill!

ALMA:

Not ill, just not very well. How you've grown up, Nellie.

NELLIE:

It's just my clothes. Since I went off to Sophie Newcombe I've picked out my own clothes, Miss Alma. When Mother had jurisdiction over my wardrobe, she tried to keep me looking like a child!

ALMA:

Your voice is grown-up, too.

NELLIE:

They're teaching me diction, Miss Alma. I'm learning to talk like you, long A's and everything, such as "cahn't" and "bahth" and "lahf" instead of "laugh." Yesterday I slipped. I said I "lahfed and lahfed till I nearly died laughing." Johnny was so amused at me!

ALMA:

Johnny?

NELLIE:

Your next-door neighbor!

ALMA:

Oh! I'm sure it must be a very fashionable school.

NELLIE:

Oh yes, they're preparing us to be young ladies in society. What a pity there's no society here to be a young lady in . . . at least not for me, with Mother's reputation!

ALMA:

You'll find other fields to conquer.

NELLIE:

What's this I hear about *you?*

ALMA:

I have no idea, Nellie.

NELLIE:

That you've quit teaching singing and gone into retirement.

ALMA:

Naturally I had to stop teaching while I was ill and as for retiring from the world . . . it's more a case of the world retiring from me.

NELLIE:

I know somebody whose feelings you've hurt badly.

ALMA:

Why, who could that be, Nellie?

NELLIE:

Somebody who regards you as an angel!

ALMA:

I can't think who might hold me in such esteem.

NELLIE:

Somebody who says that you refused to see him.

ALMA:

I saw nobody. For several months. The long summer wore me out so.

NELLIE:

Well, anyhow, I'm going to give you your present. [*She hands her a small package from the basket.*]

ALMA:

Nellie, you shouldn't have given me anything.

NELLIE:

I'd like to know why not!

ALMA:

I didn't expect it.

NELLIE:

After the trouble you took with my horrible voice?

ALMA:
It's very sweet of you, Nellie.

NELLIE:
Open it!

ALMA:
Now?

NELLIE:
Why, sure.

ALMA:
It's so prettily wrapped I hate to undo it.

NELLIE:
I love to wrap presents and since it was for you, I did a specially dainty job of it.

ALMA [*winding the ribbon about her fingers*]:
I'm going to save this ribbon. I'm going to keep this lovely paper too, with the silver stars on it. And the sprig of holly . . .

NELLIE:
Let me pin it on your jacket, Alma.

ALMA:
Yes, do. I hardly realized that Christmas was coming. . . . [*She unfolds the paper, revealing a lace handkerchief and a card.*] What an exquisite handkerchief.

NELLIE:
I hate to give people handkerchiefs, it's so unimaginative.

ALMA:
I love to get them.

NELLIE:
It comes from Maison Blanche!

ALMA:
Oh, does it really?

235

NELLIE:
Smell it!

ALMA:
Sachet *Roses!* Well, I'm just more touched and pleased than I can possibly tell you!

NELLIE:
The card!

ALMA:
Card?

NELLIE:
You dropped it. [*She snatches up the card and hands it to Alma.*]

ALMA:
Oh, how clumsy of me! Thank you, Nellie. "Joyeux Noel ... to Alma ... from Nellie and ... [*She looks up slowly.*] *John?*"

NELLIE:
He helped me wrap presents last night and when we came to yours we started talking about you. Your ears must have burned!

[*The wind blows loudly. Alma bends stiffly forward.*]

ALMA:
You mean you—spoke well of me?

NELLIE:
"Well of"! We raved, simply raved! Oh, he told me the influence you'd had on him!

ALMA:
Influence?

NELLIE:
He told me about the wonderful talks he'd had with you

236

last summer when he was so mixed up and how you in-
spired him and you more than anyone else was responsible
for his pulling himself together, after his father was killed,
and he told me about . . . [*Alma rises stiffly from the
bench.*] Where are you going, Miss Alma?

ALMA:
To drink at the fountain.

NELLIE:
He told me about how you came in the house that night
like an angel of mercy!

ALMA [*laughing harshly by the fountain*]:
This is the only angel in Glorious Hill. [*She bends to
drink.*] Her body is stone and her blood is mineral water.

[*The wind is louder.*]

NELLIE:
How penetrating the wind is!

ALMA:
I'm going home, Nellie. You run along and deliver your
presents now. . . . [*She starts away.*]

NELLIE:
But wait till I've told you the wonderfullest thing I . . .

ALMA:
I'm going home now. Goodbye.

NELLIE:
Oh— Goodbye, Miss Alma.

[*She snatches up her festive basket and rushes in the
other direction with a shrill giggle as the wind pulls at
her skirts. The lights dim out.*]

SCENE ELEVEN

An hour later. In John's office.

The interior is framed by the traceries of Victorian architecture and there is one irregular section of wall supporting the anatomy chart. Otherwise the stage is open to the cyclorama.

In the background mellow golden light touches the vane of a steeple (a gilded weathercock). Also the wings of the stone angel. A singing wind rises and falls throughout scene.

John is seated at a white enameled table examining a slide through a microscope.

[*A bell tolls the hour of five as Alma comes hesitantly in. She wears a russet suit and a matching hat with a plume. The light changes, the sun disappearing behind a cloud, fading from the steeple and the stone angel till the bell stops tolling. Then it brightens again.*]

ALMA:
No greetings? No greetings at all?

JOHN:
Hello, Miss Alma.

ALMA [*speaking with animation to control her panic*]:
How white it is here, such glacial brilliance! [*She covers her eyes, laughing.*]

JOHN:
New equipment.

ALMA:
Everything new but the chart.

JOHN:

The human anatomy's always the same old thing.

ALMA:

And such a tiresome one! I've been plagued with sore throats.

JOHN:

Everyone has here lately. These Southern homes are all improperly heated. Open grates aren't enough.

ALMA:

They burn the front of you while your back is freezing!

JOHN:

Then you go into another room and get chilled off.

ALMA:

Yes, yes, chilled to the bone.

JOHN:

But it never gets quite cold enough to convince the damn fools that a furnace is necessary so they go on building without them.

[*There is the sound of wind.*]

ALMA:

Such a strange afternoon.

JOHN:

Is it? I haven't been out.

ALMA:

The Gulf wind is blowing big, white—what do.they call them? cumulus?—clouds over! Ha-ha! It seemed determined to take the plume off my hat, like that fox terrier we had once named Jacob, snatched the plume off a hat and dashed around and around the back yard with it like a trophy!

JOHN:

I remember Jacob. What happened to him?

ALMA:

Oh, Jacob. Jacob was such a mischievous thief. We had to send him out to some friends in the country. Yes, he ended his days as—a country squire! The tales of his exploits . . .

JOHN:

Sit down, Miss Alma.

ALMA:

If I'm disturbing you . . . ?

JOHN:

No—I called the Rectory when I heard you were sick. Your father told me you wouldn't see a doctor.

ALMA:

I needed a rest, that was all. . . . You were out of town mostly. . . .

JOHN:

I was mostly in Lyon, finishing up Dad's work in the fever clinic.

ALMA:

Covering yourself with sudden glory!

JOHN:

Redeeming myself with good works.

ALMA:

It's rather late to tell you how happy I am, and also how proud. I almost feel as your father might have felt—if . . . And—are you—happy now, John?

JOHN [*uncomfortably, not looking at her*]:

I've settled with life on fairly acceptable terms. Isn't that all a reasonable person can ask for?

ALMA:

He can ask for much more than that. He can ask for the coming true of his most improbable dreams.

JOHN:

It's best not to ask for too much.

ALMA:

I disagree with you. I say, ask for all, but be prepared to get nothing! [*She springs up and crosses to the window. She continues.*] No, I haven't been well. I've thought many times of something you told me last summer, that I have a *Doppelgänger.* I looked that up and found that it means another person inside me, another self, and I don't know whether to thank you or not for making me conscious of it!—I haven't been well. . . . For a while I thought I was dying, that that was the change that was coming.

JOHN:

When did you have that feeling?

ALMA:

August. September. But now the Gulf wind has blown that feeling away like a cloud of smoke, and I know now I'm not dying, that it isn't going to turn out to be that simple. . . .

JOHN:

Have you been anxious about your heart again? [*He retreats to a professional manner and takes out a silver watch, putting his fingers on her wrist.*]

ALMA:

And now the stethoscope? [*He removes the stethoscope from the table and starts to loosen her jacket. She looks down at his bent head. Slowly, involuntarily, her gloved hands lift and descend on the crown of his head. He gets up awkwardly. She suddenly leans toward him and presses her*

241

mouth to his.] Why don't you say something? Has the cat got your tongue?

JOHN:

Miss Alma, what can I say?

ALMA:

You've gone back to calling me "Miss Alma" again.

JOHN:

We never really got past that point with each other.

ALMA:

Oh, yes, we did. We were so close that we almost breathed together!

JOHN [*with embarrassment*]:

I didn't know that.

ALMA:

No? Well, I did, I knew it. [*Her hand touches his face tenderly.*] You shave more carefully now? You don't have those little razor cuts on your chin that you dusted with gardenia talcum. . . .

JOHN:

I shave more carefully now.

ALMA:

So that explains it! [*Her fingers remain on his face, moving gently up and down it like a blind person reading Braille. He is intensely embarrassed and gently removes her hands from him.*] Is it—impossible now?

JOHN:

I don't think I know what you mean.

ALMA:

You know what I mean, all right! So be honest with me. One time I said "no" to something. You may remember the time, and all that demented howling from the cockfight?

But now I have changed my mind, or the girl who said "no," she doesn't exist any more, she died last summer —suffocated in smoke from something on fire inside her. No, she doesn't live now, but she left me her ring— You see? This one you admired, the topaz ring set in pearls. . . . And she said to me when she slipped this ring on my finger—"Remember I died empty-handed, and so make sure that your hands have *something in them!*" [*She drops her gloves. She clasps his head again in her hands.*] I said, "But what about pride?"—She said, "Forget about pride whenever it stands between you and what you must have!" [*He takes hold of her wrists.*] And then I said, "But what if he doesn't want me?" I don't know what she said then. I'm not sure whether she said anything or not— her lips stopped moving—yes, I think she stopped breathing! [*He gently removes her craving hands from his face.*] No? [*He shakes his head in dumb suffering.*] Then the answer is "no"!

JOHN [*forcing himself to speak*]:
I have a respect for the truth, and I have a respect for you— so I'd better speak honestly if you want me to speak. [*Alma nods slightly.*] You've won the argument that we had between us.

ALMA:
What—argument?

JOHN:
The one about the chart.

ALMA:
Oh—the chart!

[*She turns from him and wanders across to the chart. She gazes up at it with closed eyes, and her hands clasped in front of her.*]

243

JOHN:

It shows that we're not a package of rose leaves, that every interior inch of us is taken up with something ugly and functional and no room seems to be left for anything else in there.

ALMA:

No . . .

JOHN:

But I've come around to your way of thinking, that something else is in there, an immaterial something—as thin as smoke—which all of those ugly machines combine to produce and that's their whole reason for being. It can't be seen so it can't be shown on the chart. But it's there, just the same, and knowing it's there—why, then the whole thing—this—this unfathomable experience of ours—takes on a new value, like some—some wildly romantic work in a laboratory! Don't you see?

[*The wind comes up very loud, almost like a choir of voices. Both of them turn slightly, Alma raising a hand to her plumed head as if she were outdoors.*]

ALMA:

Yes, I see! Now that you no longer want it to be otherwise you're willing to believe that a spiritual bond can exist between us two!

JOHN:

Can't you believe that I am sincere about it?

ALMA:

Maybe you are. But I don't want to be talked to like some incurably sick patient you have to comfort. [*A harsh and strong note comes into her voice.*] Oh, I suppose I am sick, one of those weak and divided people who slip like shadows among you solid strong ones. But sometimes, out of neces-

sity, we shadowy people take on a strength of our own. I
have that now. You needn't try to deceive me.

JOHN:
I wasn't.

ALMA:
You needn't try to comfort me. I haven't come here on any
but equal terms. You said, let's talk truthfully. Well, let's
do! Unsparingly, truthfully, even shamelessly, then! It's no
longer a secret that I love you. It never was. I loved you as
long ago as the time I asked you to read the stone angel's
name with your fingers. Yes, I remember the long afternoons of our childhood, when I had to stay indoors to practice my music—and heard your playmates calling you,
"Johnny, Johnny!" How it went through me, just to hear
your name called! And how I—rushed to the window to
watch you jump the porch railing! I stood at a distance,
halfway down the block, only to keep in sight of your torn
red sweater, racing about the vacant lot you played in. Yes,
it had begun that early, this affliction of love, and has never
let go of me since, but kept on growing. I've lived next
door to you all the days of my life, a weak and divided
person who stood in adoring awe of your singleness, of your
strength. And that is my story! Now I wish *you* would tell
me—why didn't it happen between us? Why did I fail?
Why did you come almost close enough—and no closer?

JOHN:
Whenever we've gotten together, the three or four times
that we have . . .

ALMA:
As few as that?

JOHN:
It's only been three or four times that we've—come face to

245

face. And each of those times—we seemed to be trying to find something in each other without knowing what it was that we wanted to find. It wasn't a body hunger although— I acted as if I thought it might be the night I wasn't a gentleman—at the casino—it wasn't the physical you that I really wanted!

ALMA:
I know, you've already . . .

JOHN:
You didn't have that to give me.

ALMA:
Not at that time.

JOHN:
You had something else to give.

ALMA:
What did I have?

[*John strikes a match. Unconsciously he holds his curved palm over the flame of the match to warm it. It is a long kitchen match and it makes a good flame. They both stare at it with a sorrowful understanding that is still perplexed. It is about to burn his fingers. She leans forward and blows it out, then she puts on her gloves.*]

JOHN:
You couldn't name it and I couldn't recognize it. I thought it was just a Puritanical ice that glittered like flame. But now I believe it *was* flame, mistaken for ice. I still don't understand it, but I know it was there, just as I know that your eyes and your voice are the two most beautiful things I've ever known—and also the warmest, although they don't seem to be set in your body at all. . . .

ALMA:

You talk as if my body had ceased to exist for you, John, in spite of the fact that you've just counted my pulse. Yes, that's it! You tried to avoid it, but you've told me plainly. The tables have turned, yes, the tables have turned with a vengeance! You've come around to my old way of thinking and I to yours like two people exchanging a call on each other at the same time, and each one finding the other one gone out, the door locked against him and no one to answer the bell! [*She laughs.*] I came here to tell you that being a gentleman, doesn't seem so important to me any more, but you're telling me I've got to remain a lady. [*She laughs rather violently.*] The tables have turned with a vengeance! —The air in here smells of ether— It's making me dizzy . . .

JOHN:

I'll open a window.

ALMA:

Please.

JOHN:

There now.

ALMA:

Thank you, that's better. Do you remember those little white tablets you gave me? I've used them all up and I'd like to have some more.

JOHN:

I'll write the prescription for you. [*He bends to write.*]

[*Nellie is in the waiting room. They hear her voice.*]

ALMA:

Someone is waiting in the waiting room, John. One of my vocal pupils. The youngest and prettiest one with the least gift for music. The one that you helped wrap up this hand-

247

kerchief for me. [*She takes it out and touches her eyes with it.*]

[*The door opens, first a crack. Nellie peers in and giggles. Then she throws the door wide open with a peal of merry laughter. She has holly pinned on her jacket. She rushes up to John and hugs him with childish squeals.*]

NELLIE:
I've been all over town just shouting, shouting!

JOHN:
Shouting what?

NELLIE:
Glad tidings!

[*John looks at Alma over Nellie's shoulder.*]

JOHN:
I thought we weren't going to tell anyone for a while.

NELLIE:
I couldn't stop myself. [*She wheels about.*] Oh, Alma, has he told *you?*

ALMA [*quietly*]:
He didn't need to, Nellie. I guessed . . . from the Christmas card with your two names written on it!

[*Nellie rushes over to Alma and hugs her. Over Nellie's shoulder Alma looks at John. He makes a thwarted gesture as if he wanted to speak. She smiles desperately and shakes her head. She closes her eyes and bites her lips for a moment. Then she releases Nellie with a laugh of exaggerated gaiety.*]

NELLIE:
So Alma you were really the first to know!

ALMA:

I'm proud of that, Nellie.

NELLIE:

See on my finger! This was the present I couldn't tell you about!

ALMA:

Oh, what a lovely, lovely solitaire! But solitaire is such a wrong name for it. Solitaire means single and this means *two!* It's blinding, Nellie! Why it . . . hurts my eyes!

[*John catches Nellie's arm and pulls her to him. Almost violently Alma lifts her face; it is bathed in tears. She nods gratefully to John for releasing her from Nellie's attention. She picks up her gloves and purse.*]

JOHN:

Excuse her, Miss Alma. Nellie's still such a child.

ALMA [*with a breathless laugh*]:

I've got to run along now.

JOHN:

Don't leave your prescription.

ALMA:

Oh, yes, where's my prescription?

JOHN:

On the table.

ALMA:

I'll take it to the drugstore right away!

[*Nellie struggles to free herself from John's embrace which keeps her from turning to Alma.*]

NELLIE:

Alma, don't go! Johnny, let go of me, Johnny! You're hugging me so tight I can't breathe!

ALMA:

Goodbye.

NELLIE:

Alma! Alma, you know you're going to sing at the wedding! The very first Sunday in spring!—which will be Palm Sunday! "The Voice That Breathed O'er Eden."

[*Alma has closed the door. John shuts his eyes tight with a look of torment. He rains kisses on Nellie's forehead and throat and lips. The scene dims out with music.*]

SCENE TWELVE

In the park near the angel of the fountain. About dusk.

Alma enters the lighted area and goes slowly up to the fountain and bends to drink. Then she removes a small white package from her pocketbook and starts to unwrap it. While she is doing this, a Young Man comes along. He is dressed in a checked suit and a derby. He pauses by the bench. They glance at each other.

A train whistles in the distance. The Young Man clears his throat. The train whistle is repeated. The Young Man crosses toward the fountain, his eyes on Alma. She hesitates, with the unwrapped package in her hand. Then she crosses toward the bench and stands hesitantly in front of it. He stuffs his hands in his pockets and whistles. He glances with an effect of unconcern back over his shoulder.

Alma pushes her veil back with an uncertain gesture. His whistle dies out. He sways back and forth on his heels as the train whistles again. He suddenly turns to the fountain and bends to drink. Alma slips the package back into her purse. As the young man straightens up, she speaks in a barely audible voice.

ALMA:
The water—is—cool.

THE YOUNG MAN [*eagerly*]:
Did you say something?

ALMA:
I said, the water is cool.

THE YOUNG MAN:
Yes, it sure is, it's nice and cool!

ALMA:
It's always cool.

THE YOUNG MAN:
Is it?

ALMA:
Yes. Yes, even in summer. It comes from deep underground.

THE YOUNG MAN:
That's what keeps it cool.

ALMA:
Glorious Hill is famous for its artesian springs.

THE YOUNG MAN:
I didn't know that.

[*The Young Man jerkily removes his hands from his pockets. She gathers confidence before the awkwardness of his youth.*]

ALMA:
Are you a stranger in town?

THE YOUNG MAN:
I'm a traveling salesman.

ALMA:
Ah, you're a salesman who travels! [*She laughs gently.*] But you're younger than most of them are, and not so fat!

THE YOUNG MAN:
I'm just starting out. I travel for Red Goose shoes.

ALMA:
Ah! The Delta's your territory?

THE YOUNG MAN:
From the Peabody Lobby to Cat-Fish Row in Vicksburg.

[*Alma leans back and looks at him under half-closed lids, perhaps a little suggestively.*]

ALMA:
The life of a traveling salesman is interesting . . . but lonely.

THE YOUNG MAN:
You're right about that. Hotel bedrooms are lonely.

[*There is a pause. Far away the train whistles again.*]

ALMA:
All rooms are lonely where there is only one person. [*Her eyes fall shut.*]

THE YOUNG MAN [*gently*]:
You're tired, aren't you?

ALMA:
I? Tired? [*She starts to deny it; then laughs faintly and confesses the truth.*] Yes . . . a little. . . . But I shall rest now. I've just now taken one of my· sleeping tablets.

THE YOUNG MAN:
So early?

ALMA:
Oh, it won't put me to sleep. It will just quiet my nerves.

THE YOUNG MAN:
What are you nervous about?

ALMA:
I won an argument this afternoon.

THE YOUNG MAN:
That's nothing to be nervous over. You ought to be nervous if you *lost* one.

ALMA:
It wasn't the argument that I wanted to win. . . .

THE YOUNG MAN:
Well, I'm nervous too.

ALMA:
What over?

THE YOUNG MAN:
It's my first job and I'm scared of not making good.

[*That mysteriously sudden intimacy that sometimes oc-
curs between strangers more completely than old friends
or lovers moves them both. Alma hands the package of
tablets to him.*]

ALMA:
Then you must take one of my tablets.

THE YOUNG MAN:
Shall I?

ALMA:
Please take one!

THE YOUNG MAN:
Yes, I shall.

ALMA:
You'll be surprised how infinitely merciful they are. The
prescription number is 96814. I think of it as the telephone
number of God! [*They both laugh. He places one of the
tablets on his tongue and crosses to the fountain to wash it
down.*]

THE YOUNG MAN [*to the stone figure*]:
Thanks, angel. [*He gives her a little salute, and crosses back
to Alma.*]

ALMA:
Life is full of little mercies like that, not *big* mercies but
comfortable *little* mercies. And so we are able to keep on
going. . . . [*She has leaned back with half-closed eyes.*]

THE YOUNG MAN [*returning*]:
You're falling asleep.

ALMA:
Oh no, I'm not. I'm just closing my eyes. You know what
I feel like now? I feel like a water lily.

THE YOUNG MAN:
A water lily?

ALMA:
Yes, I feel like a water lily on a Chinese lagoon. Won't you
sit down? [*The Young Man does.*] My name is Alma.
Spanish for soul! What's yours?

THE YOUNG MAN:
Ha-ha! Mine's Archie Kramer. Mucho gusto, as they say in
Spain.

ALMA:
Usted habla Espanol, senor?

THE YOUNG MAN:
Un poquito! Usted habla Espanol, senorita?

ALMA:
Me tambien. Un poquito!

THE YOUNG MAN [*delightedly*]:
Ha . . . ha . . . ha! Sometimes un poquito is plenty! [*Alma
laughs . . . in a different way than she has ever laughed before, a little wearily, but quite naturally. The Young Man
leans toward her confidentially.*] What's there to do in this
town after dark?

ALMA:
There's not much to do in this town after dark, but there
are resorts on the lake that offer all kinds of after-dark en-
tertainment. There's one called Moon Lake Casino. It's

under new management, now, but I don't suppose its character has changed.

THE YOUNG MAN:
What was its character?

ALMA:
Gay, very gay, Mr. Kramer. . . .

THE YOUNG MAN:
Then what in hell are we sitting here for? Vamonos!

ALMA:
Como no, senor!

THE YOUNG MAN:
Ha-ha-ha! [*He jumps up.*] I'll call a taxi. [*He goes off shouting "Taxi."*]

[*Alma rises from the bench. As she crosses to the fountain the grave mood of the play is reinstated with a phrase of music. She faces the stone angel and raises her gloved hand in a sort of valedictory salute. Then she turns slowly about toward the audience with her hand still raised in a gesture of wonder and finality as . . . the curtain falls.*]

THE ROSE TATTOO

*O slinger! crack the nut of my eye! my heart
twittered with joy under the splendour of the
quicklime, the bird sings O Senectus! . . . the
streams are in their beds like the cries of women
and this world has more beauty than a ram's skin
painted red!*

St.-John Perse: *Anabasis*
T. S. ELIOT TRANSLATION

TO FRANK IN RETURN FOR SICILY

The Author and the Publisher express their thanks to Mr. Paul
Bigelow for valuable assistance in organizing the script of the play
for book publication.

THE TIMELESS WORLD OF A PLAY

Carson McCullers concludes one of her lyric poems with
the line: "Time, the endless idiot, runs screaming 'round the
world." It is this continual rush of time, so violent that it
appears to be screaming, that deprives our actual lives of so
much dignity and meaning, and it is, perhaps more than anything else, the *arrest of time* which has taken place in a completed work of art that gives to certain plays their feeling of
depth and significance. In the London notices of *Death of a
Salesman* a certain notoriously skeptical critic made the remark that Willy Loman was the sort of man that almost any
member of the audience would have kicked out of an office
had he applied for a job or detained one for conversation
about his troubles. The remark itself possibly holds some
truth. But the implication that Willy Loman is consequently a character with whom we have no reason to concern ourselves in drama, reveals a strikingly false conception of what plays are. Contemplation is something that exists outside of time, and so is the tragic sense. Even in the
actual world of commerce, there exists in some persons a
sensibility to the unfortunate situations of others, a capacity
for concern and compassion, surviving from a more tender
period of life outside the present whirling wire-cage of business activity. Facing Willy Loman across an office desk,
meeting his nervous glance and hearing his querulous voice,
we would be very likely to glance at our wrist watch and
our schedule of other appointments. We would not kick
him out of the office, no, but we would certainly *ease* him
out with more expedition than Willy had feebly hoped for.
But suppose there had been no wrist watch or office clock

and suppose there had *not* been the schedule of pressing appointments, and suppose that we were not actually facing Willy across a desk—and facing a person is *not* the best way to *see* him!—suppose, in other words, that the meeting with Willy Loman had somehow occurred in a world *outside* of time. Then I think we would receive him with concern and kindness and even with respect. If the world of a play did not offer us this occasion to view its characters under that special condition of a *world without time,* then, indeed, the characters and occurrences of drama would become equally pointless, equally trivial, as corresponding meetings and happenings in life.

The classic tragedies of Greece had tremendous nobility. The actors wore great masks, movements were formal, dance-like, and the speeches had an epic quality which doubtless were as removed from the normal conversation of their contemporary society as they seem today. Yet they did not seem false to the Greek audiences: the magnitude of the events and the passions aroused by them did not seem ridiculously out of proportion to common experience. And I wonder if this was not because the Greek audiences knew, instinctively or by training, that the created world of a play is removed from that element which makes people *little* and their emotions fairly inconsequential.

Great sculpture often follows the lines of the human body: yet the repose of great sculpture suddenly transmutes those human lines to something that has an absoluteness, a purity, a beauty, which would not be possible in a living mobile form.

A play may be violent, full of motion: yet it has that special kind of repose which allows contemplation and produces the climate in which tragic importance is a possible thing, provided that certain modern conditions are met.

In actual existence the moments of love are succeeded by the moments of satiety and sleep. The sincere remark is followed by a cynical distrust. Truth is fragmentary, at best: we love and betray each other not in quite the same breath but in two breaths that occur in fairly close sequence. But the fact that passion occurred in *passing,* that it then declined into a more familiar sense of indifference, should not be regarded as proof of its inconsequence. And this is the very truth that drama wishes to bring us . . .

Whether or not we admit it to ourselves, we are all haunted by a truly awful sense of impermanence. I have always had a particularly keen sense of this at New York cocktail parties, and perhaps that is why I drink the martinis almost as fast as I can snatch them from the tray. This sense is the febrile thing that hangs in the air. Horror of insincerity, of *not meaning,* overhangs these affairs like the cloud of cigarette smoke and the hectic chatter. This horror is the only thing, almost, that is left unsaid at such functions. All social functions involving a group of people not intimately known to each other are always under this shadow. They are almost always (in an unconscious way) like that last dinner of the condemned: where steak or turkey, whatever the doomed man wants, is served in his cell as a mockingly cruel reminder of what the great-big-little-transitory world had to offer.

In a play, time is arrested in the sense of being confined. By a sort of legerdemain, events are made to remain *events,* rather than being reduced so quickly to mere *occurrences.* The audience can sit back in a comforting dusk to watch a world which is flooded with light and in which emotion and action have a dimension and dignity that they would likewise have in real existence, if only the shattering intrusion of time could be locked out.

About their lives people ought to remember that when they are finished, everything in them will be contained in a marvelous state of repose which is the same as that which they unconsciously admired in drama. The rush is temporary. The great and only possible dignity of man lies in his power deliberately to choose certain moral values by which to live as steadfastly as if he, too, like a character in a play, were immured against the corrupting rush of time. Snatching the eternal out of the desperately fleeting is the great magic trick of human existence. As far as we know, as far as there exists any kind of empiric evidence, there is no way to beat the game of *being* against *nonbeing,* in which nonbeing is the predestined victor on realistic levels.

Yet plays in the tragic tradition offer us a view of certain moral values in violent juxtaposition. Because we do not participate, except as spectators, we can view them clearly, within the limits of our emotional equipment. These people on the stage do not return our looks. We do not have to answer their questions nor make any sign of being in company with them, nor do we have to compete with their virtues nor resist their offenses. All at once, for this reason, we are able to *see* them! Our hearts are wrung by recognition and pity, so that the dusky shell of the auditorium where we are gathered anonymously together is flooded with an almost liquid warmth of unchecked human sympathies, relieved of self-consciousness, allowed to function . . .

Men pity and love each other more deeply than they permit themselves to know. The moment after the phone has been hung up, the hand reaches for a scratch pad and scrawls a notation: "Funeral Tuesday at five, Church of the Holy Redeemer, don't forget flowers." And the same hand is only a little shakier than usual as it reaches, some minutes later, for a highball glass that will pour a stupefaction over the kindled nerves. Fear and evasion are the two little beasts that chase each other's tails in the revolving wire-cage of our nervous world. They distract us from feeling too much about things. Time rushes toward us with its hospital tray of infinitely varied narcotics, even while it is preparing us for its inevitably fatal operation . . .

So successfully have we disguised from ourselves the intensity of our own feelings, the sensibility of our own hearts, that plays in the tragic tradition have begun to seem untrue. For a couple of hours we may surrender ourselves to a world of fiercely illuminated values in conflict, but when the stage is covered and the auditorium lighted, almost immediately there is a recoil of disbelief. "Well, well!" we say as we shuffle back up the aisle, while the play dwindles behind us with the sudden perspective of an early Chirico painting. By the time we have arrived at Sardi's, if not as soon as we pass beneath the marquee, we have convinced ourselves once more that life has as little resemblance to the curiously stirring and meaningful occurrences on the stage as a jingle has to an elegy of Rilke.

This modern condition of his theater audience is something that an author must know in advance. The diminishing influence of life's destroyer, time, must be somehow worked into the context of his play. Perhaps it is a certain foolery, a certain distortion toward the grotesque, which will solve the problem for him. Perhaps it is only restraint, putting a mute on the strings that would like to break all bounds.

But almost surely, unless he contrives in some way to relate the dimensions of his tragedy to the dimensions of a world in which time is *included*—he will be left among his magnificent debris on a dark stage, muttering to himself: "Those fools . . ."

And if they could hear him above the clatter of tongues, glasses, chinaware and silver, they would give him this answer: "But you have shown us a world not ravaged by time. We admire your innocence. But we have seen our photographs, past and present. Yesterday evening we passed our first wife on the street. We smiled as we spoke but we didn't really see her! It's too bad, but we know what is true and not true, and at 3 A.M. your disgrace will be in print!"

—Tennessee Williams

SCENES

ACT ONE

SCENE 1   Evening
SCENE 2   Almost morning, the next day
SCENE 3   Noon of that day
SCENE 4   A late spring morning, three years later
SCENE 5   Immediately following
SCENE 6   Two hours later that day

ACT TWO

SCENE 1   Two hours later that day

ACT THREE

SCENE 1   Evening of the same day
SCENE 2   Just before dawn of the next day
SCENE 3   Morning

The Rose Tattoo was first produced by Cheryl Crawford at the Erlanger Theater in Chicago on December 29, 1950. It had its Broadway opening on February 3, 1951, at the Martin Beck Theater in New York City, with Daniel Mann as director, setting by Boris Aronson and music by David Diamond. Production Associate: Bea Lawrence. Assistant to Producer: Paul Bigelow.

Cast of the New York Production

SALVATORE	SALVATORE MINEO
VIVI	JUDY RATNER
BRUNO	SALVATORE TAORMINA
ASSUNTA	LUDMILLA TORETZKA
ROSA DELLE ROSE	PHYLLIS LOVE
SERAFINA DELLE ROSE	MAUREEN STAPLETON
ESTELLE HOHENGARTEN	SONIA SOREL
THE STREGA	DAISY BELMORE
GIUSEPPINA	ROSSANA SAN MARCO
PEPPINA	AUGUSTA MERIGHI
VIOLETTA	VIVIAN NATHAN
MARIELLA	PENNY SANTON
TERESA	NANCY FRANKLIN
FATHER DE LEO	ROBERT CARRICART
A DOCTOR	ANDREW DUGGAN
MISS YORKE	DORRIT KELTON
FLORA	JANE HOFFMAN
BESSIE	FLORENCE SUNDSTROM
JACK HUNTER	DON MURRAY
THE SALESMAN	EDDIE HYANS
ALVARO MANGIACAVALLO	ELI WALLACH
A MAN	DAVID STEWART
ANOTHER MAN	MARTIN BALSAM

AUTHOR'S PRODUCTION NOTES

The locale of the play is a village populated mostly by Sicilians somewhere along the Gulf Coast between New Orleans and Mobile. The time is the present.

As the curtain rises we hear a Sicilian folk singer with a guitar. He is singing. At each major division of the play this song is resumed and it is completed at the final curtain.

The first lighting is extremely romantic. We see a frame cottage, in a rather poor state of repair, with a palm tree leaning dreamily over one end of it and a flimsy little entrance porch, with spindling pillars, sagging steps and broken rails, at the other end. The setting seems almost tropical, for, in addition to the palm trees, there are tall canes with feathery fronds and a fairly thick growth of pampas grass. These are growing on the slope of an embankment along which runs a highway, which is not visible, but the cars passing on it can occasionally be heard. The house has a rear door which cannot be seen. The facing wall of the cottage is either a transparency that lifts for the interior scenes, or is cut away to reveal the interior.

The romantic first lighting is that of late dusk, the sky a delicate blue with an opalescent shimmer more like water than air. Delicate points of light appear and disappear like lights reflected in a twilight harbor. The curtain rises well above the low tin roof of the cottage.

We see an interior that is as colorful as a booth at a carnival. There are many religious articles and pictures of ruby and gilt, the brass cage of a gaudy parrot, a large bowl of gold-

fish, cut-glass decanters and vases, rose-patterned wallpaper and a rose-colored carpet; everything is exclamatory in its brightness like the projection of a woman's heart passionately in love. There is a small shrine against the wall between the rooms, consisting of a prie-dieu and a little statue of the Madonna in a starry blue robe and gold crown. Before this burns always a vigil light in its ruby glass cup. Our purpose is to show these gaudy, childlike mysteries with sentiment and humor in equal measure, without ridicule and with respect for the religious yearnings they symbolize.

An outdoor sign indicates that Serafina, whose home the cottage is, does "SEWING." The interior furnishings give evidence of this vocation. The most salient feature is a collection of dressmaker's dummies. There are at least seven of these life-size mannequins, in various shapes and attitudes. [They will have to be made especially for the play as their purpose is not realistic. They have pliable joints so that their positions can be changed. Their arms terminate at the wrist. In all their attitudes there is an air of drama, somewhat like the poses of declamatory actresses of the old school.] Principal among them are a widow and a bride who face each other in violent attitudes, as though having a shrill argument, in the parlor. The widow's costume is complete from black-veiled hat to black slippers. The bride's featureless head wears a chaplet of orange blossoms from which is depended a flowing veil of white marquisette, and her net gown is trimmed in white satin—lustrous, immaculate.

Most of the dummies and sewing equipment are confined to the dining room which is also Serafina's work room. In that room there is a tall cupboard on top of which are several dusty bottles of imported Sicilian spumanti.

THE SETTING BY BORIS ARONSON FOR THE BROADWAY PRODUCTION

ACT ONE

*It is the hour that the Italians call "prima sera," the begin-
ning of dusk. Between the house and the palm tree burns
the female star with an almost emerald luster.*

*The mothers of the neighborhood are beginning to call their
children home to supper, in voices near and distant, urgent
and tender, like the variable notes of wind and water. There
are three children: Bruno, Salvatore, and Vivi, ranged in
front of the house, one with a red paper kite, one with a
hoop, and the little girl with a doll dressed as a clown. They
are in attitudes of momentary repose, all looking up at something—a bird or a plane passing over—as the mothers'
voices call them.*

BRUNO:
The white flags are flying at the Coast Guard station.

SALVATORE:
That means fair weather.

VIVI:
I love fair weather.

GIUSEPPINA:
Vivi! Vieni mangiare!

PEPPINA:
Salvatore! Come home!

VIOLETTA:
Bruno! Come home to supper!

[*The calls are repeated tenderly, musically.*

[*The interior of the house begins to be visible. Serafina
delle Rose is seen on the parlor sofa, waiting for her hus-*

band Rosario's return. Between the curtains is a table set lovingly for supper; there is wine in a silver ice-bucket and a great bowl of roses.

[*Serafina looks like a plump little Italian opera singer in the role of Madame Butterfly. Her black hair is done in a high pompadour that glitters like wet coal. A rose is held in place by glittering jet hairpins. Her voluptuous figure is sheathed in pale rose silk. On her feet are dainty slippers with glittering buckles and French heels. It is apparent from the way she sits, with such plump dignity, that she is wearing a tight girdle. She sits very erect, in an attitude of forced composure, her ankles daintily crossed and her plump little hands holding a yellow paper fan on which is painted a rose. Jewels gleam on her fingers, her wrists and her ears and about her throat. Expectancy shines in her eyes. For a few moments she seems to be posing for a picture.*]

[*Rosa delle Rose appears at the side of the house, near the palm tree. Rosa, the daughter of the house, is a young girl of twelve. She is pretty and vivacious, and has about her a particular intensity in every gesture.*]

SERAFINA:
Rosa, where are you?

ROSA:
Here, Mama.

SERAFINA:
What are you doing, cara?

ROSA:
I've caught twelve lightning bugs.

[*The cracked voice of Assunta is heard, approaching.*]

274

SERAFINA:

I hear Assunta! Assunta!

[*Assunta appears and goes into the house, Rosa following her in. Assunta is an old woman in a gray shawl, bearing a basket of herbs, for she is a fattuchiere, a woman
who practices a simple sort of medicine. As she enters the
children scatter.*]

ASSUNTA:

Vengo, vengo. Buona sera. Buona sera. There is something
wild in the air, no wind but everything's moving.

SERAFINA:

I don't see nothing moving and neither do you.

ASSUNTA:

Nothing is moving so you can see it moving, but everything
is moving, and I can hear the star-noises. Hear them? Hear
the star-noises?

SERAFINA:

Naw, them ain't the star-noises. They're termites, eating the
house up. What are you peddling, old woman, in those little white bags?

ASSUNTA:

Powder, wonderful powder. You drop a pinch of it in your
husband's coffee.

SERAFINA:

What is it good for?

ASSUNTA:

What is a husband good for! I make it out of the dry blood
of a goat.

SERAFINA:

Davero!

ASSUNTA:

Wonderful stuff! But be sure you put it in his coffee at supper, not in his breakfast coffee.

SERAFINA:

My husband don't need no powder!

ASSUNTA:

Excuse me, Baronessa. Maybe he needs the opposite kind of a powder, I got that, too.

SERAFINA:

Naw, naw, *no* kind of powder at all, old woman. [*She lifts her head with a proud smile.*]

[*Outside the sound of a truck is heard approaching up on the highway.*]

ROSA [*joyfully*]:
Papa's truck!

[*They stand listening for a moment, but the truck goes by without stopping.*]

SERAFINA [*to Assunta*]:
That wasn't him. It wasn't no 10-ton truck. It didn't rattle the shutters! Assunta, Assunta, undo a couple of hooks, the dress is tight on me!

ASSUNTA:
Is it true what I told you?

SERAFINA:
Yes, it is true, but nobody needed to tell me. Assunta, I'll tell you something which maybe you won't believe.

ASSUNTA:
It is impossible to tell me anything that I don't believe.

276

SERAFINA:

Va bene! Senti, Assunta!—I knew that I had conceived on the very night of conception! [*There is a phrase of music as she says this.*]

ASSUNTA:

Ahhhh?

SERAFINA:

Senti! That night I woke up with a burning pain on me, here, on my left breast! A pain like a needle, quick, quick, hot little stitches. I turned on the light, I uncovered my breast!—On it I saw the rose tattoo of my husband!

ASSUNTA:

Rosario's tattoo?

SERAFINA:

On me, on my breast, his tattoo! And when I saw it I knew that I had conceived . . .

[*Serafina throws her head back, smiling proudly, and opens her paper fan. Assunta stares at her gravely, then rises and hands her basket to Serafina.*]

ASSUNTA:

Ecco! *You* sell the powders! [*She starts toward the door.*]

SERAFINA:

You don't believe that I saw it?

ASSUNTA [*stopping*]:
Did Rosario see it?

SERAFINA:

I screamed. But when he woke up, it was gone. It only lasted a moment. But I *did* see it, and I *did* know, when I seen it, that I had conceived, that in my body another rose was growing!

277

ASSUNTA:

Did he believe that you saw it?

SERAFINA:

No. He laughed.—He laughed and I cried . . .

ASSUNTA:

And he took you into his arms, and you stopped crying!

SERAFINA:

Si!

ASSUNTA:

Serafina, for you everything has got to be different. A sign, a miracle, a wonder of some kind. You speak to Our Lady. You say that She answers your questions. She nods or shakes Her head at you. Look, Serafina, underneath Our Lady you have a candle. The wind through the shutters makes the candle flicker. The shadows move. Our Lady seems to be nodding!

SERAFINA:

She gives me signs.

ASSUNTA:

Only to you? Because you are more important? The wife of a barone? Serafina! In Sicily they called his uncle a baron, but in Sicily everybody's a baron that owns a piece of the land and a separate house for the goats!

SERAFINA:

They said to his uncle "Voscenza!" and they kissed their hands to him! [*She kisses the back of her hand repeatedly, with vehemence.*]

ASSUNTA:

His uncle in Sicily!—Si—But *here* what's he do? Drives a truck of bananas?

278

SERAFINA [*blurting out*]:
No! *Not* bananas!

ASSUNTA:
Not bananas?

SERAFINA:
Stai zitta! [*She makes a warning gesture.*]—No—Vieni
qui, Assunta! [*She beckons her mysteriously. Assunta approaches.*]

ASSUNTA:
Cosa dici?

SERAFINA:
On top of the truck is bananas! But underneath—something
else!

ASSUNTA:
Che altre cose?

SERAFINA:
Whatever it is that the Brothers Romano want hauled out
of the state, he hauls it for them, underneath the bananas!
[*She nods her head importantly.*] And money, he gets so
much it spills from his pockets! Soon I don't have to make
dresses!

ASSUNTA [*turning away*]:
Soon I think you will have to make a black veil!

SERAFINA:
Tonight is the last time he does it! Tomorrow he quits
hauling stuff for the Brothers Romano! He pays for the 10-
ton truck and works for himself. We live with dignity in
America, then! Own truck! Own house! And in the house
will be everything electric! Stove—deep-freeze—*tutto!*—
But tonight, stay with me . . . I can't swallow my heart!—

Not till I hear the truck stop in front of the house and his key in the lock of the door!—When I call him, and him shouting back, *"Si, sono qui!"* In his hair, Assunta, he has —oil of roses. And when I wake up at night—the air, the dark room's—full of—roses . . . Each time is the first time with him. Time doesn't pass . . .

[*Assunta picks up a small clock on the cupboard and holds it to her ear.*]

ASSUNTA:
Tick, tick, tick, tick.—You say the clock is a liar.

SERAFINA:
No, the clock is a fool. I don't listen to it. My clock is my heart and my heart don't say tick-tick, it says love-love! And now I have two hearts in me, both of them saying love-love!

[*A truck is heard approaching, then passes. Serafina drops her fan. Assunta opens a bottle of spumanti with a loud pop. Serafina cries out.*]

ASSUNTA:
Stai tranquilla! Calmati! [*She pours her a glass of wine.*] Drink this wine and before the glass is empty he'll be in your arms!

SERAFINA:
I can't—swallow my heart!

ASSUNTA:
A woman must not have a heart that is too big to swallow! [*She crosses to the door.*]

SERAFINA:
Stay with me!

ASSUNTA:

I have to visit a woman who drank rat poison because of a heart too big for her to swallow.

[*Assunta leaves. Serafina returns indolently to the sofa. She lifts her hands to her great swelling breasts and murmurs aloud:*]

SERAFINA:

Oh, it's so wonderful, having *two* lives in the body, not *one* but two! [*Her hands slide down to her belly, luxuriously.*] I am heavy with life, I am big, big, big with life! [*She picks up a bowl of roses and goes into the back room.*]

[*Estelle Hohengarten appears in front of the house. She is a thin blonde woman in a dress of Egyptian design, and her blonde hair has an unnatural gloss in the clear, greenish dusk. Rosa appears from behind the house, calling out:*]

ROSA:

Twenty lightning bugs, Mama!

ESTELLE:

Little girl? Little girl?

ROSA [*resentfully*]:

Are you talking to me? [*There is a pause.*]

ESTELLE:

Come here. [*She looks Rosa over curiously.*] You're a twig off the old rosebush.—Is the lady that does the sewing in the house?

ROSA:

Mama's at home.

ESTELLE:

I'd like to see her.

281

ROSA:
Mama?

SERAFINA:
Dimi?

ROSA:
There's a lady to see you.

SERAFINA:
Oh. Tell her to wait in the parlor. [*Estelle enters and stares curiously about. She picks up a small framed picture on the cupboard. She is looking at it as Serafina enters with a bowl of roses. Serafina speaks sharply.*] That is my husband's picture.

ESTELLA:
Oh!—I thought it was Valentino.—With a mustache.

SERAFINA [*putting the bowl down on the table*]:
You want something?

ESTELLE:
Yes. I heard you do sewing.

SERAFINA:
Yes, I do sewing.

ESTELLE:
How fast can you make a shirt for me?

SERAFINA:
That all depends. [*She takes the picture from Estelle and puts it back on the cupboard.*]

ESTELLE:
I got the piece of silk with me. I want it made into a shirt for a man I'm in love with. Tomorrow's the anniversary of the day we met . . . [*She unwraps a piece of rose-colored silk which she holds up like a banner.*]

SERAFINA [*involuntarily*]:

Che bella stoffa!—Oh, that would be wonderful stuff for a
lady's blouse or for a pair of pyjamas!

ESTELLE:

I want a man's shirt made with it.

SERAFINA:

Silk this color for a shirt for a *man?*

ESTELLE:

This man is wild like a Gypsy.

SERAFINA:

A woman should not encourage a man to be wild.

ESTELLE:

A man that's wild is hard for a woman to hold, huh? But
if he was tame—would the woman want to hold him? Huh?

SERAFINA:

I am a married woman in business. I don't know nothing
about wild men and wild women and I don't have much
time—so . . .

ESTELLE:

I'll pay you twice what you ask me.

[*Outside there is the sound of the goat bleating and the
jingle of its harness; then the crash of wood splintering.*]

ROSA [*suddenly appearing at the door*]:

Mama, the black goat is loose! [*She runs down the steps
and stands watching the goat. Serafina crosses to the door.*]

THE STREGA [*in the distance*]:

Hyeh, Billy, hyeh, hyeh, Billy!

ESTELLE:

I'll pay you three times the price that you ask me for it.

SERAFINA [*shouting*]:
Watch the goat! Don't let him get in our yard! [*to Estelle*]
—If I ask you five dollars?

ESTELLE:
I will pay you fifteen. Make it twenty; money is not the
object. But it's got to be ready tomorrow.

SERAFINA:
Tomorrow?

ESTELLE:
Twenty-five dollars! [*Serafina nods slowly with a stunned
look. Estelle smiles.*] I've got the measurements with me.

SERAFINA:
Pin the measurements and your name on the silk and the
shirt will be ready tomorrow.

ESTELLE:
My name is Estelle Hohengarten.

[*A little boy races excitedly into the yard.*]

THE BOY:
Rosa, Rosa, the black goat's in your yard!

ROSA [*calling*]:
Mama, the goat's in the yard!

SERAFINA [*furiously, forgetting her visitor*]:
Il becco della strega!—Scusi! [*She runs out onto the porch.*]
Catch him, catch him before he gets at the vines!

[*Rosa dances gleefully. The Strega runs into the yard.
She has a mop of wild grey hair and is holding her black
skirts up from her bare hairy legs. The sound of the goat's
bleating and the jingling of his harness is heard in the
windy blue dusk.*

[*Serafina descends the porch steps. The high-heeled slip-pers, the tight silk skirt and the dignity of a baronessa make the descent a little gingerly. Arrived in the yard, she directs the goat-chase imperiously with her yellow paper fan, pointing this way and that, exclaiming in Italian.*]

[*She fans herself rapidly and crosses back of the house. The goat evidently makes a sudden charge. Screaming, Serafina rushes back to the front of the house, all out of breath, the glittering pompadour beginning to tumble down over her forehead.*]

SERAFINA:

Rosa! You go in the house! Don't look at the Strega!

[*Alone in the parlor, Estelle takes the picture of Rosario. Impetuously, she thrusts it in her purse and runs from the house, just as Serafina returns to the front yard.*]

ROSA [*refusing to move*]:
Why do you call her a witch?

[*Serafina seizes her daughter's arm and propels her into the house.*]

SERAFINA:

She has white eyes and every finger is crooked. [*She pulls Rosa's arm.*]

ROSA:

She has a cataract, Mama, and her fingers are crooked because she has rheumatism!

SERAFINA:

Malocchio—the evil eye—*that's* what she's got! And her fingers are crooked because she shook hands with the Devil.

285

Go in the house and wash your face with salt water and throw the salt water away! *Go in! Quick!* She's coming!

[*The boy utters a cry of triumph.*

[*Serafina crosses abruptly to the porch. At the same moment the boy runs triumphantly around the house leading the captured goat by its bell harness. It is a middle-sized black goat with great yellow eyes. The Strega runs behind with the broken rope. As the grotesque little procession runs before her—the Strega, the goat and the children—Serafina cries out shrilly. She crouches over and covers her face. The Strega looks back at her with a derisive cackle.*]

SERAFINA:
Malocchio! Malocchio!

[*Shielding her face with one hand, Serafina makes the sign of the horns with the other to ward off the evil eye. And the scene dims out.*]

SCENE TWO

It is just before dawn the next day. Father De Leo, a priest, and several black-shawled women, including Assunta, are standing outside the house. The interior of the house is very dim.

GIUSEPPINA:

There is a light in the house.

PEPPINA:

I hear the sewing machine!

VIOLETTA:

There's Serafina! She's working. She's holding up a piece of rose-colored silk.

ASSUNTA:

She hears our voices.

VIOLETTA:

She's dropped the silk to the floor and she's . . .

GIUSEPPINA:

Holding her throat! I think she . . .

PEPPINA:

Who's going to tell her?

VIOLETTA:

Father De Leo will tell her.

FATHER DE LEO:

I think a woman should tell her. I think Assunta must tell her that Rosario is dead.

ASSUNTA:

It will not be necessary to tell her. She will know when she sees us.

287

[*It grows lighter inside the house. Serafina is standing in a frozen attitude with her hand clutching her throat and her eyes staring fearfully toward the sound of voices.*]

ASSUNTA:
I think she already knows what we have come to tell her!

FATHER DE LEO:
Andiamo, Signore! We must go to the door.

[*They climb the porch steps. Assunta opens the door.*]

SERAFINA [*gasping*]:
Don't speak!

[*She retreats from the group, stumbling blindly backward among the dressmaker's dummies. With a gasp she turns and runs out the backdoor. In a few moments we see her staggering about outside near the palm tree. She comes down in front of the house, and stares blindly off into the distance.*]

SERAFINA [*wildly*]:
Don't speak!

[*The voices of the women begin keening in the house. Assunta comes out and approaches Serafina with her arms extended. Serafina slumps to her knees, whispering hoarsely: "Don't speak!" Assunta envelopes her in the gray shawl of pity as the scene dims out.*]

SCENE THREE

It is noon of the same day. Assunta is removing a funeral wreath on the door of the house. A doctor and Father De Leo are on the porch.

THE DOCTOR:

She's lost the baby. [*Assunta utters a low moan of pity and crosses herself.*] Serafina's a very strong woman and that won't kill her. But she is trying not to breathe. She's got to be watched and not allowed out of the bed. [*He removes a hypodermic and a small package from his bag and hands them to Assunta.*]—This is morphia. In the arm with the needle if she screams or struggles to get up again.

ASSUNTA:

Capisco!

FATHER DE LEO:

One thing I want to make plain. The body of Rosario must not be burned.

THE DOCTOR:

Have you seen the "body of Rosario?"

FATHER DE LEO:

Yes, I have seen his body.

THE DOCTOR:

Wouldn't you say it was burned?

FATHER DE LEO:

Of course the body was burned. When he was shot at the wheel of the truck, it crashed and caught fire. But deliberate cremation is not the same thing. It's an abomination in the sight of God.

THE DOCTOR:

Abominations are something I don't know about.

FATHER DE LEO:

The Church has set down certain laws.

THE DOCTOR:

But the instructions of a widow have to be carried out.

FATHER DE LEO:

Don't you know why she wants the body cremated? So she can keep the ashes here in the house.

THE DOCTOR:

Well, why not, if that's any comfort to her?

FATHER DE LEO:

Pagan idolatry is what I call it!

THE DOCTOR:

Father De Leo, you love your people but you don't understand them. They find God in each other. And when they lose each other, they lose God and they're lost. And it's hard to help them.—Who is that woman?

[*Estelle Hohengarten has appeared before the house. She is black-veiled, and bearing a bouquet of roses.*]

ESTELLE:

I am Estelle Hohengarten.

[*Instantly there is a great hubbub in the house. The women mourners flock out to the porch, whispering and gesticulating excitedly.*]

FATHER DE LEO:

What have you come here for?

ESTELLE:

To say good-bye to the body.

FATHER DE LEO:

The casket is closed; the body cannot be seen. And you must never come here. The widow knows nothing about you. Nothing at all.

GIUSEPPINA:

We know about you!

PEPPINA:

Va via! Sporcacciona!

VIOLETTA:

Puttana!

MARIELLA:

Assassina!

TERESA:

You sent him to the Romanos.

FATHER DE LEO:

Shhh!

[*Suddenly the women swarm down the steps like a cloud of attacking birds, all crying out in Sicilian. Estelle crouches and bows her head defensively before their savage assault. The bouquet of roses is snatched from her black-gloved hands and she is flailed with them about the head and shoulders. The thorns catch her veil and tear it away from her head. She covers her white sobbing face with her hands.*]

FATHER DE LEO:

Ferme! Ferme! Signore, fermate vi nel nome di Dio!— Have a little respect!

[*The women fall back from Estelle, who huddles weeping on the walk.*]

ESTELLE:

See him, see him, just see him . . .

FATHER DE LEO:

The body is crushed and burned. Nobody can see it. Now
go away and don't ever come here again, Estelle Hohengarten!

THE WOMEN [*in both languages, wildly*]:

Va via, va via, go way.

[*Rosa comes around the house. Estelle turns and retreats.
One of the mourners spits and kicks at the tangled veil
and roses. Father De Leo leaves. The others return inside,
except Rosa.*

[*After a few moments the child goes over to the roses.
She picks them up and carefully untangles the veil from
the thorns.*

[*She sits on the sagging steps and puts the black veil
over her head. Then for the first time she begins to weep,
wildly, histrionically. The little boy appears and gazes at
her; momentarily impressed by her performance. Then he
picks up a rubber ball and begins to bounce it.*

[*Rosa is outraged. She jumps up, tears off the veil and
runs to the little boy, giving him a sound smack and
snatching the ball away from him.*]

ROSA:

Go home! My papa is dead!

[*The scene dims out, as the music is heard again.*]

SCENE FOUR

A June day, three years later. It is morning and the light is bright. A group of local mothers are storming Serafina's house, indignant over her delay in delivering the gradua-tion dresses for their daughters. Most of the women are chattering continually in Sicilian, racing about the house and banging the doors and shutters. The scene moves swiftly and violently until the moment when Rosa finally comes out in her graduation dress.

GIUSEPPINA:
Serafina! Serafina delle Rose!

PEPPINA:
Maybe if you call her "Baronessa" she will answer the door. [*with a mocking laugh*] Call her "Baronessa" and kiss your hand to her when she opens the door.

GIUSEPPINA [*tauntingly*]:
Baronessa! [*She kisses her hand toward the door.*]

VIOLETTA:
When did she promise your dress?

PEPPINA:
All week she say, "Domani—domani—domani." But yes-tiddy I told her . . .

VIOLETTA:
Yeah?

PEPPINA:
Oh yeah. I says to her, "Serafina, domani's the high school graduation. I got to try the dress on my daughter *today*." "Domani," she says, "Sicuro! sicuro! sicuro!" So I start to

293

go away. Then I hear a voice call, "Signora! Signora!" So I turn round and I see Serafina's daughter at the window.

VIOLETTA:
Rosa?

PEPPINA:
Yeah, Rosa. An' you know how?

VIOLETTA:
How?

PEPPINA:
Naked! Nuda, nuda! [*She crosses herself and repeats a prayer.*] In nominis padri et figlio et spiritus sancti. Aaahh!

VIOLETTA:
What did she do?

PEPPINA:
Do? She say, "Signora! Please, you call this numero and ask for Jack and tell Jack my clothes are lock up so I can't get out from the house." Then Serafina come and she grab-a the girl by the hair and she pull her way from the window and she slam the shutters right in my face!

GIUSEPPINA:
Whatsa the matter the daughter?

VIOLETTA:
Who is this boy? Where did she meet him?

PEPPINA:
Boy! What boy? He's a sailor. [*At the word "sailor" the women say "Ahhh!"*] She met him at the high school dance and somebody tell Serafina. That's why she lock up the girl's clothes so she can't leave the house. She can't even go to the high school to take the examinations. Imagine!

294

VIOLETTA:

Peppina, this time *you* go to the door, yeah?

PEPPINA:

Oh yeah, I go. Now I'm getting nervous. [*The women all crowd to the door.*] Sera-feee-na!

VIOLETTA:

Louder, louder!

PEPPINA:

Apri la porta! Come on, come on!

THE WOMEN [*together*]:

Yeah, apri la porta! . . . Come on, hurry up! . . . Open up!

GIUSEPPINA:

I go get-a police.

VIOLETTA:

Whatsa matta? You want more trouble?

GIUSEPPINA:

Listen, I pay in advance five dollars and get no dress. Now what she wear, my daughter, to graduate in? A couple of towels and a rose in the hair? [*There is a noise inside: a shout and running footsteps.*]

THE WOMEN:

Something is going on in the house! I hear someone! Don't I? Don't you?

[*A scream and running footsteps are heard. The front door opens and Serafina staggers out onto the porch. She is wearing a soiled pink slip and her hair is wild.*]

SERAFINA:

Aiuto! Aiuto! [*She plunges back into the house.*]

295

[*Miss Yorke, a spinsterish high school teacher, walks quickly up to the house. The Sicilian women, now all chattering at once like a cloud of birds, sweep about her as she approaches.*]

MISS YORKE:
You ladies know I don't understand Italian! So, please . . .

[*She goes directly into the house. There are more outcries inside. The Strega comes and stands at the edge of the yard, cackling derisively.*]

THE STREGA [*calling back to someone*]:
The Wops are at it again!—She got the daughter lock up naked in there all week. Ho, ho, ho! She lock up all week —naked—shouting out the window tell people to call a number and give a message to Jack. Ho, ho, ho! I guess she's in trouble already, and only fifteen!—They ain't civilized, these Sicilians. In the old country they live in caves in the hills and the country's run by bandits. Ho, ho, ho! More of them coming over on the boats all the time. [*The door is thrown open again and Serafina reappears on the porch. She is acting wildly, as if demented.*]

SERAFINA [*gasping in a hoarse whisper*]:
She cut her wrist, my daughter, she cut her wrist! [*She runs out into the yard.*] Aiiii-eeee! Aiutatemi, aiutatemi! Call the dottore! [*Assunta rushes up to Serafina and supports her as she is about to fall to her knees in the yard.*] Get the knife away from her! Get the knife, please! Get the knife away from—she cut her wrist with—Madonna! Madonna mia . . .

ASSUNTA:
Smettila, smettila, Serafina.

296

MISS YORKE [*coming out of the back room*]:
Mrs. Delle Rose, your daughter has not cut her wrist. Now come back into the house.

SERAFINA [*panting*]:
Che dice, che dice? Che cosa? Che cosa dice?

MISS YORKE:
Your daughter's all right. Come back into the house. And you ladies please go away!

ASSUNTA:
Vieni, Serafina. Andiamo a casa. [*She supports the heavy, sagging bulk of Serafina to the steps. As they climb the steps one of the Sicilian mothers advances from the whispering group.*]

GIUSEPPINA [*boldly*]:
Serafina, we don't go away until we get our dresses.

PEPPINA:
The graduation begins and the girls ain't dressed.

[*Serafina's reply to this ill-timed request is a long, animal howl of misery as she is supported into the house. Miss Yorke follows and firmly closes the door upon the women, who then go around back of the house. The interior of the house is lighted up.*]

MISS YORKE [*to Serafina*]:
No, no, no, she's not bleeding. Rosa? Rosa, come here and show your mother that you are not bleeding to death.

[*Rosa appears silently and sullenly between the curtains that separate the two rooms. She has a small white handkerchief tied around one wrist. Serafina points at the wrist and cries out: "Aiieee!"*]

MISS YORKE [*severely*]:
Now *stop* that, Mrs. Delle Rose!

[*Serafina rushes to Rosa, who thrusts her roughly away.*]

ROSA:
Lasciami stare, Mama!—I'm so ashamed I could die. This
is the way she goes around all the time. She hasn't put on
clothes since my father was killed. For three years she sits
at the sewing machine and never puts a dress on or goes
out of the house, and now she has locked my clothes up so
I can't go out. She wants me to be like her, a freak of the
neighborhood, the way she is! Next time, next time, I won't
cut my wrist but my throat! I don't want to live locked up
with a bottle of ashes! [*She points to the shrine.*]

ASSUNTA:
Figlia, figlia, figlia, non devi parlare cosí!

MISS YORKE:
Mrs. Delle Rose, please give me the key to the closet so that
your daughter can dress for the graduation!

SERAFINA [*surrendering the key*]:
Ecco la—chiave . . . [*Rosa snatches the key and runs back
through the curtains.*]

MISS YORKE:
Now why did you lock her clothes up, Mrs. Delle Rose?

SERAFINA:
The wrist is still bleeding!

MISS YORKE:
No, the wrist is not bleeding. It's just a skin cut, a scratch.
But the child is exhausted from all this excitement and
hasn't eaten a thing in two or three days.

298

ROSA [*running into the dining room*]:
Four days! I only asked her one favor. Not to let me go out
but to let Jack come to the house so she could meet him!—
Then she locked my clothes up!

MISS YORKE:
Your daughter missed her final examinations at the high
school, but her grades have been so good that she will be
allowed to graduate with her class and take the examinations later.—You understand me, Mrs. Delle Rose!

[*Rosa goes into the back of the house.*]

SERAFINA [*standing at the curtains*]:
See the way she looks at me? I've got a wild thing in the
house, and her wrist is still bleeding!

MISS YORKE:
Let's not have any more outbursts of emotion!

SERAFINA:
Outbursts of—you make me sick! Sick! Sick at my stomach
you make me! Your school, you make all this trouble! You
give-a this dance where she gets mixed up with a sailor.

MISS YORKE:
You are talking about the Hunter girl's brother, a sailor
named Jack, who attended the dance with his sister?

SERAFINA:
"Attended with sister!"—Attended with *sister!*—My daughter, she's nobody's sister!

[*Rosa comes out of the back room. She is radiantly beautiful in her graduation gown.*]

ROSA:
Don't listen to her, don't pay any attention to her, Miss
Yorke.—I'm ready to go to the high school.

299

SERAFINA [*stunned by her daughter's beauty, and speaking with a wheedling tone and gestures, as she crouches a little.*]

O tesoro, tesoro! Vieni qua, Rosa, cara!—Come here and kiss Mama one minute!—Don't go like that, now!

ROSA:
Lasciami stare!

[*She rushes out on the porch. Serafina gazes after her with arms slowly drooping from their imploring gesture and jaw dropping open in a look of almost comic desolation.*]

SERAFINA:
Ho solo te, solo te—in questo mondo!

MISS YORKE:
Now, now, Mrs. Delle Rose, no more excitement, please!

SERAFINA [*suddenly plunging after them in a burst of fury*]:
Senti, senti, per favore!

ROSA:
Don't you dare come out on the street like that!—*Mama!*

(*She crouches and covers her face in shame, as Serafina heedlessly plunges out into the front yard in her shocking deshabille, making wild gestures.*]

SERAFINA:
You give this dance where she gets mixed up with a sailor. What do you think you want to do at this high school? [*In weeping despair, Rosa runs to the porch.*] How high is this high school? Listen, how high is this high school? Look, look, look, I will show you! It's high as that horse's

dirt out there in the street! [*Serafina points violently out in front of the house.*] Si! 'Sta fetentissima scuola! Scuola maledetta!

[*Rosa cries out and rushes over to the palm tree, leaning against it, with tears of mortification.*]

MISS YORKE:

Mrs. Delle Rose, you are talking and behaving extremely badly. I don't understand how a woman that acts like you could have such a sweet and refined young girl for a daughter!—You don't deserve it!—Really . . . [*She crosses to the palm tree.*]

SERAFINA:

Oh, you want me to talk refined to you, do you? Then do me one thing! Stop ruining the girls at the high school! [*As Serafina paces about, she swings her hips in the exaggeratedly belligerent style of a parading matador.*]

ASSUNTA:

Piantala, Serafina! Andiamo a casa!

SERAFINA:

No, no, I ain't through talking to this here teacher!

ASSUNTA:

Serafina, look at yourself, you're not dressed!

SERAFINA:

I'm dressed okay; I'm not naked! [*She glares savagely at the teacher by the palm tree. The Sicilian mothers return to the front yard.*]

ASSUNTA:

Serafina, cara? Andiamo a casa, adesso!—Basta! Basta!

SERAFINA:

Aspetta!

ROSA:

I'm so ashamed I could die, I'm so ashamed. Oh, you don't know, Miss Yorke, the way that we live. She never puts on a dress; she stays all the time in that dirty old pink slip!—And talks to my father's ashes like he was living.

SERAFINA:

Teacher! Teacher, senti! What do you think you want to do at this high school? Sentite! per favore! You give this a dance! What kind of a spring dance is it? Answer this question, please, for me! What kind of a spring dance is it? She meet this boy there who don't even go to no high school. What kind of a boy? Guardate! *A sailor that wears a gold earring!* That kind of a boy is the kind of boy she meets there!—That's why I lock her clothes up so she can't go back to the high school! [*suddenly to Assunta*] She cut her wrist! It's still bleeding! [*She strikes her forehead three times with her fist.*]

ROSA:

Mama, you look disgusting! [*She rushes away.*]

[*Miss Yorke rushes after her. Serafina shades her eyes with one hand to watch them departing down the street in the brilliant spring light.*]

SERAFINA:

Did you hear what my daughter said to me?—"You look—disgusting."—She calls me . . .

ASSUNTA:

Now, Serafina, we must go in the house. [*She leads her gently to the porch of the little house.*]

302

SERAFINA [*proudly*]:
How pretty she look, my daughter, in the white dress, like
a bride! [*to all*] Excuse me! Excuse me, please! Go away!
Get out of my yard!

GIUSEPPINA [*taking the bull by the horns*]:
No, we ain't going to go without the dresses!

ASSUNTA:
Give the ladies the dresses so the girls can get dressed for
the graduation.

SERAFINA:
That one there, she only paid for the goods. I charge for the
work.

GIUSEPPINA:
Ecco! I got the money!

THE WOMEN:
We *got* the money!

SERAFINA:
The names are pinned on the dresses. Go in and get them.
[*She turns to Assunta.*] Did you hear what my daughter
called me? She called me "disgusting!"

[*Serafina enters the house, slamming the door. After a
moment the mothers come out, cradling the white voile
dresses tenderly in their arms, murmuring "carino!" and
"bellissimo!"*]

[*As they disappear the inside light is brought up and we
see Serafina standing before a glazed mirror, looking at
herself and repeating the daughter's word.*]

SERAFINA:
Disgusting!

[*The music is briefly resumed to mark a division.*]

303

SCENE FIVE

Immediately following. Serafina's movements gather momentum. She snatches a long-neglected girdle out of a bureau drawer and holds it experimentally about her waist. She shakes her head doubtfully, drops the girdle and suddenly snatches the $8.98 hat off the millinery dummy and plants it on her head. She turns around distractedly, not remembering where the mirror is. She gasps with astonishment when she catches sight of herself, snatches the hat off and hastily restores it to the blank head of the dummy. She makes another confused revolution or two, then gasps with fresh inspiration and snatches a girlish frock off a dummy —an Alice-blue gown with daisies crocheted on it. The dress sticks on the dummy. Serafina mutters savagely in Sicilian. She finally overcomes this difficulty but in her exasperation she knocks the dummy over. She throws off the robe and steps hopefully into the gown. But she discovers it won't fit over her hips. She seizes the girdle again; then hurls it angrily away. The parrot calls to her; she yells angrily back at the parrot: "Zitto!"

In the distance the high school band starts playing. Serafina gets panicky that she will miss the graduation ceremonies, and hammers her forehead with her fist, sobbing a little. She wriggles despairingly out of the blue dress and runs out back in her rayon slip just as Flora and Bessie appear outside the house. Flora and Bessie are two female clowns of middle years and juvenile temperament. Flora is tall and angular; Bessie is rather stubby. They are dressed for a gala. Flora runs up the steps and bangs at the cottage door.

BESSIE:

I fail to understand why it's so important to pick up a polka-dot blouse when it's likely to make us miss the twelve o'clock train.

FLORA:

Serafina! Serafina!

BESSIE:

We only got fifteen minutes to get to the depot and I'll get faint on the train if I don't have m' coffee . . .

FLORA:

Git a Coke on th' train, **Bessie.**

BESSIE:

Git nothing on the train if we don't git the train!

[*Serafina runs back out of the bedroom, quite breathless, in a purple silk dress. As she passes the millinery dummy she snatches the hat off again and plants it back on her head.*]

SERAFINA:

Wrist watch! Wrist watch! Where'd I put th' wrist watch? [*She hears Flora shouting and banging and rushes to the door.*]

BESSIE:

Try the door if it ain't open.

FLORA [*pushing in*]:

Just tell me, is it ready or not?

SERAFINA:

Oh! You. Don't bother me. I'm late for the graduation of my daughter and now I can't find her graduation present.

FLORA:

You got plenty of time.

SERAFINA:

Don't you hear the band playing?

FLORA:

They're just warming up. Now, Serafina, where is my blouse?

SERAFINA:

Blouse? Not ready! I had to make fourteen graduation dresses!

FLORA:

A promise is a promise and an excuse is just an excuse!

SERAFINA:

I got to get to the high school!

FLORA:

I got to get to the depot in that blouse!

BESSIE:

We're going to the American Legion parade in New Orleans.

FLORA:

There, there, there, there it is! [*She grabs the blouse from the machine.*] Get started, woman, stitch them bandanas together! If you don't do it, I'm a-gonna report you to the Chamber of Commerce and git your license revoked!

SERAFINA [*anxiously*]:

What license you talking about? I got no license!

FLORA:

You hear that, Bessie? *She hasn't got no license!*

BESSIE:

She ain't even got a license?

SERAFINA [*crossing quickly to the machine*]:

I—I'll stitch them together! But if you make me late to my daughter's graduation, I'll make you sorry some way . . .

[*She works with furious rapidity. A train whistle is heard.*]

BESSIE [*wildly and striking at Flora with her purse*]: Train's pullin' out! Oh, God, you made us miss it!

FLORA:
Bessie, you know there's another at 12:45!

BESSIE:
It's the selfish—principle of it that makes me sick! [*She walks rapidly up and down.*]

FLORA:
Set down, Bessie. Don't wear out your feet before we git to th' city . . .

BESSIE:
Molly tole me the town was full of excitement. They're dropping paper sacks full of water out of hotel windows.

FLORA:
Which hotel are they dropping paper sacks out of?

BESSIE:
What a fool question! The Monteleone Hotel.

FLORA:
That's an old-fashioned hotel.

BESSIE:
It might be old-fashioned but you'd be surprised at some of the modern, up-to-date things that go on there.

FLORA:
I heard, I heard that the Legionnaires caught a girl on Canal Street! They tore the clothes off her and sent her home in a taxi!

BESSIE:
I double dog dare anybody to try that on me!

307

FLORA:
You?! Huh! You never need any assistance gittin' un-
dressed!

SERAFINA [*ominously*]:
You two ladies watch how you talk in there. This here is
a Catholic house. You are sitting in the same room with
Our Lady and with the blessed ashes of my husband!

FLORA [*acidly*]:
Well, ex-cuse *me!* [*She whispers maliciously to Bessie.*] It
sure is a pleasant surprise to see you wearing a dress, Serafina, but the surprise would be twice as pleasant if it was
more the right size. [*to Bessie, loudly*] She used to have a
sweet figure, a little bit plump but attractive, but setting
there at that sewing machine for three years in a kimona
and not stepping out of the house has naturally given her
hips!

SERAFINA:
If I didn't have hips I would be a very uncomfortable
woman when I set down.

[*The parrot squawks. Serafina imitates its squawk.*]

FLORA:
Polly want a cracker?

SERAFINA:
No. He don't want a cracker! What is she doing over there
at that window?

BESSIE:
Some Legionnaires are on the highway!

FLORA:
A Legionnaire? No kidding?

[*She springs up and joins her girl friend at the window. They both laugh fatuously, bobbing their heads out the window.*]

BESSIE:
He's looking this way; yell something!

FLORA [*leaning out the window*]:
Mademoiselle from Armentieres, parley-voo!

BESSIE [*chiming in rapturously*]:
Mademoiselle from Armentieres, parley-voo!

A VOICE OUTSIDE [*gallantly returning the salute*]:
Mademoiselle from Armentieres, hadn't been kissed for forty years!

BOTH GIRLS [*together; very gaily*]:
Hinky-dinky parley-voooo!

[*They laugh and applaud at the window. The Legionnaires are heard laughing. A car horn is heard as the Legionnaires drive away. Serafina springs up and rushes over to the window, jerks them away from it and slams the shutters in their faces.*]

SERAFINA [*furiously*]:
I told you wimmen that you was not in a honky-tonk! Now take your blouse and git out! Get out on the streets where you kind a wimmen belong.—This is the house of Rosario delle Rose and those are his ashes in that marble urn and I won't have—unproper things going on here or dirty talk, neither!

FLORA:
Who's talking dirty?

BESSIE:
What a helluva nerve.

309

FLORA:

I want you to listen!

SERAFINA:

You are, you are, dirty talk, all the time men, men, men!
You men-crazy things, you!

FLORA:

Sour grapes—sour grapes is your trouble! You're wild with
envy!

BESSIE:

Isn't she green with jealousy? Huh!

SERAFINA [*suddenly and religiously*]:

When I think of men I think about my husband. My husband was a Sicilian. We had love together every night of
the week, we never skipped one, from the night we was
married till the night he was killed in his fruit truck on
that road there! [*She catches her breath in a sob.*] And
maybe that is the reason I'm not man-crazy and don't like
hearing the talk of women that are. But I am interested,
now, in the happiness of my daughter who's graduating
this morning out of high school. And now I'm going to be
late, the band is playing! And I have lost her wrist watch!
—her graduation present! [*She whirls about distractedly.*]

BESSIE:

Flora, let's go!—The hell with that goddam blouse!

FLORA:

Oh, no, just wait a minute! I don't accept insults from no
one!

SERAFINA:

Go on, go on to New Orleans, you two man-crazy things,
you! And pick up a man on Canal Street but not in my
house, at my window, in front of my dead husband's ashes!

[*The high school band is playing a martial air in the distance. Serafina's chest is heaving violently; she touches her heart and momentarily seems to forget that she must go.*] I am not at all interested, I am not interested in men getting fat and bald in soldier-boy play suits, tearing the clothes off girls on Canal Street and dropping paper sacks out of hotel windows. I'm just not interested in that sort of man-crazy business. I remember my husband with a body like a young boy and hair on his head as thick and black as mine is and skin on him smooth and sweet as a yellow rose petal.

FLORA:

Oh, a *rose,* was he?

SERAFINA:

Yes, yes, a rose, a rose!

FLORA:

Yes, a rose of a Wop!—of a gangster!—shot smuggling dope under a load of bananas!

BESSIE:

Flora, Flora, let's go!

SERAFINA: ·

My folks was peasants, contadini, but he—he come from *land*owners! *Signorile,* my husband—At night I sit here and I'm satisfied to remember, because I had the best.— Not the third best and not the second best, but the *first* best, the *only* best!—So now I stay here and am satisfied now to remember, . . .

BESSIE:

Come on, come out! To the depot!

FLORA:

Just wait, I wanta hear this, it's too good to miss!

311

SERAFINA:

I count up the nights I held him all night in my arms, and I can tell you how many. Each night for twelve years. Four thousand—three hundred—and eighty. The number of nights I held him all night in my arms. Sometimes I didn't sleep, just held him all night in my arms. And I am satisfied with it. I grieve for him. Yes, my pillow at night's never dry—but I'm satisfied to remember. And I would feel cheap and degraded and not fit to live with my daughter or under the roof with the urn of his blessed ashes, those —ashes of a rose—if after that memory, after knowing that man, I went to some other, some middle-aged man, not young, not full of young passion, but getting a pot belly on him and losing his hair and smelling of sweat and liquor— and trying to fool myself that *that* was love-making! I *know* what love-making was. And I'm satisfied just to remember . . . [*She is panting as though she had run upstairs.*] Go on, you do it, you go on the streets and let them drop their sacks of dirty water on you!—I'm satisfied to remember the love of a man that was mine—*only mine!* Never touched by the hand of *nobody! Nobody* but *me!*— Just me! [*She gasps and runs out to the porch. The sun floods her figure. It seems to astonish her. She finds herself sobbing. She digs in her purse for her handkerchief.*]

FLORA [*crossing to the open door*]:
Never touched by nobody?

SERAFINA [*with fierce pride*]:
Never nobody but me!

FLORA:
I know somebody that could a tale unfold! And not so far from here neither. Not no further than the Square Roof is, that place on Esplanade!

BESSIE:

Estelle Hohengarten!

FLORA:

Estelle Hohengarten!—the blackjack dealer from Texas!

BESSIE:

Get into your blouse and let's go!

FLORA:

Everybody's known it but Serafina. I'm just telling the facts that come out at the inquest while she was in bed with her eyes shut tight and the sheet pulled over her head like a female ostrich! Tie this damn thing on me! It was a romance, not just a fly-by-night thing, but a steady affair that went on for more than a year.

[*Serafina has been standing on the porch with the door open behind her. She is in the full glare of the sun. She appears to have been struck senseless by the words shouted inside. She turns slowly about. We see that her dress is unfastened down the back, the pink slip showing. She reaches out gropingly with one hand and finds the porch column which she clings to while the terrible words strike constantly deeper. The high school band continues as a merciless counterpoint.*]

BESSIE:

Leave her in ignorance. Ignorance is bliss.

FLORA:

He had a rose tattoo on his chest, the stuck-up thing, and Estelle was so gone on him she went down to Bourbon Street and had one put on her. [*Serafina comes onto the porch and Flora turns to her, viciously.*] Yeah, a rose tattoo on her chest same as the Wop's!

SERAFINA [*very softly*]:

Liar . . . [*She comes inside; the word seems to give her strength.*]

313

BESSIE [*nervously*]:
Flora, let's go, let's go!

SERAFINA [*in a terrible voice*]:
Liar!—*Lie*-arrrrr!

[*She slams the wooden door shut with a violence that shakes the walls.*]

BESSIE [*shocked into terror*]:
Let's get outa here, Flora!

FLORA:
Let her howl her head off. I don't care.

[*Serafina has snatched up a broom.*]

BESSIE:
What's she up to?

FLORA:
I don't care what she's up to!

BESSIE:
I'm a-scared of these Wops.

FLORA:
I'm not afraid of nobody!

BESSIE:
She's gonna hit you.

FLORA:
She'd better not hit me!

[*But both of the clowns are in retreat to the door. Serafina suddenly rushes at them with the broom. She flails Flora about the hips and shoulders. Bessie gets out. But Flora is trapped in a corner. A table is turned over. Bessie, outside, screams for the police and cries: "Murder! Murder!" The high school band is playing "The Stars and*

*Stripes Forever." Flora breaks wildly past the flailing
broom and escapes out of the house. She also takes up the
cry for help. Serafina follows them out. She is flailing the
brilliant noon air with the broom. The two women run
off, screaming.*]

FLORA [*calling back*]:
I'm going to have her arrested! Police, police! I'm going to
have you arrested!

SERAFINA:
Have me arrested, *have* me, you dirt, you devil, you *liar!*
Li-i-arrrr!

[*She comes back inside the house and leans on the work
table for a moment, panting heavily. Then she rushes back
to the door, slams it and bolts it. Then she rushes to the
windows, slams the shutters and fastens them. The house
is now dark except for the vigil light in the ruby glass
cup before the Madonna, and the delicate beams admitted
through the shutter slats.*]

SERAFINA [*in a crazed manner*]:
Have me—have me—arrested—dirty slut—bitch—liar! [*She
moves about helplessly, not knowing what to do with her
big, stricken body. Panting for breath, she repeats the word
"liar" monotonously and helplessly as she thrashes about. It
is necessary for her, vitally necessary for her, to believe that
the woman's story is a malicious invention. But the words
of it stick in her mind and she mumbles them aloud as she
thrashes crazily around the small confines of the parlor.*]
Woman—Estelle—[*The sound of band music is heard.*]
Band, band, already—started.—Going to miss—graduation.
Oh! [*She retreats toward the Madonna.*] Estelle, Estelle
Hohengarten?—"A shirt for a man I'm in love with! This

315

man—is—wild like a Gypsy."—Oh, oh, Lady—The—rose-colored—silk. [*She starts toward the dining room, then draws back in terror.*] No, no, no, no, no! I don't remember! It wasn't that name, I don't remember the name! [*The band music grows louder.*] High school—graduation—late! I'll be—late for it.—Oh, Lady, give me a—*sign!* [*She cocks her head toward the statue in a fearful listening attitude.*] Che? Che dice, Signora? *Oh, Lady! Give me a sign!*

[*The scene dims out.*]

SCENE SIX

*It is two hours later. The interior of the house is in com-
plete darkness except for the vigil light. With the shutters
closed, the interior is so dark that we do not know Serafina
is present. All that we see clearly is the starry blue robe of
Our Lady above the flickering candle of the ruby glass cup.
After a few moments we hear Serafina's voice, very softly,
in the weak, breathless tone of a person near death.*

SERAFINA [*very softly*]:
Oh, Lady, give me a sign . . .

[*Gay, laughing voices are heard outside the house. Rosa
and Jack appear, bearing roses and gifts. They are shouting back to others in a car.*]

JACK:
Where do we go for the picnic?

A GIRL'S VOICE [*from the highway*]:
We're going in three sailboats to Diamond Key.

A MAN'S VOICE:
Be at Municipal Pier in half an hour.

ROSA:
Pick us up here! [*She races up the steps.*] Oh, the door's
locked! Mama's gone *out!* There's a key in that birdbath.

[*Jack opens the door. The parlor lights up faintly as they
enter.*]

JACK:
It's dark in here.

ROSA:
Yes, Mama's gone out!

317

JACK:

How do you know she's out?

ROSA:

The door was locked and all the shutters are closed! Put down those roses.

JACK:

Where shall I . . .

ROSA:

Somewhere, anywhere!—Come here! [*He approaches her rather diffidently.*] I want to teach you a little Dago word. The word is "bacio."

JACK:

What does this word mean?

ROSA:

This and this and this! [*She rains kisses upon him till he forcibly removes her face from his.*] Just think. A week ago Friday—I didn't know boys existed!—Did you know girls existed before the dance?

JACK:

Yes, I knew they existed . . .

ROSA [*holding him*]:

Do you remember what you said to me on the dance floor? "Honey, you're dancing too close?"

JACK:

Well, it was—hot in the Gym and the—floor was crowded.

ROSA:

When my girl friend was teaching me how to dance, I asked her, "How do you know which way the boy's going to move?" And she said, "You've got to feel how he's going to move with your body!" I said, "How do you feel with your body?" And she said, "By pressing up close!"—That's why I pressed up close! I didn't realize that I was—Ha, ha! Now you're blushing! Don't go *away!*—And a few minutes later you said to me, "Gee, you're beautiful!" I said, "Excuse me," and ran to the ladies' room. Do you know why? To look at myself in the mirror! And I saw that I was! For the first time in my life I was beautiful! You'd made me beautiful when you *said* that I was!

JACK [*humbly*]:
You *are* beautiful, Rosa! So much, I . . .

ROSA:
You've changed, *too.* You've stopped laughing and joking. Why have you gotten so old and serious, Jack?

JACK:
Well, honey, you're sort of . . .

ROSA:
What am I "sort of?"

JACK [*finding the exact word*]:
Wild! [*She laughs. He seizes the bandaged wrist.*] I didn't know nothing like this was going to happen.

ROSA:
Oh, that, that's nothing! I'll take the handkerchief off and you can forget it.

JACK:
How could you do a thing like that over me? I'm—nothing!

ROSA:
Everybody is nothing until you love them!

JACK:
Give me that handkerchief. I want to show it to my shipmates. I'll say, "This is the blood of a beautiful girl who cut her wrist with a knife because she loved me!"

ROSA:

Don't be so pleased with yourself. It's mostly Mercuro-chrome!

SERAFINA [*violently, from the dark room adjoining*]:
Stai zitta!—Cretina!

[*Rosa and Jack draw abruptly apart.*]

JACK [*fearfully*]:
I knew somebody was here!

ROSA [*sweetly and delicately*]:
Mama? Are you in there, Mama?

SERAFINA:
No, no, no, I'm not, I'm dead and buried!

ROSA:
Yes, Mama's in there!

JACK:
Well, I—better go and—wait outside for a—while . . .

ROSA:
You stay right here!—Mama?—Jack is with me.—Are you
dressed up nicely? [*There is no response.*] Why's it so
dark in here?—Jack, open the shutters!—I want to intro-
duce you to my mother . . .

JACK:
Hadn't I better go and . . .

ROSA:
No. Open the shutters!

[*The shutters are opened and Rosa draws apart the curtains between the two rooms. Sunlight floods the scene.
Serafina is revealed slumped in a chair at her work table
in the dining room near the Singer sewing machine. She*]

*is grotesquely surrounded by the dummies, as though she
had been holding a silent conference with them. Her appearance, in slovenly deshabille, is both comic and shocking.*]

ROSA [*terribly embarrassed*]:
Mama, Mama, you said you were dressed up pretty! Jack,
stay out for a minute! What's happened, Mama?

[*Jack remains in the parlor. Rosa pulls the curtains,
snatches a robe and flings it over Serafina. She brushes
Serafina's hair back from her sweat-gleaming face, rubs
her face with a handkerchief and dusts it with powder.
Serafina submits to this cosmetic enterprise with a dazed
look.*]

ROSA [*gesturing vertically*]:
Su, su, su, su, su, su, su, su, su!

[*Serafina sits up slightly in her chair, but she is still looking stupefied. Rosa returns to the parlor and opens the
curtains again.*]

ROSA:
Come in, Jack! Mama is ready to meet you!

[*Rosa trembles with eagerness as Jack advances nervously
from the parlor. But before he enters Serafina collapses
again into her slumped position, with a low moan.*]

ROSA [*violently*]:
Mama, Mama, su, Mama! [*Serafina sits half erect.*] She
didn't sleep good last night.—Mama, this is Jack Hunter!

JACK:
Hello, Mrs. Delle Rose. It sure is a pleasure to meet you.

321

[*There is a pause. Serafina stares indifferently at the boy.*]

ROSA:

Mama, Mama, say something!

JACK:

Maybe your Mama wants me to . . . [*He makes an awkward gesture toward the door.*]

ROSA:

No, no, Mama's just tired. Mama makes dresses; she made a whole lot of dresses for the graduation! How many, Mama, how many graduation dresses did you have to make?

SERAFINA [*dully*]:

Fa niente . . .

JACK:

I was hoping to see you at the graduation, Mrs. Delle Rose.

ROSA:

I guess that Mama was too worn out to go.

SERAFINA:

Rosa, shut the front door, shut it and lock it. There was a—policeman . . . [*There is a pause.*] What?—What?

JACK:

My sister was graduating. My mother was there and my aunt was there—a whole bunch of cousins—I was hoping that you could—all—get together . . .

ROSA:

Jack brought you some flowers.

JACK:

I hope you are partial to roses as much as I am. [*He hands her the bouquet. She takes them absently.*]

ROSA:

Mama, say something, say something simple like "Thanks."

SERAFINA:

Thanks.

ROSA:

Jack, tell Mama about the graduation; describe it to her.

JACK:

My mother said it was just like fairyland.

ROSA:

Tell her what the boys wore!

JACK:

What did—what did they wear?

ROSA:

Oh, you know what they wore. They wore blue coats and white pants and each one had a carnation! And there were three couples that did an old-fashioned dance, a minuet, Mother, to Mendelssohn's *Spring Song!* Wasn't it lovely, Jack? But one girl slipped; she wasn't used to long dresses! She slipped and fell on her—ho, ho! Wasn't it funny, Jack, wasn't it, wasn't it, Jack?

JACK [*worriedly*]:

I think that your Mama . . .

ROSA:

Oh, my prize, my prize, I have forgotten my prize!

JACK:

Where is it?

ROSA:

You set them down by the sewing sign when you looked for the key.

JACK:

Aw, excuse me, I'll get them. [*He goes out through the parlor. Rosa runs to her mother and kneels by her chair.*]

ROSA [*in a terrified whisper*]:

Mama, something has happened! What has happened, Mama? Can't you tell me, Mama? Is it because of this morning? Look. I took the bandage off, it was only a scratch! So, Mama, forget it! Think it was just a bad dream that never happened! Oh, Mama! [*She gives her several quick kisses on the forehead. Jack returns with two big books tied in white satin ribbon.*]

JACK:

Here they are.

ROSA:

Look what I got, Mama.

SERAFINA [*dully*]:

What?

ROSA:

The *Digest of Knowledge!*

JACK:

Everything's in them, from Abracadabra to Zoo! My sister was jealous. She just got a diploma!

SERAFINA [*rousing a bit*]:

Diploma, where is it? Didn't you get no diploma?

ROSA:

Si, si, Mama! Eccolo! Guarda, guarda! [*She holds up the diploma tied in ribbon.*]

SERAFINA:

Va bene.—Put it in the drawer with your father's clothes.

JACK:

Mrs. Delle Rose, you should be very, very proud of your daughter. She stood in front of the crowd and recited a poem.

ROSA:

Yes, I did. Oh, I was so excited!

JACK:

And Mrs. Delle Rose, your daughter, Rosa, was so pretty when she walked on the stage—that people went "Ooooooooooo!" —like that! Y'know what I mean? They all went— "Ooooooooo!" Like a—like a—*wind* had—blown over! Because your daughter, Rosa, was so—*lovely* looking! [*He has crouched over to Serafina to deliver this description close to her face. Now he straightens up and smiles proudly at Rosa.*] How does it feel to be the mother of the prettiest girl in the world?

ROSA [*suddenly bursting into pure delight*]:

Ha, ha, ha, ha, ha, ha! [*She throws her head back in rapture.*]

SERAFINA [*rousing*]:

Hush!

ROSA:

Ha, ha, ha, ha, ha, ha, ha, ha, ha, ha! [*She cannot control her ecstatic laughter. She presses her hand to her mouth but the laughter still bubbles out.*]

SERAFINA [*suddenly rising in anger*]:

Pazza, pazza, pazza! Finiscila! Basta, via! [*Rosa whirls around to hide her convulsions of joy. To Jack:*] Put the prize books in the parlor, and shut the front door; there was a policeman come here because of—some trouble . . . [*Jack takes the books.*]

325

ROSA:

Mama, I've never seen you like this! What will Jack think, Mama?

SERAFINA:

Why do I care what Jack thinks?—You wild, wild crazy thing, you—with the eyes of your—father . . .

JACK [*returning*]:

Yes, ma'am, Mrs. Delle Rose, you certainly got a right to be very proud of your daughter.

SERAFINA [*after a pause*]:

I am proud of the—memory of her—father.—He was a baron . . . [*Rosa takes Jack's arm.*] And who are *you?* What are you?—per piacere!

ROSA:

Mama, I just introduced him; his name is Jack Hunter.

SERAFINA:

Hunt-er?

JACK:

Yes, ma'am, Hunter. Jack Hunter.

SERAFINA:

What are you hunting?—Jack?

ROSA:

Mama!

SERAFINA:

What all of 'em are hunting? To have a good time, and the Devil cares who pays for it? I'm sick of men, I'm almost as sick of men as I am of wimmen.—Rosa, get out while I talk to this boy!

ROSA:

I didn't bring Jack here to be insulted!

JACK:

Go on, honey, and let your Mama talk to me. I think your Mama has just got a slight wrong—impression . . .

SERAFINA [*ominously*]:
Yes, I got an impression!

ROSA:

I'll get dressed! Oh, Mama, don't spoil it for me!—the happiest day of my life! [*She goes into the back of the house.*]

JACK [*after an awkward pause*]:
Mrs. Delle Rose . . .

SERAFINA [*correcting his pronunciation*]:
Delle Rose!

JACK: ˙

Mrs. Delle Rose, I'm sorry about all this. Believe me, Mrs. Delle Rose, the last thing I had in mind was getting mixed up in a family situation. I come home after three months to sea, I docked at New Orleans, and come here to see my folks. My sister was going to a high school dance. She took me with her, and there I met your daughter.

SERAFINA:
What did you do?

JACK:

At the high school dance? We danced! My sister had told me that Rose had a very strict mother and wasn't allowed to go on dates with boys so when it was over, I said, "I'm sorry you're not allowed to go out." And she said, "Oh! What gave you the idea I *wasn't!*" So then I thought my sister had made a mistake and I made a date with her for the next night.

SERAFINA:
What did you do the next night?

JACK:

The next night we went to the movies.

SERAFINA:

And what did you do—that night?

JACK:

At the movies? We ate a bag of popcorn and watched the movie!

SERAFINA:

She come home at midnight and said she had been with a girl friend studying "civics."

JACK:

Whatever story she told you, it ain't my fault!

SERAFINA:

And the night after that?

JACK:

Last Tuesday? We went roller skating!

SERAFINA:

And afterward?

JACK:

After the skating? We went to a drugstore and had an ice cream soda!

SERAFINA:

Alone?

JACK:

At the drugstore? No. It was crowded. And the skating rink was full of people skating!

SERAFINA:

You mean that you haven't been alone with my Rosa?

JACK:

Alone or not alone, what's the point of that question? I still don't see the point of it.

SERAFINA:

We are Sicilians. We don't leave the girls with the boys they're not engaged to!

JACK:

Mrs. Delle Rose, this is the United States.

SERAFINA:

But we are Sicilians, and we are not cold-blooded.—My girl is a *virgin!* She *is*—or she *was*—I would like to know—*which!*

JACK:

Mrs. Delle Rose! I got to tell you something. You might not believe it. It is a hard thing to say. But I am—*also* a—*virgin* . . .

SERAFINA:

What? No. I do not believe it.

JACK:

Well, it's true, though. This is the first time—I . . .

SERAFINA:

First time you *what?*

JACK:

The first time I really wanted to . . .

SERAFINA:

Wanted to what?

JACK:

Make—love . . .

SERAFINA:

You? A sailor?

JACK [*sighing deeply*]:
Yes, ma'am. I had opportunities to!—But I—always thought
of my mother . . . I always asked myself, would she or
would she not—think—this or that person was—decent!

SERAFINA:
But with my daughter, my Rosa, your mother tells you
okay?—go ahead, son!

JACK:
Mrs. Delle Rose! [*with embarrassment*]—Mrs. Delle Rose,
I . . .

SERAFINA:
Two weeks ago I was slapping her hands for scratching
mosquito bites. She rode a bicycle to school. Now all at
once—I've got a wild thing in the house. She says she's in
love. And you? Do you say *you're* in love?

JACK [*solemnly*]:
Yes, ma'am, I do, I'm in love!—very much . . .

SERAFINA:
Bambini, tutti due, bambini!

[*Rosa comes out, dressed for the picnic.*]

ROSA:
I'm ready for Diamond Key!

SERAFINA:
Go out on the porch. Diamond Key!

ROSA [*with a sarcastic curtsy*]:
Yes, Mama!

SERAFINA:
What are you? Catholic?

JACK:

Me? Yes, ma'am, Catholic.

SERAFINA:

You don't look Catholic to me!

ROSA [*shouting, from the door*]:

Oh, God, Mama, how do Catholics look? How do they look different from anyone else?

SERAFINA:

Stay out till I call you! [*Rosa crosses to the birdbath and prays. Serafina turns to Jack.*] Turn around, will you?

JACK:

Do what, ma'am?

SERAFINA:

I said, *turn around!* [*Jack awkwardly turns around.*] Why do they make them Navy pants so tight?

ROSA [*listening in the yard*]:

Oh, my God . . .

JACK [*flushing*]:

That's a question you'll have to ask the Navy, Mrs. Delle Rose.

SERAFINA:

And that gold earring, what's the gold earring for?

ROSA [*yelling from the door*]:

For crossing the equator, Mama; he crossed it three times. He was initiated into the court of Neptune and gets to wear a gold earring! He's a shellback!

[*Serafina springs up and crosses to slam the porch door. Rosa runs despairingly around the side of the house and leans, exhausted with closed eyes, against the trunk of a palm tree. The Strega creeps into the yard, listening.*]

SERAFINA:

You see what I got. A wild thing in the house!

JACK:

Mrs. Delle Rose, I guess that Sicilians are very emotional people . . .

SERAFINA:

I want nobody to take advantage of that!

JACK:

You got the wrong idea about me, Mrs. Delle Rose.

SERAFINA:

I know what men want—not to eat popcorn with girls or to slide on ice! And boys are the same, only younger.— Come here. Come here!

[*Rosa hears her mother's passionate voice. She rushes from the palm tree to the backdoor and pounds on it with both fists.*]

ROSA:

Mama! Mama! Let me in the door, Jack!

JACK:

Mrs. Delle Rose, your daughter is calling you.

SERAFINA:

Let her call!—Come here. [*She crosses to the shrine of Our Lady.*] *Come here!*

[*Despairing of the backdoor, Rosa rushes around to the front. A few moments later she pushes open the shutters of the window in the wall and climbs half in. Jack crosses apprehensively to Serafina before the Madonna.*]

SERAFINA:

You said you're Catholic, ain't you?

JACK:
Yes, ma'am.

SERAFINA:
Then kneel down in front of Our Lady!

JACK:
Do—do what, did you say?

SERAFINA:
I said to get down on your knees in front of Our Lady!

[*Rosa groans despairingly in the window. Jack kneels
awkwardly upon the hassock.*]

ROSA:
Mama, Mama, *now* what?!

[*Serafina rushes to the window, pushes Rosa out and
slams the shutters.*]

SERAFINA [*returning to Jack*]:
Now say after me what I say!

JACK:
Yes, ma'am.

[*Rosa pushes the shutters open again.*]

SERAFINA:
I promise the Holy Mother that I will respect the innocence
of the daughter of . . .

ROSA [*in anguish*]:
Ma-*maaa!*

SERAFINA:
Get back out of that window!—Well? Are you gonna say it?

JACK:
Yes, ma'am. What was it, again?

SERAFINA:

I promise the Holy Mother . . .

JACK:

I promise the Holy Mother . . .

SERAFINA:

As I hope to be saved by the Blessed Blood of Jesus . . .

JACK:

As I hope to be saved by the . . .

SERAFINA:

Blessed Blood of . . .

JACK:

Jesus . . .

SERAFINA:

That I will respect the innocence of the daughter, Rosa, of Rosario delle Rose.

JACK:

That I will respect the innocence—of—Rosa . . .

SERAFINA:

Cross yourself! [*He crosses himself.*] Now get up, get up, get up! I am satisfied now . . .

[*Rosa jumps through the window and rushes to Serafina with arms outflung and wild cries of joy.*]

SERAFINA:

Let me go, let me breathe! [*Outside the Strega cackles derisively.*]

ROSA:

Oh, wonderful Mama, don't breathe! Oh, Jack! *Kiss* Mama! *Kiss Mama!* Mama, please kiss Jack!

SERAFINA:

Kiss? Me? No, no, no, no!—Kiss my *hand* . . .

[*She offers her hand, shyly, and Jack kisses it with a loud smack. Rosa seizes the wine bottle.*]

ROSA:

Mama, get some wine glasses!

[*Serafina goes for the glasses, and Rosa suddenly turns to Jack. Out of her mother's sight, she passionately grabs hold of his hand and presses it, first to her throat, then to her lips and finally to her breast. Jack snatches her hand away as Serafina returns with the glasses. Voices are heard calling from the highway.*]

VOICES OUTSIDE:

Ro-osa!—Ro-osa!—Ro-osa!

[*A car horn is heard blowing.*]

SERAFINA:

Oh, I forgot the graduation present.

[*She crouches down before the bureau and removes a fancily wrapped package from its bottom drawer. The car horn is honking, and the voices are calling.*]

ROSA:

They're calling for us! *Coming!* Jack! [*She flies out the door, calling back to her mother.*] G'bye, Mama!

JACK [*following Rosa*]:

Good-bye, Mrs. Delle Rose!

SERAFINA [*vaguely*]:

It's a Bulova wrist watch with seventeen jewels in it . . . [*She realizes that she is alone.*] Rosa! [*She goes to the door, still holding out the present. Outside the car motor roars, and the voices shout as the car goes off. Serafina stumbles outside, shielding her eyes with one hand, extending the gift with the other.*] Rosa, Rosa, your present! Regalo, regalo—tesoro!

[*But the car has started off, with a medley of voices shouting farewells, which fade quickly out of hearing. Serafina turns about vaguely in the confusing sunlight and gropes for the door. There is a derisive cackle from the witch next door. Serafina absently opens the package and removes the little gold watch. She winds it and then holds it against her ear. She shakes it and holds it again to her ear. Then she holds it away from her and glares at it fiercely.*]

SERAFINA [*pounding her chest three times*]:
Tick—tick—tick! [*She goes to the Madonna and faces it.*]
Speak to me, Lady! Oh, Lady, give me a sign!

[*The scene dims out.*]

ACT TWO

It is two hours later the same day.

Serafina comes out onto the porch, barefooted, wearing a rayon slip. Great shadows have appeared beneath her eyes; her face and throat gleam with sweat. There are dark stains of wine on the rayon slip. It is difficult for her to stand, yet she cannot sit still. She makes a sick moaning sound in her throat almost continually.

A hot wind rattles the canebrake. Vivi, the little girl, comes up to the porch to stare at Serafina as at a strange beast in a cage. Vivi is chewing a licorice stick which stains her mouth and her fingers. She stands chewing and staring. Serafina evades her stare. She wearily drags a broken gray wicker chair down off the porch, all the way out in front of the house, and sags heavily into it. It sits awry on a broken leg.

Vivi sneaks toward her. Serafina lurches about to face her angrily. The child giggles and scampers back to the porch.

SERAFINA [*sinking back into the chair*]:
Oh, Lady, Lady, Lady, give me a—sign . . . [*She looks up at the white glare of the sky.*]

[*Father De Leo approaches the house. Serafina crouches low in the chair to escape his attention. He knocks at the door. Receiving no answer, he looks out into the yard, sees her, and approaches her chair. He comes close to address her with a gentle severity.*]

FATHER DE LEO:
Buon giorno, Serafina.

SERAFINA [*faintly, with a sort of disgust*]:
Giorno . . .

FATHER DE LEO:
I'm surprised to see you sitting outdoors like this. What is
that thing you're wearing?—I think it's an undergarment!
—It's hanging off one shoulder, and your head, Serafina,
looks as if you had stuck it in a bucket of oil. Oh, I see now
why the other ladies of the neighborhood aren't taking
their afternoon naps! They find it more entertaining to sit
on the porches and watch the spectacle you are putting on
for them!—Are you listening to me?—I must tell you that
the change in your appearance and behavior since Rosario's
death is shocking—shocking! A woman can be dignified in
her grief but when it's carried too far it becomes a sort of
self-indulgence. Oh, I knew this was going to happen when
you broke the Church law and had your husband cremated!
[*Serafina lurches up from the chair and shuffles back to the
porch. Father De Leo follows her.*]—Set up a little idola-
trous shrine in your house and give worship to a bottle of
ashes. [*She sinks down upon the steps.*]—Are you listening
to me?

[*Two women have appeared on the embankment and
descend toward the house. Serafina lurches heavily up to
meet them, like a weary bull turning to face another attack.*]

SERAFINA:
You ladies, what you want? I don't do sewing! Look, I quit
doing sewing. [*She pulls down the "SEWING" sign and
hurls it away.*] Now you got places to go, you ladies, go
places! Don't hang around front of my house!

FATHER DE LEO:
The ladies want to be friendly.

SERAFINA:
Naw, they don't come to be friendly. They think they know something that Serafina don't know; they think I got *these* on my head! [*She holds her fingers like horns at either side of her forehead.*] Well, I ain't got them! [*She goes padding back out in front of the house. Father De Leo follows.*]

FATHER DE LEO:
You called me this morning in distress over something.

SERAFINA:
I called you this morning but now it is afternoon.

FATHER DE LEO:
I had to christen the grandson of the Mayor.

SERAFINA:
The Mayor's important people, not Serafina!

FATHER DE LEO:
You don't come to confession.

SERAFINA [*starting back toward the porch*]:
No, I don't come, I don't go, I—Ohhh! [*She pulls up one foot and hops on the other.*]

FATHER DE LEO:
You stepped on something?

SERAFINA [*dropping down on the steps*]:
No, no, no, no, no, I don't step on—noth'n . . .

FATHER DE LEO:
Come in the house. We'll wash it with antiseptic. [*She lurches up and limps back toward the house.*] Walking barefooted you will get it infected.

SERAFINA:
Fa niente . . .

[*At the top of the embankment a little boy runs out with a red kite and flourishes it in the air with rigid gestures, as though he were giving a distant signal. Serafina shades her eyes with a palm to watch the kite, and then, as though its motions conveyed a shocking message, she utters a startled soft cry and staggers back to the porch. She leans against a pillar, running her hand rapidly and repeatedly through her hair. Father De Leo approaches her again, somewhat timidly.*]

FATHER DE LEO:
Serafina?

SERAFINA:
Che, che, che cosa vuole?

FATHER DE LEO:
I am thirsty. Will you go in the house and get me some water?

SERAFINA:
Go in. Get you some water. The faucet is working.—I can't go in the house.

FATHER DE LEO:
Why can't you go in the house?

SERAFINA:
The house has a tin roof on it. I got to breathe.

FATHER DE LEO:
You can breathe in the house.

SERAFINA:
No, I can't breathe in the house. The house has a tin roof on it and I . . .

340

[*The Strega has been creeping through the canebrake pretending to search for a chicken.*]

THE STREGA:

Chick, chick, chick, chick, chick? [*She crouches to peer under the house.*]

SERAFINA:

What's that? Is that the . . . ? Yes, the Strega! [*She picks up a flower pot containing a dead plant and crosses the yard.*] Strega! Strega! [*The Strega looks up, retreating a little.*] Yes, you, I mean you! You ain't look for no chick! Getta hell out of my yard! [*The Strega retreats, viciously muttering, back into the canebrake. Serafina makes the protective sign of the horns with her fingers. The goat bleats.*]

FATHER DE LEO:

You have no friends, Serafina.

SERAFINA:

I don't want friends.

FATHER DE LEO:

You are still a young woman. Eligible for—loving and— bearing again! I remember you dressed in pale blue silk at Mass one Easter morning, yes, like a lady wearing a—piece of the—weather! Oh, how proudly you walked, *too* proudly! —But now you crouch and shuffle about barefooted; you live like a convict, dressed in the rags of a convict. You have no companions; women you don't mix with. You . . .

SERAFINA:

No, I don't mix with them women. [*glaring at the women on the embankment*] The dummies I got in my house, I mix with them better because they don't make up no lies!— What kind of women are them? [*mimicking fiercely*]

341

"Eee, Papa, eeee, baby, eee, me, me, me! At thirty years old they got no more use for the letto matrimoniale, no. The big bed goes to the basement! They get little beds from Sears Roebuck and sleep on their bellies!

FATHER DE LEO:
Attenzione!

SERAFINA:
They make the life without glory. Instead of the heart they got the deep-freeze in the house. The men, they don't feel no glory, not in the house with them women; they go to the bars, fight in them, get drunk, get fat, put horns on the women because the women don't give them the love which is glory.—I did, I give him the glory. To me the big bed was beautiful like a religion. Now I lie on it with dreams, with memories only! But it is still beautiful to me and I don't believe that the man in my heart gave me horns! [*The women whisper.*] What, what are they saying? Does ev'rybody know something that I don't know?—No, all I want is a sign, a sign from Our Lady, to tell me the lie is a lie! And then I . . . [*The women laugh on the embankment. Serafina starts fiercely toward them. They scatter.*] Squeak, squeak, squawk, squawk! Hens—like water thrown on them! [*There is the sound of mocking laughter.*]

FATHER DE LEO:
People are laughing at you on all the porches.

SERAFINA:
I'm laughing, too. Listen to me, I'm laughing! [*She breaks into loud, false laughter, first from the porch, then from the foot of the embankment, then crossing in front of the house.*]

Ha, ha, ha, ha, ha, ha, ha! Now ev'rybody is laughing. Ha, ha, ha, ha, ha, ha!

FATHER DE LEO:

Zitta ora!—Think of your daughter.

SERAFINA [*understanding the word "daughter"*]:

You, *you* think of my daughter! Today you give out the diplomas, today at the high school you give out the prizes, diplomas! You give to my daughter a set of books call the *Digest of Knowledge!* What does she know? How to be cheap already?—Oh, yes, that is what to learn, how to be cheap and to cheat!—You know what they do at this high school? They ruin the girls there! They give the spring dance because the girls are man-crazy. And there at that dance my daughter goes with a sailor that has in his ear a gold ring! And pants so tight that a woman ought not to look at him! This morning, this morning she cuts with a knife her wrist if I don't let her go!—Now all of them gone to some island, they call it a picnic, all of them, gone in a—boat!

FATHER DE LEO:

There *was* a school picnic, chaperoned by the teachers.

SERAFINA:

Oh, lo so, lo so! The man-crazy old-maid teachers!—They all run wild on the island!

FATHER DE LEO:

Serafina delle Rose! [*He picks up the chair by the back and hauls it to the porch when she starts to resume her seat.*]—I *command* you to go in the house.

SERAFINA:

Go in the house? I will. I will go in the house if you will answer one question.—Will you answer one question?

FATHER DE LEO:

I will if I know the answer.

SERAFINA:

Aw, you know the answer!—You used to hear the confessions of my husband. [*She turns to face the priest.*]

FATHER DE LEO:

Yes, I heard his confessions . . .

SERAFINA [*with difficulty*]:

Did he ever speak to you of a *woman*?

[*A child cries out and races across in front of the house. Father De Leo picks up his panama hat. Serafina paces slowly toward him. He starts away from the house.*]

SERAFINA [*rushing after him*]:

Aspettate! Aspettate un momento!

FATHER DE LEO [*fearfully, not looking at her*]:

Che volete?

SERAFINA:

Rispondetemi! [*She strikes her breast.*] Did he speak of a woman to you?

FATHER DE LEO:

You know better than to ask me such a question. I don't break the Church laws. The secrets of the confessional are sacred to me. [*He walks away.*]

SERAFINA [*pursuing and clutching his arm*]:

I got to know. You could tell me.

FATHER DE LEO:

Let go of me, Serafina!

SERAFINA:

Not till you tell me, Father. Father, you tell me, please tell me! Or I will go mad! [*in a fierce whisper*] I will go back

in the house and smash the urn with the ashes—if you
don't tell me! I will go mad with the doubt in my heart
and I will smash the urn and scatter the ashes—of my husband's body!

FATHER DE LEO:
What could I tell you? If you would not believe the known
facts about him . . .

SERAFINA:
Known facts, who knows the known facts?

[*The neighbor women have heard the argument and
begin to crowd around, muttering in shocked whispers at
Serafina's lack of respect.*]

FATHER DE LEO [*frightened*]:
Lasciatemi, lasciatemi stare!—Oh, Serafina, I am too old for
this—please!—Everybody is . . .

SERAFINA [*in a fierce, hissing whisper*]:
Nobody knew my rose of the world but me and now they
can lie because the rose ain't living. They want the marble
urn broken; they want me to smash it. They want the rose
ashes scattered because I had too much glory. They don't
want glory like *that* in nobody's heart. They want—mouse-
squeaking!—known facts.—Who knows the known facts?
You—padres—wear black because of the fact that the facts
are known by nobody!

FATHER DE LEO:
Oh, Serafina! There are people watching!

SERAFINA:
Let them watch something. That will be a change for them.
—It's been a long time I wanted to break out like this and
now I . . .

FATHER DE LEO:

I am too old a man; I am not strong enough. I am sixty-seven years old! Must I call for help, now?

SERAFINA:

Yes, call! Call for help, but I won't let you go till you tell me!

FATHER DE LEO:

You're not a respectable woman.

SERAFINA:

No, I'm not a respectable; I'm a woman.

FATHER DE LEO:

No, you are not a woman. You are an animal!

SERAFINA:

Si, si, animale! Sono animale! Animale. Tell them all, shout it all to them, up and down the whole block! The Widow Delle Rose is not respectable, she is not even a woman, she is an animal! She is attacking the priest! She will tear the black suit off him unless he tells her the whores in this town are lying to her!

[*The neighbor women have been drawing closer as the argument progresses, and now they come to Father De Leo's rescue and assist him to get away from Serafina, who is on the point of attacking him bodily. He cries out, "Officer! Officer!" but the women drag Serafina from him and lead him away with comforting murmurs.*]

SERAFINA [*striking her wrists together*]:

Yes, it's me, it's me!! Lock me up, lock me, lock me up! Or I will—*smash!*—the marble . . . [*She throws her head far back and presses her fists to her eyes. Then she rushes crazily to the steps and falls across them.*]

ASSUNTA:

Serafina! Figlia! Figlia! Andiamo a casa!

SERAFINA:

Leave me alone, old woman.

[*She returns slowly to the porch steps and sinks down on them, sitting like a tired man, her knees spread apart and her head cupped in her hands. The children steal back around the house. A little boy shoots a beanshooter at her. She starts up with a cry. The children scatter, shrieking. She sinks back down on the steps, then leans back, staring up at the sky, her body rocking.*]

SERAFINA:

Oh, Lady, Lady, Lady, give me a sign!

[*As if in mocking answer, a novelty salesman appears and approaches the porch. He is a fat man in a seersucker suit and a straw hat with a yellow, red and purple band. His face is beet-red and great moons of sweat have soaked through the armpits of his jacket. His shirt is lavender, and his tie, pale blue with great yellow polka dots, is a butterfly bow. His entrance is accompanied by a brief, satiric strain of music.*]

THE SALESMAN:

Good afternoon, lady. [*She looks up slowly. The salesman talks sweetly, as if reciting a prayer.*] I got a little novelty here which I am offering to just a few lucky people at what we call an introductory price. Know what I mean? Not a regular price but a price which is less than what it costs to manufacture the article, a price we are making for the sake of introducing the product in the Gulf Coast territory. Lady, this thing here that I'm droppin' right in youah lap is bigger than television; it's going to revolutionize the

347

domestic life of America.—Now I don't do house to house
canvassing. I sell directly to merchants but when I stopped
over there to have my car serviced, I seen you taking the
air on the steps and I thought I would just drop over and . . .

[*There is the sound of a big truck stopping on the highway, and a man's voice, Alvaro's, is heard, shouting.*]

ALVARO:
Hey! Hey, you road hog!

THE SALESMAN [*taking a sample out of his bag*]:
Now, lady, this little article has a deceptive appearance. First
of all, I want you to notice how *compact* it is. It takes up
no more space than . . .

[*Alvaro comes down from the embankment. He is about
twenty-five years old, dark and very good-looking. He is
one of those Mediterranean types that resemble glossy
young bulls. He is short in stature, has a massively sculp-
tural torso and bluish-black curls. His face and manner
are clownish; he has a charming awkwardness. There is
a startling, improvised air about him; he frequently seems
surprised at his own speeches and actions, as though he
had not at all anticipated them. At the moment when we
first hear his voice the sound of timpani begins, at first
very pianissimo, but building up as he approaches, till it
reaches a vibrant climax with his appearance to Serafina
beside the house.*]

ALVARO:
Hey.

THE SALESMAN [*without glancing at him*]:
Hay is for horses!—Now, madam, you see what happens
when I press this button?

348

[*The article explodes in Serafina's face. She slaps it away with an angry cry. At the same time Alvaro advances, trembling with rage, to the porch steps. He is sweating and stammering with pent-up fury at a world of frustrations which are temporarily localized in the gross figure of this salesman.*]

ALVARO:

Hey, you! Come here! What the hell's the idea, back there at that curve? You make me drive off the highway!

THE SALESMAN [*to Serafina*]:

Excuse me for just one minute. [*He wheels menacingly about to face Alvaro.*] Is something giving you gas pains, Maccaroni?

ALVARO:

My name is not Maccaroni.

THE SALESMAN:

All right. Spaghetti.

ALVARO [*almost sobbing with passion*]:

I am not maccaroni. I am not spaghetti. I am a human being that drives a truck of bananas. I drive a truck of bananas for the Southern Fruit Company for a living, not to play cowboys and Indians on no highway with no rotten road hog. You got a 4-lane highway between Pass Christian and here. I give you the sign to pass me. You tail me and give me the horn. You yell "Wop" at me and "Dago." "Move over, Wop, move over, Dago." Then at the goddam curve, you go pass me and make me drive off the highway and yell back "Son of a bitch of a Dago!" I don't like that, no, no! And I am glad you stop here. Take the cigar from your mouth, take out the cigar!

349

THE SALESMAN:

Take it out for me, greaseball.

ALVARO:

If I take it out I will push it down your throat. I got three
dependents! If I fight, I get fired, but I will fight and get
fired. Take out the cigar!

[*Spectators begin to gather at the edge of the scene. Serafina stares at the truck driver, her eyes like a somnam-
bule's. All at once she utters a low cry and seems about
to fall.*]

ALVARO:

Take out the cigar, take out, take out the cigar!

[*He snatches the cigar from the salesman's mouth and
the salesman brings his knee up violently into Alvaro's
groin. Bending double and retching with pain, Alvaro
staggers over to the porch.*]

THE SALESMAN [*shouting, as he goes off*]:

I got your license number, Maccaroni! I know your boss!

ALVARO [*howling*]:

Drop dead! [*He suddenly staggers up the steps.*] Lady,
lady, I got to go in the house!

[*As soon as he enters, he bursts into rending sobs, leaning against a wall and shaking convulsively. The spectators outside laugh as they scatter. Serafina slowly enters
the house. The screen door rasps loudly on its rusty
springs as she lets it swing gradually shut behind her, her
eyes remaining fixed with a look of stupefied wonder
upon the sobbing figure of the truck driver. We must understand her profound unconscious response to this sudden contact with distress as acute as her own. There is a*

*long pause as the screen door makes its whining, catlike
noise swinging shut by degrees.*]

SERAFINA:

Somebody's—in my house? [*finally, in a hoarse, tremulous
whisper*] What are you—doing in here? Why have you—
come in my house?

ALVARO:

Oh, lady—leave me alone!—Please—now!

SERAFINA:

You—got no business—in here . . .

ALVARO:

I got to cry after a fight. I'm sorry, lady. I . . .
[*The sobs still shake him. He leans on a dummy.*]

SERAFINA:

Don't lean on my dummy. Sit down if you can't stand up.
—What is the matter with you?

ALVARO:

I always cry after a fight. But I don't want people to see
me. It's not like a man. [*There is a long pause; Serafina's
attitude seems to warm toward the man.*]

SERAFINA:

A man is not no different from no one else . . . [*All at once
her face puckers up, and for the first time in the play Serafina begins to weep, at first soundlessly, then audibly. Soon
she is sobbing as loudly as Alvaro. She speaks between sobs.*]
—I always cry—when somebody else is crying . . .

ALVARO:

No, no, lady, *don't* cry! Why should *you* cry? I will stop. I
will stop in a minute. This is not like a man. I am ashame
of myself. I will stop now; please, lady . . .

[*Still crouching a little with pain, a hand clasped to his abdomen, Alvaro turns away from the wall. He blows his nose between two fingers. Serafina picks up a scrap of white voile and gives it to him to wipe his fingers.*]

SERAFINA:
Your jacket is torn.

ALVARO [*sobbing*]:
My company jacket is torn?

SERAFINA:
Yes . . .

ALVARO:
Where is it torn?

SERAFINA [*sobbing*]:
Down the—back.

ALVARO:
Oh, Dio!

SERAFINA:
Take it off. I will sew it up for you. I do—sewing.

ALVARO:
Oh, Dio! [*sobbing*] I got three dependents! [*He holds up three fingers and shakes them violently at Serafina.*]

SERAFINA:
Give me—give me your jacket.

ALVARO:
He took down my license number!

SERAFINA:
People are always taking down license numbers and telephone numbers and numbers that don't mean nothing—all them numbers . . .

ALVARO:

Three, three dependents! Not citizens, even! No relief
checks, no nothing! [*Serafina sobs.*] He is going to com-
plain to the boss.

SERAFINA:

I wanted to cry all day.

ALVARO:

He said he would fire me if I don't stop fighting!

SERAFINA:

Stop crying so I can stop crying.

ALVARO:

I am a sissy. Excuse me. I am ashame.

SERAFINA:

Don't be ashame of nothing, the world is too crazy for
people to be ashame in it. I'm not ashame and I had two
fights on the street and my daughter called me "disgusting."
I got to sew this by hand; the machine is broke in a fight
with two women.

ALVARO:

That's what—they call a cat fight . . . [*He blows his nose.*]

SERAFINA:

Open the shutters, please, for me. I can't see to work. [*She
has crossed to her work table. He goes over to the window.
As he opens the shutters, the light falls across his fine torso,
the undershirt clinging wetly to his dark olive skin. Serafina is struck and murmurs: "Ohhh . . ." There is the
sound of music.*]

ALVARO:

What, lady?

SERAFINA [*in a strange voice*]:
The light on the body was like a man that lived here . . .

ALVARO:
Che dice?

SERAFINA:
Niente.—Ma com'è strano!—Lei è Napoletano? [*She is threading a needle.*]

ALVARO:
Io sono Siciliano! [*Serafina sticks her finger with her needle and cries out.*] Che fa?

SERAFINA:
I—stuck myself with the—needle!—You had—better wash up . . .

ALVARO:
Dov'è il gabinetto?

SERAFINA [*almost inaudibly*]:
Dietro. [*She points vaguely back.*]

ALVARO:
Con permesso! [*He moves past her. As he does so, she picks up a pair of broken spectacles on the work table. Holding them up by the single remaining side piece, like a lorgnette, she inspects his passing figure with an air of stupefaction. As he goes out, he says:*] A kick like that can have serious consequences! [*He goes into the back of the house.*]

SERAFINA [*after a pause*]: Madonna Santa!—*My husband's body*, with the head of a *clown!* [*She crosses to the Madonna.*] O Lady, O Lady! [*She makes an imploring gesture.*] Speak to me!—What are you saying?—Please, Lady, I can't hear you! Is it a sign? Is it a sign of something?

354

What does it mean? Oh, *speak to me,* Lady!—Everything is too strange!

[*She gives up the useless entreaty to the impassive statue. Then she rushes to the cupboard, clambers up on a chair and seizes a bottle of wine from the top shelf. But she finds it impossible to descend from the chair. Clasping the dusty bottle to her breast, she crouches there, helplessly whimpering like a child, as Alvaro comes back in.*]

ALVARO:

Ciao!

SERAFINA:

I can't get up.

ALVARO:

You mean you can't get down?

SERAFINA:

I mean I—can't get down . . .

ALVARO:

Con permesso, Signora! [*He lifts her down from the chair.*]

SERAFINA:

Grazie.

ALVARO:

I am ashame of what happen. Crying is not like a man. Did anyone see me?

SERAFINA:

Nobody saw you but me. To me it don't matter.

ALVARO:

You are simpatica, molto!—It was not just the fight that makes me break down. I was like this all today! [*He shakes his clenched fists in the air.*]

355

SERAFINA:

You and—me, too!—What was the trouble today?

ALVARO:

My name is Mangiacavallo which means "Eat-a-horse." It's a comical name, I know. Maybe two thousand and seventy years ago one of my grandfathers got so hungry that he ate up a horse! That ain't my fault. Well, today at the Southern Fruit Company I find on the pay envelope not "Mangiacavallo" but "EAT A HORSE" in big print! Ha, ha, ha, very funny!—I open the pay envelope! In it I find a notice.—The wages have been *garnishee!* You know what garnishee is? [*Serafina nods gravely.*] Garnishee!—Eat a horse!—Road hog!—All in one day is too much! I go crazy, I boil, I cry, and I am ashame but I am not able to help it!—Even a Wop truck driver's a human being! And human beings must cry . . .

SERAFINA:

Yes, they must cry. I couldn't cry all day but now I have cried and I am feeling much better.—I will sew up the jacket . . .

ALVARO [*licking his lips*]:

What is that in your hand? A bottle of vino?

SERAFINA:

This is spumanti. It comes from the house of the family of my husband. The Delle Rose! A very great family. I was a peasant, but I married a baron!—No, I still don't believe it! I married a baron when I didn't have shoes!

ALVARO:

Excuse me for asking—but where is the Baron, now? [*Serafina points gravely to the marble urn.*] Where did you say?

SERAFINA:

Them're his ashes in that marble urn.

356

ALVARO:

Ma! Scusatemi! Scusatemi! [*crossing himself*]—I hope he is resting in peace.

SERAFINA:

It's him you reminded me of—when you opened the shutters. Not the face but the body.—Please get me some ice from the icebox in the kitchen. I had a—very bad day . . .

ALVARO:

Oh, ice! Yes—ice—I'll get some . . . [*As he goes out, she looks again through the broken spectacles at him.*]

SERAFINA:

Non posso crederlo!—A clown of a face like that with my husband's body!

[*There is the sound of ice being chopped in the kitchen. She inserts a corkscrew in the bottle but her efforts to open it are clumsily unsuccessful. Alvaro returns with a little bowl of ice. He sets it down so hard on the table that 'a piece flies out. He scrambles after it, retrieves it and wipes it off on his sweaty undershirt.*]

SERAFINA:

I think the floor would be cleaner!

ALVARO:

Scusatemi!—I wash it again?

SERAFINA:

Fa niente!

ALVARO:

I am a—clean!—I . . .

SERAFINA:

Fa niente, niente!—The bottle should be in the ice but the next best thing is to pour the wine over the bottle.

357

ALVARO:

You mean over the ice?

SERAFINA:

I mean over the . . .

ALVARO:

Let me open the bottle. Your hands are not used to rough work. [*She surrenders the bottle to him and regards him through the broken spectacles again.*]

SERAFINA:

These little bits of white voile on the floor are not from a snowstorm. I been making voile dresses for high school graduation.—One for my daughter and for thirteen other girls.—All of the work I'm not sure didn't kill me!

ALVARO:

The wine will make you feel better.

[*There is a youthful cry from outside.*]

SERAFINA:

There is a wild bunch of boys and girls in this town. In Sicily the boys would dance with the boys because a girl and a boy could not dance together unless they was going to be married. But here they run wild on islands!—boys, girls, man-crazy teachers . . .

ALVARO:

Ecco! [*The cork comes off with a loud pop. Serafina cries out and staggers against the table. He laughs. She laughs with him, helplessly, unable to stop, unable to catch her breath.*]—I like a woman that laughs with all her heart.

SERAFINA:

And a woman that cries with her heart?

ALVARO:

I like everything that a woman does with her heart.

[*Both are suddenly embarrassed and their laughter dies out. Serafina smooths down her rayon slip. He hands her a glass of the sparkling wine with ice in it. She murmurs "Grazie."*

[*Unconsciously the injured finger is lifted again to her lip and she wanders away from the table with the glass held shakily.*]

ALVARO [*continuing nervously*]:
I see you had a bad day.

SERAFINA:
Sono così—stanca . . .

ALVARO [*suddenly springing to the window and shouting*]:
Hey, you kids, git down off that truck! Keep your hands off them bananas! [*At the words "truck" and "bananas" Serafina gasps again and spills some wine on her slip.*] Little buggers!—Scusatemi . . .

SERAFINA:
You haul—you haul bananas?

ALVARO:
Si, Signora.

SERAFINA:
Is it a 10-ton truck?

ALVARO:
An 8-ton truck.

SERAFINA:
My husband hauled bananas in a 10-ton truck.

ALVARO:
Well, he was a baron.

SERAFINA:
Do you haul just bananas?

ALVARO:
Just bananas. What else would I haul?

SERAFINA:
My husband hauled bananas, but underneath the bananas was something else. He was—wild like a—Gypsy.—"Wild —like a—Gypsy?" Who said that?—I hate to start to re-member, and then not remember . . .

[*The dialogue between them is full of odd hesitations, broken sentences and tentative gestures. Both are nerv-ously exhausted after their respective ordeals. Their fum-bling communication has a curious intimacy and sweet-ness, like the meeting of two lonely children for the first time. It is oddly luxurious to them both, luxurious as the first cool wind of evening after a scorching day. Serafina idly picks up a little Sicilian souvenir cart from a table.*]

SERAFINA:
The priest was against it.

ALVARO:
What was the priest against?

SERAFINA:
Me keeping the ashes. It was against the Church law. But I had to have something and that was all I could have. [*She sets down the cart.*]

ALVARO:
I don't see nothing wrong with it.

SERAFINA:
You don't?

ALVARO:

No! Niente!—The body would've decayed, but ashes always stay clean.

SERAFINA [*eagerly*]:

Si, si, bodies decay, but ashes always stay clean! Come here. I show you this picture—my wedding. [*She removes a picture tenderly from the wall.*] Here's me a bride of fourteen, and this—this—*this!* [*drumming the picture with her finger and turning her face to Alvaro with great lustrous eyes*] My husband! [*There is a pause. He takes the picture from her hand and holds it first close to his eyes, then far back, then again close with suspirations of appropriate awe.*] Annnh?—Annnnh?—Che dice!

ALVARO [*slowly, with great emphasis*]:

Che bell' uomo! Che bell' uomo!

SERAFINA [*replacing the picture*]:

A rose of a man. On his chest he had the tattoo of a rose. [*then, quite suddenly*]—Do you believe strange things, or do you doubt them?

ALVARO:

If strange things didn't happen, I wouldn't be here. You wouldn't be here. We wouldn't be talking together.

SERAFINA:

Davvero! I'll tell you something about the tattoo of my husband. My husband, he had this rose tattoo on his chest. One night I woke up with a burning pain on me here. I turn on the light. I look at my naked breast and on it I see the rose tattoo of my husband, on me, on *my* breast, *his* tattoo.

ALVARO:

Strano!

SERAFINA:

And that was the night that—I got to speak frankly to tell you . . .

ALVARO:

Speak frankly! We're grown-up people.

SERAFINA:

That was the night I conceived my son—the little boy that was lost when I lost my husband . . .

ALVARO:

Che cosa—strana!—Would you be willing to show me the rose tattoo?

SERAFINA:

Oh, it's gone now, it only lasted a moment. But I did see it. I saw it clearly.—Do you believe me?

ALVARO:

Lo credo!

SERAFINA:

I don't know why I told you. But I like what you said. That bodies decay but ashes always stay clean—immacolate!—But, you know, there are some people that want to make everything dirty. Two of them kind of people come in the house today and told me a terrible lie in front of the ashes.—So awful a lie that if I thought it was true—I would smash the urn—and throw the ashes away! [*She hurls her glass suddenly to the floor.*] Smash it, *smash it like that!*

ALVARO:

Ma!—Baronessa!

[*Serafina seizes a broom and sweeps the fragments of glass away.*]

362

SERAFINA:

And take this broom and sweep them out the backdoor like so much trash!

ALVARO [*impressed by her violence and a little awed*]: What lie did they tell you?

SERAFINA:

No, no, no! I don't want to talk about it! [*She throws down the broom.*] I just want to forget it; it wasn't true, it was false, false, false!—as the hearts of the bitches that told it . . .

ALVARO:

Yes. I would forget anything that makes you unhappy.

SERAFINA:

The memory of a love don't make you unhappy unless you believe a lie that makes it dirty. I don't believe in the lie. The ashes are clean. The memory of the rose in my heart is perfect!—Your glass is weeping . . .

ALVARO:

Your glass is weeping too.

[*While she fills his glass, he moves about the room, looking here and there. She follows him. Each time he picks up an article for inspection she gently takes it from him and examines it herself with fresh interest.*]

ALVARO:

Cozy little homelike place you got here.

SERAFINA:

Oh, it's—molto modesto.—You got a nice place too?

ALVARO:

I got a place with three dependents in it.

363

SERAFINA:

What—dependents?

ALVARO [*counting them on his fingers*]:

One old maid sister, one feeble-minded grandmother, one
lush of a pop that's not worth the powder it takes to blow
him to hell.—They got the parchesi habit. They play the
game of parchesi, morning, night, noon. Passing a bucket
of beer around the table . . .

SERAFINA:

They got the beer habit, too?

ALVARO:

Oh, yes. And the numbers habit. This spring the old maid
sister gets female trouble—mostly mental, I think—she turns
the housekeeping over to the feeble-minded grandmother,
a very sweet old lady who don't think it is necessary to pay
the grocery bill so long as there's money to play the numbers. She plays the numbers. She has a perfect system except it don't ever work. And the grocery bill goes up, up,
up, up, up!—so high you can't even see it!—Today the
Ideal Grocery Company garnishees my wages . . . There,
now! I've told you my life . . . [*The parrot squawks. He
goes over to the cage.*] Hello, Polly, how's tricks?

SERAFINA:

The name ain't Polly. It ain't a she; it's a he.

ALVARO:

How can you tell with all them tail feathers? [*He sticks
his finger in the cage, pokes at the parrot and gets bitten.*]
Owww!

SERAFINA [*vicariously*]:

Ouuu . . . [*Alvaro sticks his injured finger in his mouth.
Serafina puts her corresponding finger in her mouth. He*

crosses to the telephone.] I told you watch out.—What are you calling, a doctor?

ALVARO:

I am calling my boss in Biloxi to explain why I'm late.

SERAFINA:

The call to Biloxi is a ten-cent call.

ALVARO:

Don't worry about it.

SERAFINA:

I'm not worried about it. You will pay it.

ALVARO:

You got a sensible attitude toward life . . . Give me the Southern Fruit Company in Biloxi—seven-eight-seven!

SERAFINA:

You are a bachelor. With three dependents? [*She glances below his belt.*]

ALVARO:

I'll tell you my hopes and dreams!

SERAFINA:

Who? Me?

ALVARO:

I am hoping to meet some sensible older lady. Maybe a lady a little bit older than me.—I don't care if she's a little too plump or not such a stylish dresser! [*Serafina self-consciously pulls up a dangling strap.*] The important thing in a lady is understanding. Good sense. And I want her to have a well-furnished house and a profitable little business of some kind . . . [*He looks about him significantly.*]

SERAFINA:

And such a lady, with a well-furnished house and business, what does she want with a man with three dependents with the parchesi and the beer habit, playing the numbers!

ALVARO:

Love and affection!—in a world that is lonely—and cold!

SERAFINA:

It might be lonely but I would not say "cold" on this particular day!

ALVARO:

Love and affection is what I got to offer on hot or cold days in this lonely old world and is what I am looking for. I got nothing else. Mangiacavallo has nothing. In fact, he is the grandson of the village idiot of Ribera!

SERAFINA [*uneasily*]:

I see you like to make—jokes!

ALVARO:

No, no joke!—Davvero!—He chased my grandmother in a flooded rice field. She slip on a wet rock.—Ecco! Here I am.

SERAFINA:

You ought to be more respectful.

ALVARO:

What have I got to respect? The rock my grandmother slips on?

SERAFINA:

Yourself at least! Don't you work for a living?

ALVARO:

If I *don't* work for a living I would respect myself *more*. Baronessa, I am a healthy young man, existing without no love life. I look at the magazine pictures. Them girls in the

advertisement—you know what I mean? A little bitty thing
here? A little bitty thing there?

[*He touches two portions of his anatomy. The latter por-
tion embarrasses Serafina, who quietly announces:*]

SERAFINA:
The call is ten cents for three minutes. Is the line busy?

ALVARO:
Not the line, but the boss.

SERAFINA:
And the charge for the call goes higher. That ain't the
phone of a millionaire you're using!

ALVARO:
I think you talk a poor mouth. [*He picks up the piggy
bank and shakes it.*] This pig sounds well fed to me.

SERAFINA:
Dimes and quarters.

ALVARO:
Dimes and quarters're better than nickels and dimes. [*Serafina rises severely and removes the piggy bank from his
grasp.*] Ha, ha, ha! You think I'm a bank robber?

SERAFINA:
I think you are maleducato! Just get your boss on the
phone or hang the phone up.

ALVARO:
What, what! Mr. Siccardi? How tricks at the Southern
Fruit Comp'ny this hot afternoon? Ha, ha, ha!—Mangiacavallo!—What? You got the complaint already? Sentite,
per favore! This road hog was—Mr. Siccardi? [*He jiggles
the hook; then slowly hangs up.*] A man with three dependents!—out of a job . . . [*There is a pause.*]

SERAFINA:

Well, you better ask the operator the charges.

ALVARO:

Oofla! A man with three dependents—out of a job!

SERAFINA:

I can't see to work no more. I got a suggestion to make. Open the bottom drawer of that there bureau and you will find a shirt in white tissue paper and you can wear that one while I am fixing this. And call for it later. [*He crosses to the bureau.*]—It was made for somebody that never called for it. [*He removes the package.*] Is there a name pinned to it?

ALVARO:

Yes, it's . . .

SERAFINA [*fiercely, but with no physical movement*]:

Don't tell me the name! Throw it away, out the window!

ALVARO:

Perchè?

SERAFINA:

Throw it, throw it away!

ALVARO [*crumpling the paper and throwing it through the window*]:

Ecco fatto! [*There is a distant cry of children as he unwraps the package and holds up the rose silk shirt, exclaiming in Latin delight at the luxury of it.*] Colore di rose! Seta! Seta pura!—Oh, this shirt is too good for Mangiacavallo! Everything here is too good for Mangiacavallo!

SERAFINA:

Nothing's too good for a man if the man is good.

ALVARO:

The grandson of a village idiot is not that good.

SERAFINA:

No matter whose grandson you are, put it on; you are welcome to wear it.

ALVARO [*slipping voluptuously into the shirt*]:
Sssssssss!

SERAFINA:

How does it feel, the silk, on you?

ALVARO:

It feels like a girl's hands on me! [*There is a pause, while he shows her the whiteness of his teeth.*]

SERAFINA [*holding up her broken spectacles*]:
It will make you less trouble.

ALVARO:

There is nothing more beautiful than a gift between people!
—Now you are smiling!—You like me a little bit better?

SERAFINA [*slowly and tenderly*]:
You know what they should of done when you was a baby? They should of put tape on your ears to hold them back so when you grow up they wouldn't stick out like the wings of a little kewpie! [*She touches his ear, a very slight touch, betraying too much of her heart. Both laugh a little and she turns away, embarrassed.*]

[*Outside the goat bleats and there is the sound of splintering timber. One of the children races into the front yard, crying out.*]

SALVATORE:

Mizz' Dell' Rose! The black goat's in your yard!

SERAFINA:

Il becco della strega!

369

[*Serafina dashes to the window, throws the shutters violently open and leans way out. This time, she almost feels
relief in this distraction. The interlude of the goat chase
has a quality of crazed exaltation. Outside is heard the
wild bleating of the goat and the jingling of his harness.*]

SERAFINA:
Miei pomodori! Guarda i miei pomodori!

THE STREGA [*entering the front yard with a broken length
of rope, calling out*]:
Heyeh, Billy! Heyeh. Heyeh, Billy!

SERAFINA [*making the sign of horns with her fingers*]:
There is the Strega! She lets the goat in my yard to eat my
tomatoes! [*backing from the window*] She has the eye;
she has the malocchio, and so does the goat! The goat has
the evil eye, too. He got in my yard the night that I lost
Rosario and my boy! Madonna, Madonna mia! Get that
goat out of my yard! [*She retreats to the Madonna, making
the sign of the horns with her fingers, while the goat chase
continues outside.*]

ALVARO:
Now take it easy! I will catch the black goat and give him
a kick that he will never forget!

[*Alvaro runs out the front door and joins in the chase.
The little boy is clapping together a pair of tin pan lids
which sound like cymbals. The effect is weird and beautiful with the wild cries of the children and the goat's
bleating. Serafina remains anxiously halfway between
the shutters and the protecting Madonna. She gives a
furious imitation of the bleating goat, contorting her face
with loathing. It is the fury of woman at the desire she
suffers. At last the goat is captured.*]

BRUNO:

Got him, got him, got him!

ALVARO:

Vieni presto, Diavolo!

[Alvaro appears around the side of the house with a tight hold on the broken rope around the goat's neck. The boy follows behind, gleefully clapping the tin lids together, and further back follows the Strega, holding her broken length of rope, her gray hair hanging into her face and her black skirts caught up in one hand, revealing bare feet and hairy legs. Serafina comes out on the porch as the grotesque little procession passes before it, and she raises her hand with the fingers making horns as the goat and the Strega pass her. Alvaro turns the goat over to the Strega and comes panting back to the house.]

ALVARO:

Niente paura!—I got to go now.—You have been troppo gentile, Mrs. . . .

SERAFINA:

I am the widow of the Baron Delle Rose.—Excuse the way I'm—not dressed . . . *[He keeps hold of her hand as he stands on the porch steps. She continues very shyly, panting a little.]* I am not always like this.—Sometimes I fix myself up!—When my husband was living, when my husband comes home, when he was living—I had a clean dress on! And sometimes even, I—put a rose in my hair . . .

ALVARO:

A rose in your hair would be pretty!

SERAFINA:

But for a widow—it ain't the time of roses . . .

371

[*The sound of music is heard, of a mandolin playing.*]

ALVARO:

Naw, you make a mistake! It's always for everybody the time of roses! The rose is the heart of the world like the heart is the—heart of the—body! But you, Baronessa—you know what I think you have done?

SERAFINA:

What—what have I—done?

ALVARO: ·

You have put your heart in the marble urn with the ashes. [*Now singing is heard along with the music, which continues to the end of the scene.*] And if in a storm sometime, or sometime when a 10-ton truck goes down the highway —the marble urn was to *break!* [*He suddenly points up at the sky.*] Look! Look, Baronessa!

SERAFINA [*startled*]:
Look? Look? I don't see!

ALVARO:

I was pointing at your heart, broken out of the urn and away from the ashes!—*Rondinella felice!* [*He makes an airy gesture toward the fading sky.*]

SERAFINA:

Oh! [*He whistles like a bird and makes graceful winglike motions with his hands.*] Buffone, buffone—piantatela! I take you serious—then you make it a joke . . . [*She smiles involuntarily at his antics.*]

ALVARO:
When can I bring the shirt back?

SERAFINA:
When do you pass by again?

ALVARO:

I will pass by tonight for supper. Volete?

SERAFINA:

Then look at the window tonight. If the shutters are open and there is a light in the window, you can stop by for your —jacket—but if the shutters are closed, you better not stop because my Rosa will be home. Rosa's my daughter. She has gone to a picnic—maybe—home early—but you know how picnics are. They—wait for the moon to—start singing.— Not that there's nothing wrong in two grown-up people having a quiet conversation!—but Rosa's fifteen—I got to be careful to set her a perfect example.

ALVARO:

I will look at the window.—I will look at the win-dooow! [*He imitates a bird flying off with gay whistles.*]

SERAFINA:

Buffone!

ALVARO [*shouting from outside*]:

Hey, you little buggers, climb down off that truck! Lay offa them bananas!

[*His truck is heard starting and pulling away. Serafina stands motionless on the porch, searching the sky with her eyes.*]

SERAFINA:

Rosario, forgive me! Forgive me for thinking the awful lie could be true!

[*The light in the house dims out. A little boy races into the yard holding triumphantly aloft a great golden bunch of bananas. A little girl pursues him with shrill cries. He eludes her. They dash around the house. The light fades and the curtain falls.*]

373

It is the evening of the same day. The neighborhood children are playing games around the house. One of them is counting by fives to a hundred, calling out the numbers, as he leans against the palm tree.

Serafina is in the parlor, sitting on the sofa. She is seated stiffly and formally, wearing a gown that she has not worn since the death of her husband, and with a rose in her hair. It becomes obvious from her movements that she is wearing a girdle that constricts her unendurably.

[*There is the sound of a truck approaching up on the highway. Serafina rises to an odd, crouching position. But the truck passes by without stopping. The girdle is becoming quite intolerable to Serafina and she decides to take it off, going behind the sofa to do so. With much grunting, she has gotten it down as far as her knees, when there is the sound outside of another truck approaching. This time the truck stops up on the highway, with a sound of screeching brakes. She realizes that Alvaro is coming, and her efforts to get out of the girdle, which is now pinioning her legs, become frantic. She hobbles from behind the sofa as Alvaro appears in front of the house.*]

ALVARO [*gaily*]:
Rondinella felice! I will look at win-dooooo! Signora Delle Rose!

[*Serafina's response to this salutation is a groan of anguish. She hobbles and totters desperately to the curtains between the rooms and reaches them just in time to hide*

374

*herself as Alvaro comes into the parlor from the porch
through the screen door. He is carrying a package and a
candy box.*]

ALVARO:
C'è nessuno?

SERAFINA [*at first inaudibly*]:
Si, si, sono qui. [*then loudly and hoarsely, as she finally
gets the girdle off her legs*] Si, si, sono qui! [*To cover her
embarrassment, she busies herself with fixing wineglasses
on a tray.*]

ALVARO:
I hear the rattle of glasses! Let me help you! [*He goes
eagerly through the curtain but stops short, astonished.*]

SERAFINA:
Is—something the—matter?

ALVARO:
I didn't expect to see you looking so pretty! You are a
young little widow!

SERAFINA:
You are—fix yourself up . . .

ALVARO:
I been to The Ideal Barber's! I got the whole works!

SERAFINA [*faintly, retreating from him a little*]:
You got—rose oil—in your hair . . .

ALVARO:
Olio di rose! You like the smell of it? [*Outside there is a
wild, distant cry of children, and inside a pause. Serafina
shakes her head slowly with the infinite wound of a recollection.*]—You—*don't*—like—the smell of it? Oh, then I
wash the smell *out*, I go and . . . [*He starts toward the
back. She raises her hand to stop him.*]

SERAFINA:

No, no, no, fa—niente.—I—*like* the smell of it . . .

[*A little boy races into the yard, ducks some invisible missile, sticks out his tongue and yells: "Yahhhhh!" Then he dashes behind the house.*]

SERAFINA:

Shall we—set down in the parlor?

ALVARO:

I guess that's better than standing up in the dining room. [*He enters formally.*]—Shall we set down on the sofa?

SERAFINA:

You take the sofa. I will set down on this chair.

ALVARO [*disappointed*]:

You don't like to set on a sofa?

SERAFINA:

I lean back too far on that sofa. I like a straight back behind me . . .

ALVARO:

That chair looks not comfortable to me.

SERAFINA:

This chair is a comfortable chair.

ALVARO:

But it's more easy to talk with two on a sofa!

SERAFINA:

I talk just as good on a chair as I talk on a sofa . . . [*There is a pause. Alvaro nervously hitches his shoulder.*] Why do you hitch your shoulders like that?

ALVARO:

Oh, that!—That's a—nervous—habit . . .

SERAFINA:

I thought maybe the suit don't fit you good . . .

ALVARO:

I bought this suit to get married in four years ago.

SERAFINA:

But didn't get married?

ALVARO:

I give her, the girl, a zircon instead of a diamond. She had it examined. The door was slammed in my face.

SERAFINA:

I think that maybe I'd do the same thing myself.

ALVARO:

Buy the zircon?

SERAFINA:

No, slam the door.

ALVARO:

Her eyes were not sincere-looking. You've got sincere-looking eyes. Give me your hand so I can tell your fortune! [*She pushes her chair back from him.*] I see two men in your life. One very handsome. One not handsome. His ears are too big but not as big as his heart! He has three dependents.—In fact he has four dependents! Ha, ha, ha!

SERAFINA:

What is the fourth dependent?

ALVARO:

The one that every man's got, his biggest expense, worst troublemaker and chief liability! Ha, ha, ha!

SERAFINA:

I hope you are not talking vulgar. [*She rises and turns her back to him. Then she discovers the candy box.*] What's that fancy red box?

377

ALVARO:

A present I bought for a nervous but nice little lady!

SERAFINA:

Chocolates? Grazie! Grazie! But I'm too fat.

ALVARO:

You are not fat, you are just pleasing and plump. [*He reaches way over to pinch the creamy flesh of her upper arm.*]

SERAFINA:

No, please. Don't make me nervous. If I get nervous again I will start to cry . . .

ALVARO:

Let's talk about something to take your mind off your troubles. You say you got a young daughter?

SERAFINA [*in a choked voice*]:

Yes. I got a young daughter. Her name is Rosa.

ALVARO:

Rosa, Rosa! She's pretty?

SERAFINA:

She has the eyes of her father, and his wild, stubborn blood! Today was the day of her graduation from high school. She looked so pretty in a white voile dress with a great big bunch of—roses . . .

ALVARO:

Not no prettier than her Mama, I bet—with that rose in your hair!

SERAFINA:

She's only fifteen.

ALVARO:

Fifteen?

SERAFINA [*smoothing her blue silk lap with a hesitant hand*]:
Yes, only fifteen . . .

ALVARO:
But has a boy friend, does she?

SERAFINA:
She met a sailor.

ALVARO:
Oh, Dio! No wonder you seem to be nervous.

SERAFINA:
I didn't want to let her go out with this sailor. He had a gold ring in his ear.

ALVARO:
Madonna Santa!

SERAFINA:
This morning she cut her wrist—not much but enough to bleed—with a kitchen knife!

ALVARO:
Tch, tch! A very wild girl!

SERAFINA:
I had to give in and let her bring him to see me. He said he was Catholic. I made him kneel down in front of Our Lady there and give Her his promise that he would respect the innocence of my Rosa!—But how do I know that he was a Catholic, *really?*

ALVARO [*taking her hand*]:
Poor little worried lady! But you got to face facts. Sooner or later the innocence of your daughter cannot be respected. —Did he—have a—tattoo?

379

SERAFINA [*startled*]:
Did who have—what?

ALVARO:
The sailor friend of your daughter, did he have a tattoo?

SERAFINA:
Why do you ask me that?

ALVARO:
Just because most sailors have a tattoo.

SERAFINA:
How do I know if he had a tattoo or not!

ALVARO:
I got a tattoo!

SERAFINA:
You got a tattoo?

ALVARO:
Si, si, veramente!

SERAFINA:
What kind of tattoo you got?

ALVARO:
What kind you think?

SERAFINA:
Oh, I think—you have got—a South Sea girl without clothes
on . . .

ALVARO:
No South Sea girl.

SERAFINA:
Well, maybe a big red heart with MAMA written across it.

ALVARO:
Wrong again, Baronessa.

[*He takes off his tie and slowly unbuttons his shirt, gazing at her with an intensely warm smile. He divides the unbuttoned shirt, turning toward her his bare chest. She utters a gasp and rises.*]

SERAFINA:

No, no, no!—*Not a rose!* [*She says it as if she were evading her feelings.*]

ALVARO:

Si, si, una rosa!

SERAFINA:

I—don't feel good! The air is . . .

ALVARO:

Che fate, che fate, che dite?

SERAFINA:

The house has a tin roof on it!—The air is—I got to go outside the house to breathe! Scu—scusatemi! [*She goes out onto the porch and clings to one of the spindling porch columns for support, breathing hoarsely with a hand to her throat. He comes out slowly.*]

ALVARO [*gently*]:

I didn't mean to surprise you!—Mi dispiace molto!

SERAFINA [*with enforced calm*]:

Don't—talk about it! Anybody could have a rose tattoo.—It don't mean nothing.—You know how a tin roof is. It catches the heat all day and it don't cool off until—midnight . . .

ALVARO:

No, no, not until midnight. [*She makes a faint laughing sound, is quite breathless and leans her forehead against the porch column. He places his fingers delicately against the*

381

small of her back.] It makes it hot in the bedroom—so that you got to sleep without nothing on you . . .

SERAFINA:
No, you—can't stand the covers . . .

ALVARO:
You can't even stand a—*nightgown!* [*His fingers press her back.*]

SERAFINA:
Please. There is a strega next door; she's always watching!

ALVARO:
It's been so long since I felt the soft touch of a woman! [*She gasps loudly and turns to the door.*] Where are you going?

SERAFINA:
I'm going back in the house! [*She enters the parlor again, still with forced calm.*]

ALVARO [*following her inside*]:
Now, now, what is the matter?

SERAFINA:
I got a feeling like I have—forgotten something.

ALVARO:
What?

SERAFINA:
I can't remember.

ALVARO:
It couldn't be nothing important if you can't remember. Let's open the chocolate box and have some candy.

SERAFINA [*eager for any distraction*]:
Yes! Yes, open the box!

[*Alvaro places a chocolate in her hand. She stares at it blankly.*]

ALVARO:

Eat it, eat the chocolate. If you don't eat it, it will melt in your hand and make your fingers all gooey!

SERAFINA:

Please, I . . .

ALVARO:

Eat it!

SERAFINA [*weakly and gagging*]:

I can't, I can't, I would choke! Here, you eat it.

ALVARO:

Put it in my mouth! [*She puts the chocolate in his mouth.*] Now, look. Your fingers are gooey!

SERAFINA:

Oh!—I better go wash them! [*She rises unsteadily. He seizes her hands and licks her fingers.*]

ALVARO:

Mmmm! Mmmmm! Good, very good!

SERAFINA:

Stop that, stop that, stop that! That—ain't—nice . . .

ALVARO:

I'll lick off the chocolate for you.

SERAFINA:

No, no, no!—I am the mother of a fifteen-year-old girl!

ALVARO:

You're as old as your arteries, Baronessa. Now set back down. The fingers are now white as snow!

383

SERAFINA:
You don't—understand—how I feel . . .

ALVARO:
You don't understand how *I* feel.

SERAFINA [*doubtfully*]:
How do you—feel? [*In answer, he stretches the palms of his hands out toward her as if she were a fireplace in a freezing-cold room.*]—What does—*that*—mean?

ALVARO:
The night is warm but I feel like my hands are—freezing!

SERAFINA:
Bad—circulation . . .

ALVARO:
No, too *much* circulation! [*Alvaro becomes tremulously pleading, shuffling forward a little, slightly crouched like a beggar.*] Across the room I feel the sweet warmth of a lady!

SERAFINA [*retreating, doubtfully*]:
Oh, you talk a sweet mouth. I think you talk a sweet mouth to fool a woman.

ALVARO:
No, no, I know—I know that's what warms the world, that is what makes it the summer! [*He seizes the hand she hold defensively before her and presses it to his own breast in a crushing grip.*] Without it, the rose—the rose would not grow on the bush; the fruit would not grow on the tree!

SERAFINA:
I know, and the truck—the truck would not haul the bananas! But, Mr. Mangiacavallo, that is my hand, not a sponge. I got bones in it. Bones break!

384

ALVARO:

Scusatemi, Baronessa! [*He returns her hand to her with a bow.*] For me it is winter, because I don't have in my life the sweet warmth of a lady. I live with my hands in my pockets! [*He stuffs his hands violently into his pants' pockets, then jerks them out again. A small cellophane-wrapped disk falls on the floor, escaping his notice, but not Serafina's.*]—You don't like the poetry!—How can a man talk to you?

SERAFINA [*ominously*]:

I like the poetry good. Is that a piece of the poetry that you dropped out of your pocket? [*He looks down.*]—No, no, right by your foot!

ALVARO [*aghast as he realizes what it is that she has seen*]:

Oh, that's—that's nothing! [*He kicks it under the sofa.*]

SERAFINA [*fiercely*]:

You talk a sweet mouth about women. Then drop such a thing from your pocket?—Va via, vigliacco! [*She marches grandly out of the room, pulling the curtains together behind her. He hangs his head despairingly between his hands. Then he approaches the curtains timidly.*]

ALVARO [*in a small voice*]:

Baronessa?

SERAFINA:

Pick up what you dropped on the floor and go to the Square Roof with it. Buona notte!

ALVARO:

Baronessa! [*He parts the curtains and peeks through them.*]

SERAFINA:

I told you good night. Here is no casa privata. Io, non sono puttana!

ALVARO:

Understanding is—very—necessary!

SERAFINA:

I understand plenty. You think you got a good thing, a thing that is cheap!

ALVARO:

You make a mistake, Baronessa! [*He comes in and drops to his knees beside her, pressing his cheek to her flank. He speaks rhapsodically.*] So soft is a lady! So, so, so, so, so *soft* —is a lady!

SERAFINA:

Andate via, sporcaccione, andate a casa! Lasciatemi! Lasciatemi stare!

[*She springs up and runs into the parlor. He pursues. The chase is grotesquely violent and comic. A floor lamp is overturned. She seizes the chocolate box and threatens to slam it into his face if he continues toward her. He drops to his knees, crouched way over, and pounds the floor with his fists, sobbing.*]

ALVARO:

Everything in my life turns out like this!

SERAFINA:

Git up, git up, git up!—you village idiot's grandson! There is people watching you through that window, the—Strega next door . . . [*He rises slowly.*] And where is the shirt that I loaned you? [*He shuffles abjectly across the room, then hands her a neatly wrapped package.*]

ALVARO:

My sister wrapped it up for you.—My sister was very happy I met this *nice* lady!

386

SERAFINA:

Maybe she thinks I will pay the grocery bill while she plays
the numbers!

ALVARO:

She don't think nothing like that. She is an old maid, my
sister. She wants—nephews—nieces . . .

SERAFINA:

You tell her for me I don't give nephews and nieces!

[*Alvaro hitches his shoulders violently in his embarrassment and shuffles over to where he had left his hat. He
blows the dust off it and rubs the crown on his sleeve.
Serafina presses a knuckle to her lips as she watches his
awkward gestures. She is a little abashed by his humility.
She speaks next with the great dignity of a widow whose
respectability has stood the test.*]

SERAFINA:

Now, Mr. Mangiacavallo, please tell me the truth about
something. *When* did you get the tattoo put on your chest?

ALVARO [*shyly and sadly, looking down at his hat*]:
I got it tonight—after supper . . .

SERAFINA:

That's what I thought. You had it put on because I told
you about my husband's tattoo.

ALVARO:

I wanted to be—close to you . . . to make you—happy . . .

SERAFINA:

Tell it to the marines! [*He puts on his hat with an apologetic gesture.*] You got the tattoo and the chocolate box
after supper, and then you come here to fool me!

ALVARO:

I got the chocolate box a long time ago.

387

SERAFINA:

How long ago? If that is not too much a personal question!

ALVARO:

I got it the night the door was slammed in my face by the girl that I give—the zircon . . .

SERAFINA:

Let that be a lesson. Don't try to fool women. You are not smart enough!—Now take the shirt back. You can keep it.

ALVARO:

Huh?

SERAFINA:

Keep it. I don't want it back.

ALVARO:

You just now said that you did.

SERAFINA:

It's a man's shirt, ain't it?

ALVARO:

You just now accused me of trying to steal it off you.

SERAFINA:

Well, you been making me nervous!

ALVARO:

Is it my fault you been a widow too long?

SERAFINA:

You make a mistake!

ALVARO:

You make a mistake!

SERAFINA:

Both of us make a mistake!

[*There is a pause. They both sigh profoundly.*]

ALVARO:

We should of have been friends, but I think we meet the
wrong day.—Suppose I go out and come in the door again
and we start all over?

SERAFINA:

No, I think it's no use. The day was wrong to begin with,
because of two women. Two women, they told me today
that my husband had put on my head the nanny-goat's
horns!

ALVARO:

How is it possible to put horns on a widow?

SERAFINA:

That was before, before! They told me my husband was
having a steady affair with a woman at the Square Roof.
What was the name on the shirt, on the slip of paper? Do
you remember the name?

ALVARO:

You told me to . . .

SERAFINA:

Tell me! Do you remember?

ALVARO:

I remember the name because I know the woman. The
name was Estelle Hohengarten.

SERAFINA:

Take me there! Take me to the Square Roof!—Wait, wait!

[*She plunges into the dining room, snatches a knife out
of the sideboard drawer and thrusts it in her purse. Then
she rushes back, with the blade of the knife protruding
from the purse.*]

389

ALVARO [*noticing the knife*]:
They—got a cover charge there . . .

SERAFINA:
I will charge them a cover! Take me there now, this minute!

ALVARO:
The fun don't start till midnight.

SERAFINA:
I will start the fun sooner.

ALVARO:
The floor show commences at midnight.

SERAFINA:
I will commence it! [*She rushes to the phone.*] Yellow Cab,
please, Yellow Cab. I want to go to the Square Roof out of
my house! Yes, you come to my house and take me to the
Square Roof right this minute! My number is—what is my
number? Oh my God, what is my number?—64 is my
number on Front Street! Subito, subito—quick!

[*The goat bleats outside.*]

ALVARO:
Baronessa, the knife's sticking out of your purse. [*He grabs
the purse.*] What do you want with this weapon?

SERAFINA:
To cut the lying tongue out of a woman's mouth! Saying
she has on her breast the tattoo of my husband because he
had put on me the horns of a goat! I cut the heart out of
that woman, she cut the heart out of me!

ALVARO:
Nobody's going to cut the heart out of nobody!

[*A car is heard outside, and Serafina rushes to the porch.*]

SERAFINA [*shouting*]:
Hey, Yellow Cab, Yellow Cab, Yellow—Cab . . . [*The car passes by without stopping. With a sick moan she wanders into the yard. He follows her with a glass of wine.*]—Something hurts—in my heart . . .

ALVARO [*leading her gently back to the house*]:
Baronessa, drink this wine on the porch and keep your eyes on that star. [*He leads her to a porch pillar and places the glass in her trembling hand. She is now submissive.*] You know the name of that star? That star is Venus. She is the only female star in the sky. Who put her up there? Mr. Siccardi, the transportation manager of the Southern Fruit Company? No. She was put there by God. [*He enters the house and removes the knife from her purse.*] And yet there's some people that don't believe in nothing. [*He picks up the telephone.*] Esplanade 9-7-0.

SERAFINA:
What are you doing?

ALVARO:
Drink that wine and I'll settle this whole problem for you. [*on the telephone*] I want to speak to the blackjack dealer, please, Miss Estelle Hohengarten . . .

SERAFINA:
Don't talk to that woman, she'll lie!

ALVARO:
Not Estelle Hohengarten. She deals a straight game of cards.—Estelle? This is Mangiacavallo. I got a question to ask you which is a personal question. It has to do with a very good-looking truck driver, not living now but once on a time thought to have been a very well-known character at the Square Roof. His name was . . . [*He turns ques-*

391

tioningly to the door where Serafina is standing.] What was his name, Baronessa?

SERAFINA [*hardly breathing*]:
Rosario delle Rose!

ALVARO:
Rosario delle Rose was the name. [*There is a pause.*]—È vero?—Mah! Che peccato . . .

[*Serafina drops her glass and springs into the parlor with a savage outcry. She snatches the phone from Alvaro and screams into it.*]

SERAFINA [*wildly*]:
This is the wife that's speaking! What do you know of my husband, what is the lie?

[*A strident voice sounds over the wire.*]

THE VOICE [*loud and clear*]:
Don't you remember? I brought you the rose-colored silk to make him a shirt. You said, "For a man?" and I said, "Yes, for a man that's wild like a Gypsy!" But if you think I'm a liar, come here and let me show you his rose tattooed on my chest!

[*Serafina holds the phone away from her as though it had burst into flame. Then, with a terrible cry, she hurls it to the floor. She staggers dizzily toward the Madonna. Alvaro seizes her arm and pushes her gently onto the sofa.*]

ALVARO:
Piano, piano, Baronessa! This will be gone, this will pass in a moment. [*He puts a pillow behind her, then replaces the telephone.*]

SERAFINA [*staggering up from the sofa*]:
The room's—going round . . .

ALVARO:
You ought to stay lying down a little while longer. I know,
I know what you need! A towel with some ice in it to put
on your forehead—Baronessa.—You stay right there while
I fix it! [*He goes into the kitchen, and calls back.*] Torno
subito, Baronessa!

[*The little boy runs into the yard. He leans against the
bending trunk of the palm, counting loudly.*]

THE LITTLE BOY:
Five, ten, fifteen, twenty, twenty-five, thirty . . .

[*There is the sound of ice being chopped in the kitchen.*]

SERAFINA:
Dove siete, dove siete?

ALVARO:
In cucina!—Ghiaccio . . .

SERAFINA:
Venite qui!

ALVARO:
Subito, subito . . . .

SERAFINA [*turning to the shrine, with fists knotted*]:
Non voglio, non voglio farlo!

[*But she crosses slowly, compulsively toward the shrine,
with a trembling arm stretched out.*]

THE LITTLE BOY:
Seventy-five, eighty, eighty-five, ninety, ninety-five, one hundred! [*then, wildly*] *Ready or not you shall be caught!*

393

[*At this cry, Serafina seizes the marble urn and hurls it violently into the furthest corner of the room. Then, instantly, she covers her face. Outside the mothers are heard calling their children home. Their voices are tender as music, fading in and out. The children appear slowly at the side of the house, exhausted from their wild play.*]

GIUSEPPINA:
Vivi! Vi-vi!

PEPINA:
Salvatore!

VIOLETTA:
Bruno! Come home, come home!

[*The children scatter. Alvaro comes in with the ice pick.*]

ALVARO:
I broke the point of the ice pick.

SERAFINA [*removing her hands from her face*]:
I don't want ice ... [*She looks about her, seeming to gather a fierce strength in her body. Her voice is hoarse, her body trembling with violence, eyes narrow and flashing, her fists clenched.*] Now I show you how wild and strong like a man a woman can be! [*She crosses to the screen door, opens it and shouts.*] Buona notte, Mr. Mangiacavallo!

ALVARO:
You—you make me go *home,* now?

SERAFINA:
No, no; senti, cretino! [*in a strident whisper*] You make out like you are going. You drive the truck out of sight where the witch can't see it. Then you come back and I leave the backdoor open for you to come in. Now, tell me good-bye so all the neighbors can hear you! [*She shouts.*] Arrivederci!

ALVARO:

Ha, ha! Capish! [*He shouts too.*] Arrivederci! [*He runs to the foot of the embankment steps.*]

SERAFINA [*still more loudly*]:
Buona notte!

ALVARO:
Buona notte, Baronessa!

SERAFINA [*in a choked voice*]:
Give them my love; give everybody—my love . . . Arrivederci!

ALVARO:
Ciao!

[*Alvaro scrambles on down the steps and goes off. Serafina comes down into the yard. The goat bleats. She mutters savagely to herself.*]

SERAFINA:
Sono una bestia, una bestia feroce!

[*She crosses quickly around to the back of the house. As she disappears, the truck is heard driving off; the lights sweep across the house. Serafina comes in through the backdoor. She is moving with great violence, gasping and panting. She rushes up to the Madonna and addresses her passionately with explosive gestures, leaning over so that her face is level with the statue's.*]

SERAFINA:
Ora, ascolta, Signora! You hold in the cup of your hand this little house and you smash it! You break this little house like the shell of a bird in your hand, because you have hate Serafina?—Serafina that *loved* you!—No, no, no, you don't speak! I don't believe in you, Lady! You're just

395

a poor little doll with the paint peeling off, and now I blow out the light and I forget you the way you forget Serafina! [*She blows out the vigil light.*] Ecco—fatto!

[*But now she is suddenly frightened; the vehemence and boldness have run out. She gasps a little and backs away from the shrine, her eyes rolling apprehensively this way and that. The parrot squawks at her. The goat bleats. The night is full of sinister noises, harsh bird cries, the sudden flapping of wings in the canebrake, a distant shriek of Negro laughter. Serafina retreats to the window and opens the shutters wider to admit the moonlight. She stands panting by the window with a fist pressed to her mouth. In the back of the house a door slams open. Serafina catches her breath and moves as though for protection behind the dummy of the bride. Alvaro enters through the backdoor, calling out softly and hoarsely, with great excitement.*]

ALVARO:
Dove? Dove sei, cara?

SERAFINA [*faintly*]:
Sono qui . . .

ALVARO:
You have turn out the light!

SERAFINA:
The moon is enough . . . [*He advances toward her. His white teeth glitter as he grins. Serafina retreats a few steps from him. She speaks tremulously, making an awkward gesture toward the sofa.*] Now we can go on with our— conversation . . . [*She catches her breath sharply.*]

[*The curtain comes down.*]

It is just before daybreak of the next day. Rosa and Jack appear at the top of the embankment steps.

ROSA:

I thought they would never leave. [*She comes down the steps and out in front of the house, then calls back to him.*] Let's go down there.

[*He obeys hesitatingly. Both are very grave. The scene is played as close as possible to the audience. She sits very straight. He stands behind her with his hands on her shoulders.*]

ROSA [*leaning her head back against him*]:

This was the happiest day of my life, and this is the saddest night . . . [*He crouches in front of her.*]

SERAFINA [*from inside the house*]:

Aaaaaahhhhhhhh!

JACK [*springing up, startled*]:

What's that?

ROSA [*resentfully*]:

Oh! That's Mama dreaming about my father.

JACK:

I—feel like a—*heel!* I feel like a rotten heel!

ROSA:

Why?

JACK:

That promise I made your mother.

ROSA:

I hate her for it.

JACK:

Honey—Rosa, she—wanted to protect you.

[*There is a long-drawn cry from the back of the house:* "*Ohhhh—Rosario!*"]

ROSA:

She wanted me not to have what she's dreaming about . . .

JACK:

Naw, naw, honey, she—wanted to—protect you . . .

[*The cry from within is repeated softly.*]

ROSA:

Listen to her making love in her sleep! Is that what she wants *me* to do, just—*dream* about it?

JACK [*humbly*]:

She knows that her Rosa *is* a rose. And she wants her rose to have someone—better than *me* . . .

ROSA:

Better than—*you!* [*She speaks as if the possibility were too preposterous to think of.*]

JACK:

You see me through—rose-colored—glasses . . .

ROSA:

I see you with love!

JACK:

Yes, but your Mama sees me with—common sense . . . [*Serafina cries out again.*] I got to be going! [*She keeps a tight hold on him. A rooster crows.*] Honey, it's so late the roosters are crowing!

ROSA:

They're fools, they're fools, it's early!

JACK:

Honey, on that island I almost forgot my promise. Almost, but not quite. Do you understand, honey?

ROSA:

Forget the promise!

JACK:

I made it on my knees in front of Our Lady. I've got to leave now, honey.

ROSA [*clasping him fiercely*]:

You'd have to break my arms to!

JACK:

Rosa, Rosa! You want to drive me crazy?

ROSA:

I want you not to remember.

JACK:

You're a very young girl! Fifteen—fifteen is too young!

ROSA:

Caro, caro, carissimo!

JACK:

You got to save some of those feelings for when you're grown up!

ROSA:

Carissimo!

JACK:

Hold some of it back until you're grown!

ROSA:

I have been grown for two years!

JACK:

No, no, that ain't what I . . .

ROSA:

Grown enough to be married, and have a—baby!

JACK [*springing up*]:

Oh, good—Lord! [*He circles around her, pounding his palm repeatedly with his fist and champing his teeth together with a grimace. Suddenly he speaks.*] I got to be going!

ROSA:

You want me to scream? [*He groans and turns away from her to resume his desperate circle. Rosa is blocking the way with her body.*]—I know, I know! You don't want me! [*Jack groans through his gritting teeth.*] No, no, you don't want me . . .

JACK:

Now you listen to me! You almost got into trouble today on that island! You almost did, but not quite!—But it didn't quite happen and no harm is done and you can just—forget it . . .

ROSA:

It is the only thing in my life that I want to remember!— When are you going back to New Orleans?

JACK:

Tomorrow.

ROSA:

When does your—ship sail?

JACK:

Tomorrow.

ROSA:
Where to?

JACK:
Guatemala.

SERAFINA [*from the house*]:
Aahh!

ROSA:
Is that a long trip?

JACK:
After Guatemala, Buenos Aires. After Buenos Aires, Rio.
Then around the Straits of Magellan and back up the west
coast of South America, putting in at three ports before we
dock at San Francisco.

ROSA:
I don't think I will—ever see you again . . .

JACK:
The ship won't sink!

ROSA [*faintly and forlornly*]:
No, but—I think it could just happen once, and if it don't
happen that time, it never can—later . . . [*A rooster crows.
They face each other sadly and quietly.*] You don't need
to be very old to understand how it works out. One time,
one time, only once, it could be—God!—to remember.—
Other times? Yes—they'd be something.—But only once,
God—to remember . . . [*With a little sigh she crosses to
pick up his white cap and hand it gravely to him.*]—I'm
sorry to you it didn't—mean—that much . . .

JACK [*taking the cap and hurling it to the ground*]:
Look! Look at my knuckles! You see them scabs on my
knuckles? You know how them scabs got there? They got

401

there because I banged my knuckles that hard on the deck of the sailboat!

ROSA:

Because it—didn't quite happen? [*Jack jerks his head up and down in grotesquely violent assent to her question. Rosa picks up his cap and returns it to him again.*]—Because of the promise to Mama! I'll never forgive her . . . [*There is a pause.*] What time in the afternoon must you be on the boat?

JACK:

Why?

ROSA:

Just tell me what time.

JACK:

Five!—Why?

ROSA:

What will you be doing till five?

JACK:

Well, I could be a goddam liar and tell you I was going to —pick me a hatful of daisies in—Audubon Park.—Is that what you want me to tell you?

ROSA:

No, tell me the truth.

JACK:

All right, I'll tell you the truth. I'm going to check in at some flea-bag hotel on North Rampart Street. Then I'm going to get loaded! And then I'm going to get . . . [*He doesn't complete the sentence but she understands him. She places the hat more becomingly on his blond head.*]

402

ROSA:

Do me a little favor. [*Her hand slides down to his cheek and then to his mouth.*] Before you get loaded and before you—before you—

JACK:

Huh?

ROSA:

Look in the waiting room at the Greyhound bus station, please. At twelve o'clock, noon!

JACK:

Why?

ROSA:

You might find me there, waiting for you . . .

JACK:

What—what good would that do?

ROSA:

I never been to a hotel but I know they have numbers on doors and sometimes—numbers are—lucky.—Aren't they? —Sometimes?—Lucky?

JACK:

You want to buy me a ten-year stretch in the brig?

ROSA:

I want you to give me that little gold ring on your ear to put on my finger.—I want to give you my heart to keep forever! And ever! And ever! [*Slowly and with a barely audible sigh she leans her face against him.*] Look for me! I will be there!

JACK [*breathlessly*]:

In all of my life, I never felt nothing so sweet as the feel of your little warm body in my arms . . .

[*He breaks away and runs toward the road. From the foot of the steps he glares fiercely back at her like a tiger through the bars of a cage. She clings to the two porch pillars, her body leaning way out.*]

ROSA:
Look for me! I will be there!

[*Jack runs away from the house. Rosa returns inside. Listlessly she removes her dress and falls on the couch in her slip, kicking off her shoes. Then she begins to cry, as one cries only once in a lifetime, and the scene dims out.*]

SCENE THREE

The time is three hours later.

We see first the exterior view of the small frame building against a night sky which is like the starry blue robe of Our Lady. It is growing slightly paler.

[*The faint light discloses Rosa asleep on the couch. The covers are thrown back for it has been a warm night, and on the concave surface of the white cloth, which is like the dimly lustrous hollow of a shell, is the body of the sleeping girl which is clad only in a sheer white slip.*

[*A cock crows. A gentle wind stirs the white curtains inward and the tendrils of vine at the windows, and the sky lightens enough to distinguish the purple trumpets of the morning glory against the very dim blue of the sky in which the planet Venus remains still undimmed.*

[*In the back of the cottage someone is heard coughing hoarsely and groaning in the way a man does who has drunk very heavily the night before. Bedsprings creak as a heavy figure rises. Light spills dimly through the curtains, now closed, between the two front rooms.*

[*There are heavy, padding footsteps and Alvaro comes stumbling rapidly into the dining room with the last bottle of spumanti in the crook of an arm, his eyes barely open, legs rubbery, saying, "Wuh-wuh-wuh-wuh-wuh-wuh . . ." like the breathing of an old dog. The scene should be played with the pantomimic lightness, almost fantasy, of an early Chaplin comedy. He is wearing only his trousers and his chest is bare. As he enters he collides*

405

*with the widow dummy, staggers back, pats her inflated
bosom in a timid, apologetic way, remarking:*]

ALVARO:

Scusami, Signora, I am the grandson of the village idiot of
Ribera!

[*Alvaro backs into the table and is propelled by the im-
pact all the way to the curtained entrance to the parlor. He
draws the curtains apart and hangs onto them, peering
into the room. Seeing the sleeping girl, he blinks several
times, suddenly makes a snoring sound in his nostrils and
waves one hand violently in front of his eyes as if to dis-
pel a vision. Outside the goat utters a long "Baaaaaaa-
aaaa!" As if in response, Alvaro whispers, in the same
basso key, "Che bella!" The first vowel of "bella" is enor-
mously prolonged like the "baaa" of the goat. On his rubbery legs he shuffles forward a few steps and leans over to
peer more intently at the vision. The goat bleats again.
Alvaro whispers more loudly: "Che bel-la!" He drains
the spumanti, then staggers to his knees, the empty bottle
rolling over the floor. He crawls on his knees to the foot
of the bed, then leans against it like a child peering into
a candy shop window, repeating: "Che bel-la, che
bel-la!" with antiphonal responses from the goat outside.
Slowly, with tremendous effort, as if it were the sheer side
of a precipice, he clambers upon the couch and crouches
over the sleeping girl in a leapfrog position, saying "Che
bel-la!" quite loudly, this time, in a tone of innocently
joyous surprise. All at once Rosa wakens. She screams,
even before she is quite awake, and springs from the couch
so violently that Alvaro topples over to the floor.*

[*Serafina cries out almost instantly after Rosa. She lunges
through the dining room in her torn and disordered*

*nightgown. At the sight of the man crouched by the couch
a momentary stupefaction turns into a burst of savage
fury. She flies at him like a great bird, tearing and claw-
ing at his stupefied figure. With one arm Alvaro wards
off her blows, plunging to the floor and crawling into the
dining room. She seizes a broom with which she flails
him about the head, buttocks and shoulders while he
scrambles awkwardly away. The assault is nearly word-
less. Each time she strikes at him she hisses: "Sporcaccione!" He continually groans: "Dough, dough, dough!"
At last he catches hold of the widow dummy which he
holds as a shield before him while he entreats the two
women.*]

ALVARO:

Senti, Baronessa! Signorina! I didn't know what I was
doin', I was dreamin', I was just dreamin'! I got turn
around in the house; I got all twisted! I thought that you
was your Mama!—Sono ubriaco! Per favore!

ROSA [*seizing the broom*]:
That's enough, Mama!

SERAFINA [*rushing to the phone*]:
Police!

ROSA [*seizing the phone*]:
No, no, no, no, no, no!—You want everybody to know?

SERAFINA [*weakly*]:
Know?—Know *what,* cara?

ROSA:

Just give him his clothes, now, Mama, and let him get out!
[*She is clutching a bedsheet about herself.*]

ALVARO:

Signorina—young lady! I swear I was *dreaming!*

SERAFINA:

Don't speak to my daughter! [*then, turning to Rosa*]—
Who is this man? How did this man get here?

ROSA [*coldly*]:

Mama, don't say any more. Just give him his clothes in the
bedroom so he can get out!

ALVARO [*still crouching*]:

I am so sorry, so sorry! I don't remember a thing but that
I was dreaming!

SERAFINA [*shoving him toward the back of the room with
her broom*]:

Go on, go get your clothes on, you—idiot's grandson, you!
—Svelto, svelto, più svelto! [*Alvaro continues his apologetic mumbling in the back room.*] Don't talk to me, don't
say nothing! Or I will kill you!

[*A few moments later Alvaro rushes around the side of
the house, his clothes half buttoned and his shirttails out.*]

ALVARO:

But, Baronessa, I *love* you! [*A teakettle sails over his head
from behind the house. The Strega bursts into laughter.
Despairingly, Alvaro retreats, tucking his shirttails in and
shaking his head.*] Baronessa, Baronessa, I love you!

[*As Alvaro runs off, the Strega is heard cackling:*]

THE STREGA'S VOICE:

The Wops are at it again. Had a truck driver in the house
all night!

[*Rosa is feverishly dressing. From the bureau she has
snatched a shimmering white satin slip, disappearing for
a moment behind a screen to put it on as Serafina comes*]

408

padding sheepishly back into the room, her nightgown now covered by a black rayon kimona sprinkled with poppies, her voice tremulous with fear, shame and apology.]

ROSA [*behind the screen*]:
Has the man gone?

SERAFINA:
That—man?

ROSA:
Yes, "that man!"

SERAFINA [*inventing desperately*]:
I don't know how he got in. Maybe the backdoor was open.

ROSA:
Oh, yes, maybe it was!

SERAFINA:
Maybe he—climbed in a window . . .

ROSA:
Or fell down the chimney, maybe! [*She comes from behind the screen, wearing the white bridal slip.*]

SERAFINA:
Why you put on the white things I save for your wedding?

ROSA:
Because I want to. That's a good enough reason. [*She combs her hair savagely.*]

SERAFINA:
I want you to understand about that man. That was a man that—that was—that was a man that . . .

ROSA:
You can't think of a lie?

SERAFINA:
He was a—truck driver, cara. He got in a fight, he was chase by—policemen!

ROSA:
They chased him into your bedroom?

SERAFINA:
I took pity on him, I give him first aid, I let him sleep on the floor. He give me his promise—he . . .

ROSA:
Did he kneel in front of Our Lady? Did he promise that he would respect your innocence?

SERAFINA:
Oh, cara, cara! [*abandoning all pretense*] He was Sicilian; he had rose oil in his hair and the rose tattoo of your father. In the dark room I couldn't see his clown face. I closed my eyes and dreamed that he was your father! I closed my eyes! I dreamed that he was your father . . .

ROSA:
Basta, basta, non voglio sentire più niente! The only thing worse than a liar is a liar that's also a hypocrite!

SERAFINA:
Senti, per favore! [*Rosa wheels about from the mirror and fixes her mother with a long and withering stare. Serafina cringes before it.*] Don't look at me like that with the eyes of your father! [*She shields her face as from a terrible glare.*]

410

ROSA:

Yes, I am looking at you with the eyes of my father. I see you the way *he* saw you. [*She runs to the table and seizes the piggy bank.*] Like this, this *pig!* [*Serafina utters a long, shuddering cry like a cry of childbirth.*] I need five dollars. I'll take it out of this! [*Rosa smashes the piggy bank to the floor and rakes some coins into her purse. Serafina stoops to the floor. There is the sound of a train whistle. Rosa is now fully dressed, but she hesitates, a little ashamed of her cruelty—but only a little. Serafina cannot meet her daughter's eyes. At last the girl speaks.*]

SERAFINA:

How beautiful—is my daughter! Go to the boy!

ROSA [*as if she might be about to apologize*]:
Mama? He didn't touch me—he just said—"Che bella!"

[*Serafina turns slowly, shamefully, to face her. She is like a peasant in the presence of a young princess. Rosa stares at her a moment longer, then suddenly catches her breath and runs out of the house. As the girl leaves, Serafina calls:*]

SERAFINA:

Rosa, Rosa, the—wrist watch! [*Serafina snatches up the little gift box and runs out onto the porch with it. She starts to call her daughter again, holding the gift out toward her, but her breath fails her.*] Rosa, Rosa, the—wrist watch . . . [*Her arms fall to her side. She turns, the gift still ungiven. Senselessly, absently, she holds the watch to her ear again. She shakes it a little, then utters a faint, startled laugh.*]

[*Assunta appears beside the house and walks directly in, as though Serafina had called her.*]

SERAFINA:

Assunta, the urn is broken. The ashes are spilt on the floor and I can't touch them.

[*Assunta stoops to pick up the pieces of the shattered urn. Serafina has crossed to the shrine and relights the candle before the Madonna.*]

ASSUNTA:

There are no ashes.

SERAFINA:

Where—where are they? Where have the ashes gone?

ASSUNTA [*crossing to the shrine*]:

The wind has blown them away.

[*Assunta places what remains of the broken urn in Serafina's hands. Serafina turns it tenderly in her hands and then replaces it on the top of the prie-dieu before the Madonna.*]

SERAFINA:

A man, when he burns, leaves only a handful of ashes. No woman can hold him. The wind must blow him away.

[*Alvaro's voice is heard, calling from the top of the highway embankment.*]

ALVARO'S VOICE:

Rondinella felice!

[*The neighborhood women hear Alvaro calling, and there is a burst of mocking laughter from some of them. Then they all converge on the house from different directions and gather before the porch.*]

PEPPINA:

Serafina delle Rose!

GIUSEPPINA:

Baronessa! Baronessa delle Rose!

PEPPINA:

There is a man on the road without the shirt!

GIUSEPPINA [*with delight*]:
Si, si! Senza camicia!

PEPPINA:

All he got on his chest is a rose tattoo! [*to the women*] She
lock up his shirt so he can't go to the high school?

[*The women shriek with laughter. In the house Serafina
snatches up the package containing the silk shirt, while
Assunta closes the shutters of the parlor windows.*]

SERAFINA:

Un momento! [*She tears the paper off the shirt and rushes
out onto the porch, holding the shirt above her head defiantly.*] Ecco la camicia!

[*With a soft cry, Serafina drops the shirt, which is immediately snatched up by Peppina. At this point the music
begins again, with a crash of percussion, and continues
to the end of the play. Peppina flourishes the shirt in
the air like a banner and tosses it to Giuseppina, who
is now on the embankment. Giuseppina tosses it on to
Mariella, and she in her turn to Violetta, who is above
her, so that the brilliantly colored shirt moves in a zigzag
course through the pampas grass to the very top of the
embankment, like a streak of flame shooting up a dry
hill. The women call out as they pass the shirt along:*]

PEPPINA:

Guardate questa camicia! Coloro di rose!

413

MARIELLA [*shouting up to Alvaro*]:
Corragio, signor!

GIUSEPPINA:
Avanti, avanti, signor!

VIOLETTA [*at the top of the embankment, giving the shirt a final flourish above her*]:
Corragio, corragio! The Baronessa is waiting!

[*Bursts of laughter are mingled with the cries of the women. Then they sweep away like a flock of screaming birds, and Serafina is left upon the porch, her eyes closed, a hand clasped to her breast. In the meanwhile, inside the house, Assunta has poured out a glass of wine. Now she comes to the porch, offering the wine to Serafina and murmuring:*]

ASSUNTA:
Stai tranquilla.

SERAFINA [*breathlessly*]:
Assunta, I'll tell you something that maybe you won't believe.

ASSUNTA [*with tender humor*]:
It is impossible to tell me anything that I don't believe.

SERAFINA:
Just now I felt on my breast the burning again of the rose. I know what it means. It means that I have conceived! [*She lifts the glass to her lips for a moment and then returns it to Assunta.*] Two lives again in the body! Two, two lives again, two!

ALVARO'S VOICE [*nearer now, and sweetly urgent*]:
Rondinella felice!

[*Alvaro is not visible on the embankment but Serafina begins to move slowly toward his voice.*]

ASSUNTA:
Dove vai, Serafina?

SERAFINA [*shouting now, to Alvaro*]:
Vengo, vengo, amore!

[*She starts up the embankment toward Alvaro and the curtain falls as the music rises with her in great glissandi of sound.*]

CAMINO REAL*

"*In the middle of the journey of our life
I came to myself in a dark wood where the
straight way was lost.*"

CANTO I, DANTE'S *Inferno*

*Use Anglicized pronunciation: *Cá*-mino *Ré*al

FOR ELIA KAZAN

,

FOREWORD*

It is amazing and frightening how completely one's whole being becomes absorbed in the making of a play. It is almost as if you were frantically constructing another world while the world that you live in dissolves beneath your feet, and that your survival depends on completing this construction at least one second before the old habitation collapses.

More than any other work that I have done, this play has seemed to me like the construction of another world, a separate existence. Of course, it is nothing more nor less than my conception of the time and world that I live in, and its people are mostly archetypes of certain basic attitudes and qualities with those mutations that would occur if they had continued along the road to this hypothetical terminal point in it.

A convention of the play is existence outside of time in a place of no specific locality. If you regard it that way, I suppose it becomes an elaborate allegory, but in New Haven we opened directly across the street from a movie theatre that was showing *Peter Pan* in Technicolor and it did not seem altogether inappropriate to me. Fairy tales nearly always have some simple moral lesson of good and evil, but that is not the secret of their fascination any more, I hope, than the philosophical import that might be distilled from the fantasies of *Camino Real* is the principal element of its appeal.

To me the appeal of this work is its unusual degree of freedom. When it began to get under way I felt a new sensation of release, as if I could "ride out" like a tenor sax taking the breaks in a Dixieland combo or a piano in a bop session. You may call it self-indulgence, but I was not doing it merely for

---

* Written prior to the Broadway premiere of *Camino Real* and published in *The New York Times* on Sunday, March 15, 1953.

myself. I could not have felt a purely private thrill of release unless I had hope of sharing this experience with lots and lots of audiences to come.

My desire was to give these audiences my own sense of something wild and unrestricted that ran like water in the mountains, or clouds changing shape in a gale, or the continually dissolving and transforming images of a dream. This sort of freedom is not chaos nor anarchy. On the contrary, it is the result of painstaking design, and in this work I have given more conscious attention to form and construction than I have in any work before. Freedom is not achieved simply by working freely.

Elia Kazan was attracted to this work mainly, I believe, for the same reason—its freedom and mobility of form. I know that we have kept saying the word "flight" to each other as if the play were merely an abstraction of the impulse to fly, and most of the work out of town, his in staging, mine in cutting and revising, has been with this impulse in mind: the achievement of a continual flow. Speech after speech and bit after bit that were nice in themselves have been remorselessly blasted out of the script and its staging wherever they seemed to obstruct or divert this flow.

There have been plenty of indications already that this play will exasperate and confuse a certain number of people which we hope is not so large as the number it is likely to please. At each performance a number of people have stamped out of the auditorium, with little regard for those whom they have had to crawl over, almost as if the building had caught on fire, and there have been sibilant noises on the way out and demands for money back if the cashier was foolish enough to remain in his box.

I am at a loss to explain this phenomenon, and if I am being facetious about one thing, I am being quite serious about another when I say that I had never for one minute supposed that the play would seem obscure and confusing to anyone who was willing to meet it even less than halfway. It was a costly production, and for this reason I had to read it aloud, together with a few of the actors on one occasion, before large groups of prospective backers, before the funds to produce it were in the till. It was only then that I came up against the disconcerting surprise that some people would think that the play needed clarification.

My attitude is intransigent. I still don't agree that it needs any explanation. Some poet has said that a poem should not mean but be. Of course, a play is not a poem, not even a poetic play has quite the same license as a poem. But to go to *Camino Real* with the inflexible demands of a logician is unfair to both parties.

In Philadelphia a young man from a literary periodical saw the play and then cross-examined me about all its dreamlike images. He had made a list of them while he watched the play, and afterward at my hotel he brought out the list and asked me to explain the meaning of each one. I can't deny that I use a lot of those things called symbols but being a self-defensive creature, I say that symbols are nothing but the natural speech of drama.

We all have in our conscious and unconscious minds a great vocabulary of images, and I think all human communication is based on these images as are our dreams; and a symbol in a play has only one legitimate purpose which is to say a thing more directly and simply and beautifully than it could be said in words.

I hate writing that is a parade of images for the sake of images; I hate it so much that I close a book in disgust when

421

it keeps on saying one thing is like another; I even get disgusted with poems that make nothing but comparisons between one thing and another. But I repeat that symbols, when used respectfully, are the purest language of plays. Sometimes it would take page after tedious page of exposition to put across an idea that can be said with an object or a gesture on the lighted stage.

To take one case in point: the battered portmanteau of Jacques Casanova is hurled from the balcony of a luxury hotel when his remittance check fails to come through. While the portmanteau is still in the air, he shouts: "Careful, I have—" —and when it has crashed to the street he continues—"fragile—mementos . . ." I suppose that is a symbol, at least it is an object used to express as directly and vividly as possible certain things which could be said in pages of dull talk.

As for those patrons who departed before the final scene, I offer myself this tentative bit of solace: that these theatregoers may be a little domesticated in their theatrical tastes. A cage represents security as well as confinement to a bird that has grown used to being in it; and when a theatrical work kicks over the traces with such apparent insouciance, security seems challenged and, instead of participating in its sense of freedom, one out of a certain number of playgoers will rush back out to the more accustomed implausibility of the street he lives on.

To modify this effect of complaisance I would like to admit to you quite frankly that I can't say with any personal conviction that I have written a good play, I only know that I have felt a release in this work which I wanted you to feel with me.

Tennessee Williams

AFTERWORD

Once in a while someone will say to me that he would rather wait for a play to come out as a book than see a live performance of it, where he would be distracted from its true values, if it has any, by so much that is mere spectacle and sensation and consequently must be meretricious and vulgar. There are plays meant for reading. I have read them. I have read the works of "thinking playwrights" as distinguished from us who are permitted only to feel, and probably read them earlier and appreciated them as much as those who invoke their names nowadays like the incantation of Aristophanes' frogs. But the incontinent blaze of a live theatre, a theatre meant for seeing and for feeling, has never been and never will be extinguished by a bucket brigade of critics, new or old, bearing vessels that range from cut-glass punch bowl to Haviland teacup. And in my dissident opinion, a play in a book is only the shadow of a play and not even a clear shadow of it. Those who did not like *Camino Real* on the stage will not be likely to form a higher opinion of it in print, for of all the works I have written, this one was meant most for the vulgarity of performance. The printed script of a play is hardly more than an architect's blueprint of a house not yet built or built and destroyed.

The color, the grace and levitation, the structural pattern in motion, the quick interplay of live beings, suspended like fitful lightning in a cloud, these things are the play, not words on paper, nor thoughts and ideas of an author, those shabby things snatched off basement counters at Gimbel's.

My own creed as a playwright is fairly close to that expressed by the painter in Shaw's play *The Doctor's Dilemma*: "I believe in Michelangelo, Velasquez and Rembrandt; in the might of design, the mystery of color, the redemption of all things by beauty everlasting and the message of art that has made these hands blessed. Amen."

How much art his hands were blessed with or how much mine are, I don't know, but that art is a blessing is certain and that it contains its message is also certain, and I feel, as the painter did, that the message lies in those abstract beauties of form and color and line, to which I would add light and motion.

In these following pages are only the formula by which a play could exist.

Dynamic is a word in disrepute at the moment, and so, I suppose, is the word *organic,* but those terms still define the dramatic values that I value most and which I value more as they are more deprecated by the ones self-appointed to save what they have never known.

> *Tennessee Williams*
> June 1, 1953

EDITOR'S NOTE

The version of *Camino Real* here published is considerably revised over the one presented on Broadway. Following the opening there, Mr. Williams went to his home at Key West and continued to work on this play. When he left six weeks later to direct Donald Windham's *The Starless Air* in Houston, Texas, he took the playing version with him and reworked it whenever time allowed. It was with him when he drove in leisurely fashion back to New York. As delivered to the publisher, the manuscript of *Camino Real* was typed on three different typewriters and on stationery of hotels across the country.

Three characters, a prologue and several scenes that were not in the Broadway production have been added, or reinstated from earlier, preproduction versions, while other scenes have been deleted.

Camino Real is divided into a Prologue and Sixteen "Blocks," scenes with no perceptible time lapse between them for the most part. There are intermissions indicated after Block Six and Block Eleven.

The action takes place in an unspecified Latin-American country.

Camino Real was first produced by Cheryl Crawford and Ethel Reiner, in association with Walter P. Chrysler, Jr., and following tryouts in New Haven and Philadelphia, it had its Broadway premiere on March 19, 1953, at the Martin Beck Theatre. The production was directed by Elia Kazan, with the assistance of Anna Sokolow; the setting and costumes were designed by Lemuel Ayers; and incidental music was contributed by Bernardo Ségall. Production associate: Anderson Lawler. Tennessee Williams was represented by Liebling-Wood.

Cast of the Broadway Production

GUTMAN	FRANK SILVERA
SURVIVOR	GUY THOMAJAN
ROSITA	AZA BARD
FIRST OFFICER	HENRY SILVA
JACQUES CASANOVA	JOSEPH ANTHONY
LA MADRECITA DE LOS PERDIDOS	VIVIAN NATHAN
HER SON	ROLANDO VALDEZ
KILROY	ELI WALLACH
FIRST STREETCLEANER	NEHEMIAH PERSOFF
SECOND STREETCLEANER	FRED SADOFF
ABDULLAH	ERNESTO GONZALEZ
A BUM IN A WINDOW	MARTIN BALSAM
A. RATT	MIKE GAZZO
THE LOAN SHARK	SALEM LUDWIG
BARON DE CHARLUS	DAVID J. STEWART
LOBO	RONNE AUL
SECOND OFFICER	WILLIAM LENNARD
A GROTESQUE MUMMER	GLUCK SANDOR
MARGUERITE GAUTIER	JO VAN FLEET

LADY MULLIGAN	Lucille Patton
WAITER	Page Johnson
LORD BYRON	Hurd Hatfield
NAVIGATOR OF THE FUGITIVO	Antony Vorno
PILOT OF THE FUGITIVO	Martin Balsam
MARKET WOMAN	Charlotte Jones
SECOND MARKET WOMAN	Joanna Vischer
STREET VENDOR	Ruth Volner
LORD MULLIGAN	Parker Wilson
THE GYPSY	Jennie Goldstein
HER DAUGHTER, ESMERALDA	Barbara Baxley
NURSIE	Salem Ludwig
EVA	Mary Grey
THE INSTRUCTOR	David J. Stewart
ASSISTANT INSTRUCTOR	Parker Wilson
MEDICAL STUDENT	Page Johnson
DON QUIXOTE	Hurd Hatfield
SANCHO PANZA	(*Not in production*)
PRUDENCE DUVERNOY	(*Not in production*)
OLYMPE	(*Not in production*)

Street Vendors: Aza Bard, Ernesto Gonzalez, Charlotte Jones, Gluck Sandor, Joanna Vischer, Ruth Volner, Antony Vorno.

Guests: Martin Balsam, Mary Grey, Lucille Patton, Joanna Vischer, Parker Wilson.

Passengers: Mike Gazzo, Mary Grey, Page Johnson, Charlotte Jones, William Lennard, Salem Ludwig, Joanna Vischer, Ruth Volner.

At the Fiesta: Ronne Aul, Martin Balsam, Aza Bard, Mike Gazzo, Ernesto Gonzalez, Mary Grey, Charlotte Jones, William Lennard, Nehemiah Persoff, Fred Sadoff, Gluck Sandor, Joanna Vischer, Antony Vorno, Parker Wilson.

THE NEW YORK PRODUCTION SET BY LEMUEL AYERS

PROLOGUE

As the curtain rises, on an almost lightless stage, there is a loud singing of wind, accompanied by distant, measured reverberations like pounding surf or distant shellfire. Above the ancient wall that backs the set and the perimeter of mountains visible above the wall, are flickers of a white radiance as though daybreak were a white bird caught in a net and struggling to rise.

The plaza is seen fitfully by this light. It belongs to a tropical seaport that bears a confusing, but somehow harmonious, resemblance to such widely scattered ports as Tangiers, Havana, Vera Cruz, Casablanca, Shanghai, New Orleans.

On stage left is the luxury side of the street, containing the façade of the Siete Mares Hotel and its low terrace on which are a number of glass-topped white iron tables and chairs. In the downstairs there is a great bay window in which are seen a pair of elegant "dummies," one seated, one standing behind, looking out into the plaza with painted smiles. Upstairs is a small balcony and behind it a large window exposing a wall on which is hung a phoenix painted on silk: this should be softly lighted now and then in the play, since resurrections are so much a part of its meaning.

Opposite the hotel is Skid Row which contains the Gypsy's gaudy stall, the Loan Shark's establishment with a window containing a variety of pawned articles, and the "Ritz Men Only" which is a flea-bag hotel or flophouse and which has a practical window above its downstairs entrance, in which a bum will appear from time to time to deliver appropriate or contrapuntal song titles.

Upstage is a great flight of stairs that mount the ancient wall to a sort of archway that leads out into "Terra Incognita,"

431

as it is called in the play, a wasteland between the walled town and the distant perimeter of snow-topped mountains.

Downstage right and left are a pair of arches which give entrance to dead-end streets.

Immediately after the curtain rises a shaft of blue light is thrown down a central aisle of the theatre, and in this light, advancing from the back of the house, appears Don Quixote de la Mancha, dressed like an old "desert rat." As he enters the aisle he shouts, "Hola!", in a cracked old voice which is still full of energy and is answered by another voice which is impatient and tired, that of his squire, Sancho Panza. Stumbling with a fatigue which is only physical, the old knight comes down the aisle, and Sancho follows a couple of yards behind him, loaded down with equipment that ranges from a medieval shield to a military canteen or Thermos bottle. Shouts are exchanged between them.

QUIXOTE [*ranting above the wind in a voice which is nearly as old*]:
Blue is the color of distance!

SANCHO [*wearily behind him*]:
Yes, distance is blue.

QUIXOTE:
Blue is also the color of nobility.

SANCHO:
Yes, nobility's blue.

QUIXOTE:
Blue is the color of distance and nobility, and that's why an old knight should always have somewhere about him a bit of blue ribbon . . .

[*He jostles the elbow of an aisle-sitter as he staggers with fatigue; he mumbles an apology.*]

SANCHO:
Yes, a bit of blue ribbon.

QUIXOTE:
A bit of faded blue ribbon, tucked away in whatever remains of his armor, or borne on the tip of his lance, his—unconquerable lance! It serves to remind an old knight of distance that he has gone and distance he has yet to go . . .

[*Sancho mutters the Spanish word for excrement as several pieces of rusty armor fall into the aisle.*

[*Quixote has now arrived at the foot of the steps onto the forestage. He pauses there as if wandering out of or into a dream. Sancho draws up clanking behind him.*

[*Mr. Gutman, a lordly fat man wearing a linen suit and a pith helmet, appears dimly on the balcony·of the Siete Mares, a white cockatoo on his wrist. The bird cries out harshly.*]

GUTMAN:
Hush, Aurora.

QUIXOTE:
It also reminds an old knight of that green country he lived in which was the youth of his heart, before such singing words as *Truth!*

SANCHO [*panting*]:
—Truth.

QUIXOTE:
Valor!

SANCHO:
—Valor.

QUIXOTE [*elevating his lance*]:
Devoir!

SANCHO:
—Devoir ...

QUIXOTE:
—turned into the meaningless mumble of some old monk
hunched over cold mutton at supper!

[*Gutman alerts a pair of Guards in the plaza, who cross
with red lanterns to either side of the proscenium where
they lower black and white striped barrier gates as if the
proscenium marked a frontier. One of them, with a hand
on his holster, advances toward the pair on the steps.*]

GUARD:
Vien aquí.

[*Sancho hangs back but Quixote stalks up to the barrier
gate. The Guard turns a flashlight on his long and exceed-
ingly grave red face, "frisks" him casually for concealed
weapons, examines a rusty old knife and tosses it contemptuously away.*]

Sus papeles! Sus documentos!

[*Quixote fumblingly produces some tattered old papers
from the lining of his hat.*]

GUTMAN [*impatiently*]:
Who is it?

GUARD:
An old desert rat named Quixote.

GUTMAN:

Oh!—Expected!—Let him in.

[*The Guards raise the barrier gate and one sits down to smoke on the terrace. Sancho hangs back still. A dispute takes place on the forestage and steps into the aisle.*]

QUIXOTE:

Forward!

SANCHO:

Aw, naw. I know this place. [*He produces a crumpled parchment.*] Here it is on the chart. Look, it says here: "Continue until you come to the square of a walled town which is the end of the *Ca*mino Re*al* and the beginning of the *Ca*mino *Re*al. Halt there," it says, "and turn back, Traveler, for the spring of humanity has gone dry in this place and—"

QUIXOTE [*He snatches the chart from him and reads the rest of the inscription.*]:

"—there are no birds in the country except wild birds that are tamed and kept in—" [*He holds the chart close to his nose.*]

—*Cages!*

SANCHO [*urgently*]:

Let's go back to La Mancha!

QUIXOTE:

Forward!

SANCHO:

The time has come for retreat!

QUIXOTE:

The time for retreat never comes!

435

SANCHO:
I'm going back to *La Mancha!*
[*He dumps the knightly equipment into the orchestra pit.*]

QUIXOTE:
Without me?

SANCHO [*bustling up the aisle*]:
With you or without you, old tireless and tiresome master!

QUIXOTE [*imploringly*]:
Saaaaaan-chooooooooo!

SANCHO [*near the top of the aisle*]:
I'm going back to La *Maaaaaaaaan-chaaaaaaa . . .*

[*He disappears as the blue light in the aisle dims out. The Guard puts out his cigarette and wanders out of the plaza. The wind moans and Gutman laughs softly as the Ancient Knight enters the plaza with such a desolate air.*]

QUIXOTE [*looking about the plaza*]:
—Lonely . . .

[*To his surprise the word is echoed softly by almost unseen figures huddled below the stairs and against the wall of the town. Quixote leans upon his lance and observes with a wry smile—*]

—When so many are lonely as seem to be lonely, it would be inexcusably selfish to be lonely alone.

[*He shakes out a dusty blanket. Shadowy arms extend toward him and voices murmur.*]

VOICE:
Sleep. Sleep. Sleep.

QUIXOTE [*arranging his blanket*]:
Yes, I'll sleep for a while, I'll sleep and dream for a while
against the wall of this town ...

[*A mandolin or guitar plays "The Nightingale of France."*]

—And my dream will be a pageant, a masque in which old
meanings will be remembered and possibly new ones discovered, and when I wake from this sleep and this disturbing
pageant of a dream, I'll choose one among its shadows to take
along with me in the place of Sancho ...

[*He blows his nose between his fingers and wipes them on
his shirttail.*]

—For new companions are not as familiar as old ones but all
the same—they're old ones with only slight differences of face
and figure, which may or may not be improvements, and it
would be selfish of me to be lonely alone ...

[*He stumbles down the incline into the Pit below the stairs
where most of the Street People huddle beneath awnings of
open stalls.*

[*The white cockatoo squawks.*]

GUTMAN:
Hush, Aurora.

QUIXOTE:
And tomorrow at this same hour, which we call madrugada,
the loveliest of all words, except the word alba, and that word
also means daybreak—

—Yes, at daybreak tomorrow I will go on from here with a
new companion and this old bit of blue ribbon to keep me
in mind of distance that I have gone and distance I have yet
to go, and also to keep me in mind of—

[*The cockatoo cries wildly.*

[*Quixote nods as if in agreement with the outcry and folds himself into his blanket below the great stairs.*]

GUTMAN [*stroking the cockatoo's crest*]:
Be still, Aurora. I know it's morning, Aurora.

[*Daylight turns the plaza silver and slowly gold. Vendors rise beneath white awnings of stalls. The Gypsy's stall opens. A tall, courtly figure, in his late middle years (Jacques Casanova) crosses from the Siete Mares to the Loan Shark's, removing a silver snuffbox from his pocket as Gutman speaks. His costume, like that of all the legendary characters in the play (except perhaps Quixote) is generally "modern" but with vestigial touches of the period to which he was actually related. The cane and the snuff-box and perhaps a brocaded vest may be sufficient to give this historical suggestion in Casanova's case. He bears his hawklike head with a sort of anxious pride on most occasions, a pride maintained under a steadily mounting pressure.*]

—It's morning and after morning. It's afternoon, ha ha! And now I must go downstairs to announce the beginning of that old wanderer's dream ...

[*He withdraws from the balcony as old Prudence Duvernoy stumbles out of the hotel, as if not yet quite awake from an afternoon siesta. Chattering with beads and bracelets, she wanders vaguely down into the plaza, raising a faded green silk parasol, damp henna-streaked hair slipping under a monstrous hat of faded silk roses; she is searching for a lost poodle.*]

PRUDENCE:
Trique? Trique?

[Jacques comes out of the Loan Shark's replacing his case angrily in his pocket.]

JACQUES:
Why, I'd rather give it to a street beggar! This case is a Boucheron, I won it at faro at the summer palace, at Tsarskoe Selo in the winter of—

[The Loan Shark slams the door. Jacques glares, then shrugs and starts across the plaza. Old Prudence is crouched over the filthy gray bundle of a dying mongrel by the fountain.]

PRUDENCE:
Trique, oh, Trique!

[The Gypsy's son, Abdullah, watches, giggling.]

JACQUES *[reproving]*:
It is a terrible thing for an old woman to outlive her dogs.

[He crosses to Prudence and gently disengages the animal from her grasp.]

Madam, that is not Trique.

PRUDENCE:
—When I woke up she wasn't in her basket ...

JACQUES:
Sometimes we sleep too long in the afternoon and when we wake we find things changed, Signora.

PRUDENCE:
Oh, you're Italian!

JACQUES:
I am from Venice, Signora.

PRUDENCE:
Ah, Venice, city of pearls! I saw you last night on the terrace

dining with—Oh, I'm so worried about her! I'm an old friend of hers, perhaps she's mentioned me to you. Prudence Duvernoy? I was her best friend in the old days in Paris, but now she's forgotten so much ...

I hope you have influence with her!

[*A waltz of Camille's time in Paris is heard.*]

I want you to give her a message from a certain wealthy old gentleman that she met at one of those watering places she used to go to for her health. She resembled his daughter who died of consumption and so he adored Camille, lavished everything on her! What did she do? Took a young lover who hadn't a couple of pennies to rub together, disinherited by his father because of *her!* Oh, you can't do that, not now, not any more, you've got to be realistic on the Camino Real!

[*Gutman has come out on the terrace: he announces quietly—*]

GUTMAN:
Block One on the Camino Real.

PRUDENCE [*continuing*]:

Yes, you've got to be practical on it! Well, give her this message, please, Sir. He wants her back on any terms whatsoever! [*Her speech gathers furious momentum.*] Her evenings will be free. He wants only her mornings, mornings are hard on old men because their hearts beat slowly, and he wants only her mornings! Well, that's how it should be! A sensible arrangement! Elderly gentlemen have to content themselves with a lady's spare time before supper! Isn't that so? Of course so! And so I told him! I told him, Camille isn't well! She requires delicate care! Has many debts, creditors storm her door! "How much does she owe?" he asked me, and, oh, did I do some lightning mathematics! Jewels in pawn, I told him, pearls, rings, necklaces, bracelets, diamond eardrops are in pawn! Horses put up for sale at a public auction!

JACQUES [*appalled by this torrent*]:
Signora, Signora, all of these things are—

PRUDENCE:
—What?

JACQUES:
Dreams!

[*Gutman laughs. A woman sings at a distance.*]

PRUDENCE [*continuing with less assurance*]:
—You're not so young as I thought when I saw you last night on the terrace by candlelight on the—Oh, but—Ho ho!—I bet there is *one* old fountain in this plaza that hasn't gone dry!

[*She pokes him obscenely. He recoils. Gutman laughs. Jacques starts away but she seizes his arm again, and the torrent of speech continues.*]

PRUDENCE:

Wait, wait, listen! Her candle is burning low. But how can you tell? She might have a lingering end, and charity hospitals? Why, you might as well take a flying leap into the Streetcleaners' barrel. Oh, I've told her and told her not to live in a dream! A dream is nothing to live in, why, it's gone like a—

Don't let her elegance fool you! That girl has done the Camino in carriages but she has also done it on foot! She knows every stone the Camino is paved with! So tell her this. You tell her, she won't listen to me!—Times and conditions have undergone certain changes since we were friends in Paris, and now we dismiss young lovers with skins of silk and eyes like a child's first prayer, we put them away as lightly as we put away white gloves meant only for summer, and pick up a pair of black ones, suitable for winter . . .

[*The singing voice rises: then subsides.*]

JACQUES:

Excuse me, Madam.

[*He tears himself from her grasp and rushes into the Siete Mares.*]

PRUDENCE [*dazed, to Gutman*]:

—What block is this?

GUTMAN:

Block One.

PRUDENCE:

I didn't hear the announcement . . .

GUTMAN [*coldly*]:

Well, now you do.

[*Olympe comes out of the lobby with a pale orange silk parasol like a floating moon.*]

OLYMPE:
Oh, there you are, I've looked for you high and low!—mostly low ...

[*They float vaguely out into the dazzling plaza as though a capricious wind took them, finally drifting through the Moorish arch downstage right.*

[*The song dies out.*]

GUTMAN [*lighting a thin cigar*]:
Block Two on the Camino Real.

BLOCK TWO

After Gutman's announcement, a hoarse cry is heard. A
figure in rags, skin blackened by the sun, tumbles crazily
down the steep alley to the plaza. He turns about blindly,
murmuring: "A donde la fuente?" He stumbles against
the hideous old prostitute Rosita who grins horribly and
whispers something to him, hitching up her ragged, filthy
skirt. Then she gives him a jocular push toward the fountain. He falls upon his belly and thrusts his hands into the
dried-up basin. Then he staggers to his feet with a despairing cry.

THE SURVIVOR:
La fuente está seca!

[Rosita laughs madly but the other Street People moan. A
dry gourd rattles.]

ROSITA:
The fountain is dry, but there's plenty to drink in the Siete
Mares!

[She shoves him toward the hotel. The proprietor, Gutman,
steps out, smoking a thin cigar, fanning himself with a
palm leaf. As the Survivor advances, Gutman whistles. A
man in military dress comes out upon the low terrace.]

OFFICER:
Go back!

[The Survivor stumbles forward. The Officer fires at him.
He lowers his hands to his stomach, turns slowly about with
a lost expression, looking up at the sky, and stumbles toward
the fountain. During the scene that follows, until the entrance of La Madrecita and her Son, the Survivor drags

himself slowly about the concrete rim of the fountain, almost entirely ignored, as a dying pariah dog in a starving country. Jacques Casanova comes out upon the terrace of the Siete Mares. Now he passes the hotel proprietor's impassive figure, descending a step beneath and a little in advance of him, and without looking at him.]

JACQUES [*with infinite weariness and disgust*]:
What has happened?

GUTMAN [*serenely*]:

We have entered the second in a progress of sixteen blocks on the Camino Real. It's five o'clock. That angry old lion, the Sun, looked back once and growled and then went switching his tail toward the cool shade of the Sierras. Our guests have taken their afternoon siestas . . .

[*The Survivor has come out upon the forestage, now, not like a dying man but like a shy speaker who has forgotten the opening line of his speech. He is only a little crouched over with a hand obscuring the red stain over his belly. Two or three Street People wander about calling their wares: "Tacos, tacos, fritos . . ."—"Lotería, lotería"—Rosita shuffles around, calling "Love? Love?"—pulling down the filthy décolletage of her blouse to show more of her sagging bosom. The Survivor arrives at the top of the stairs descending into the orchestra of the theatre, and hangs onto it, looking out reflectively as a man over the rail of a boat coming into a somewhat disturbingly strange harbor.*]

GUTMAN [*continuing*]:
—They suffer from extreme fatigue, our guests at the Siete Mares, all of them have a degree or two of fever. Questions are passed amongst them like something illicit and shameful, like counterfeit money or drugs or indecent post cards—

445

[*He leans forward and whispers:*]

—"What is this place? Where are we? What is the meaning of—*Shhhh!*"—Ha ha . . .

THE SURVIVOR [*very softly to the audience*]:
I once had a pony named Peeto. He caught in his nostrils the scent of thunderstorms coming even before the clouds had crossed the Sierra . . .

VENDOR:
Tacos, tacos, fritos . . .

ROSITA:
Love? Love?

LADY MULLIGAN [*to waiter on terrace*]:
Are you sure no one called me? I was expecting a call . . .

GUTMAN [*smiling*]:
My guests are confused and exhausted but at this hour they pull themselves together, and drift downstairs on the wings of gin and the lift, they drift into the public rooms and exchange notes again on fashionable couturiers and custom tailors, restaurants, vintages of wine, hairdressers, plastic surgeons, girls and young men susceptible to offers . . .

[*There is a hum of light conversation and laughter within.*]

—Hear them? They're exchanging notes . . .

JACQUES [*striking the terrace with his cane*]:
I asked you what has happened in the plaza!

GUTMAN:
Oh, in the plaza, ha ha!—Happenings in the plaza don't concern us . . .

JACQUES:
I heard shots fired.

GUTMAN:
Shots were fired to remind you of your good fortune in staying here. The public fountains have gone dry, you know, but the Siete Mares was erected over the only perpetual never-dried-up spring in Tierra Caliente, and of course that advantage has to be—protected—sometimes by—martial law . . .

[*The guitar resumes.*]

THE SURVIVOR:
When Peeto, my pony, was born—he stood on his four legs at once, and accepted the world!—He was wiser than I . . .

VENDOR:
Fritos, fritos, tacos!

ROSITA:
Love!

THE SURVIVOR:
—When Peeto was one year old he was wiser than God!

[*A wind sings across the plaza; a dry gourd rattles.*]

"Peeto, Peeto!" the Indian boys call after him, trying to stop him—trying to stop the wind!

[*The Survivor's head sags forward. He sits down as slowly as an old man on a park bench. Jacques strikes the terrace again with his cane and starts toward the Survivor. The Guard seizes his elbow.*]

JACQUES:
Don't put your hand on *me*!

GUARD:
Stay here.

GUTMAN:
Remain on the terrace, please, Signor Casanova.

JACQUES [*fiercely*]:
—*Cognac!*

[*The Waiter whispers to Gutman. Gutman chuckles.*]

GUTMAN:
The Maître 'D' tells me that your credit has been discontinued in the restaurant and bar, he says that he has enough of your tabs to pave the terrace with!

JACQUES:
What a piece of impertinence! I told the man that the letter that I'm expecting has been delayed in the mail. The postal service in this country is fantastically disorganized, and you know it! You also know that Mlle. Gautier will guarantee my tabs!

GUTMAN:
Then let her pick them up at dinner tonight if you're hungry!

JACQUES:
I'm not accustomed to this kind of treatment on the Camino Real!

GUTMAN:
Oh, you'll be, you'll be, after a single night at the "Ritz Men Only." That's where you'll have to transfer your patronage if the letter containing the remittance check doesn't arrive tonight.

JACQUES:

I assure you that I shall do nothing of the sort!—Tonight or ever!

GUTMAN:

Watch out, old hawk, the wind is ruffling your feathers!

[*Jacques sinks trembling into a chair.*]

—Give him a thimble of brandy before he collapses . . . Fury is a luxury of the young, their veins are resilient, but his are brittle . . .

JACQUES:

Here I sit, submitting to insult for a thimble of brandy— while directly in front of me—

[*The singer, La Madrecita, enters the plaza. She is a blind woman led by a ragged Young Man. The Waiter brings Jacques a brandy.*]

—a man in the plaza dies like a pariah dog!—I take the brandy! I sip it!—My heart is too tired to break, my heart is too tired to—break . . .

[*La Madrecita chants softly. She slowly raises her arm to point at the Survivor crouched on the steps from the plaza.*]

GUTMAN [*suddenly*]:

Give me the phone! Connect me with the Palace. Get me the Generalissimo, quick, quick, quick!

[*The Survivor rises feebly and shuffles very slowly toward the extended arms of "The Little Blind One."*]

Generalissimo? Gutman speaking! Hello, sweetheart. There has been a little incident in the plaza. You know that party of

449

young explorers that attempted to cross the desert on foot?
Well, one of them's come back. He was very thirsty. He
found the fountain dry. He started toward the hotel. He was
politely advised to advance no further. But he disregarded this
advice. Action had to be taken. And now, and now—that old
blind woman they call "La Madrecita"?—She's come into the
plaza with the man called "The Dreamer" . . .

SURVIVOR:
Donde?

THE DREAMER:
Aquí!

GUTMAN [*continuing*]:
You remember those two! I once mentioned them to you.
You said "They're harmless dreamers and they're loved by the
people."—"What," I asked you, "is harmless about a dreamer,
and what," I asked you, "is harmless about the love of the
people?—Revolution only needs good dreamers who remember
their dreams, and the love of the people belongs safely only
to you—their Generalissimo!"—Yes, now the blind woman
has recovered her sight and is extending her arms to the
wounded Survivor, and the man with the guitar is leading
him to her . . .

[*The described action is being enacted.*]

Wait one moment! There's a possibility that the forbidden
word may be spoken! Yes! The forbidden word is about to
be spoken!

[*The Dreamer places an arm about the blinded Survivor,
and cries out:*]

THE DREAMER:
Hermano!

450

[*The cry is repeated like springing fire and a loud murmur sweeps the crowd. They push forward with cupped hands extended and the gasping cries of starving people at the sight of bread. Two Military Guards herd them back under the colonnades with clubs and drawn revolvers. La Madrecita chants softly with her blind eyes lifted. A Guard starts toward her. The People shout "NO!"*]

LA MADRECITA [*chanting*]:
"Rojo está el sol! Rojo está el sol de sangre! Blanca está la luna! Blanca está la luna de miedo!"

[*The crowd makes a turning motion.*]

GUTMAN [*to the waiter*]:
Put up the ropes!

[*Velvet ropes are strung very quickly about the terrace of the Siete Mares. They are like the ropes on decks of steamers in rough waters. Gutman shouts into the phone again:*]

The word was spoken. The crowd is agitated. Hang on!

[*He lays down instrument.*]

JACQUES [*hoarsely, shaken*]:
He said "Hermano." That's the word for brother.

GUTMAN [*calmly*]:
Yes, the most dangerous word in any human tongue is the word for brother. It's inflammatory.—I don't suppose it can be struck out of the language altogether but it must be reserved for strictly private usage in back of soundproof walls. Otherwise it disturbs the population . . .

JACQUES:
The people need the word. They're thirsty for it!

451

GUTMAN:

What are these creatures? Mendicants. Prostitutes. Thieves and petty vendors in a bazaar where the human heart is a part of the bargain.

JACQUES:

Because they need the word and the word is forbidden!

GUTMAN:

The word is said in pulpits and at tables of council where its volatile essence can be contained. But on the lips of these creatures, what is it? A wanton incitement to riot, without understanding. For what is a brother to them but someone to get ahead of, to cheat, to lie to, to undersell in the market. Brother, you say to a man whose wife you sleep with!—But now, you see, the word has disturbed the people and made it necessary to invoke martial law!

[*Meanwhile the Dreamer has brought the Survivor to La Madrecita, who is seated on the cement rim of the fountain. She has cradled the dying man in her arms in the attitude of a* Pietà. *The Dreamer is crouched beside them, softly playing a guitar. Now he springs up with a harsh cry:*]

THE DREAMER:
Muerto!

[*The Streetcleaners' piping commences at a distance. Gut-man seizes the phone again.*]

GUTMAN [*into phone*]:
Generalissimo, the Survivor is no longer surviving. I think we'd better have some public diversion right away. Put the Gypsy on! Have her announce the Fiesta!

452

LOUDSPEAKER [*responding instantly*]:
Damas y Caballeros! The next voice you hear will be the
voice of—the Gypsy!

GYPSY [*over loudspeaker*]:
Hoy! Noche de Fiesta! Tonight the moon will restore the
virginity of my daughter!

GUTMAN:
Bring on the Gypsy's daughter, Esmeralda. Show the virgin-
to-be!

[*Esmeralda is led from the Gypsy's stall by a severe duenna,
"Nursie," out upon the forestage. She is manacled by the
wrist to the duenna. Her costume is vaguely Levantine.*

[*Guards are herding the crowd back again.*]

GUTMAN:
Ha ha! Ho ho ho! Music!

[*There is gay music. Rosita dances.*]

Abdullah! You're on!

[*Abdullah skips into the plaza, shouting histrionically.*]

ABDULLAH:
Tonight the moon will restore the virginity of my sister,
Esmeralda!

GUTMAN:
Dance, boy!

[*Esmeralda is led back into the stall. Throwing off his
burnoose, Abdullah dances with Rosita. Behind their dance,
armed Guards force La Madrecita and the Dreamer to
retreat from the fountain, leaving the lifeless body of the*

453

Survivor. All at once there is a discordant blast of brass instruments.

[*Kilroy comes into the plaza. He is a young American vagrant, about twenty-seven. He wears dungarees and a skivvy shirt, the pants faded nearly white from long wear and much washing, fitting him as closely as the clothes of sculpture. He has a pair of golden boxing gloves slung about his neck and he carries a small duffle bag. His belt is ruby-and-emerald-studded with the word CHAMP in bold letters. He stops before a chalked inscription on a wall downstage which says: "Kilroy Is Coming!" He scratches out "Coming" and over it prints "Here!"*]

GUTMAN:

Ho ho!—a clown! The Eternal Punchinella! That's exactly what's needed in a time of crisis!

Block Three on the Camino Real.

KILROY [*genially, to all present*]:
Ha ha!

[*Then he walks up to the Officer by the terrace of the Siete Mares.*]

Buenas dias, señor.

[*He gets no response—barely even a glance.*]

Habla Inglesia? Usted?

OFFICER:
What is it you want?

KILROY:
Where is Western Union or Wells-Fargo? I got to send a wire to some friends in the States.

OFFICER:
No hay Western Union, no hay Wells-Fargo.

KILROY:
That is very peculiar. I never struck a town yet that didn't have one or the other. I just got off a boat. Lousiest frigging tub I ever shipped on, one continual hell it was, all the way up from Rio. And me sick, too. I picked up one of those tropical fevers. No sick bay on that tub, no doctor, no medicine or nothing, not even one quinine pill, and I was burning up with Christ knows how much fever. I couldn't make them understand I was sick. I got a bad heart, too. I had to retire from the prize ring because of my heart. I was the light heavyweight champion of the West Coast, won these gloves! —before my ticker went bad.—Feel my chest! Go on, feel it! Feel it. I've got a heart in my chest as big as the head of a baby. Ha ha! They stood me in front of a screen that makes

you transparent and that's what they seen inside me, a heart in my chest as big as the head of a baby! With something like that you don't need the Gypsy to tell you, "Time is short, Baby —get ready to hitch on wings!" The medics wouldn't okay me for no more fights. They said to give up liquor and smoking and sex!—To give up sex!—I used to believe a man couldn't live without sex—but he can—if he wants to! My real true woman, my wife, she would of stuck with me, but it was all spoiled with her being scared and me, too, that a real hard kiss would kill me!—So one night while she was sleeping I wrote her good-bye . . .

[*He notices a lack of attention in the Officer: he grins.*]

No comprendo the lingo?

OFFICER:
What is it you want?

KILROY:
Excuse my ignorance, but what place is this? What is this country and what is the name of this town? I know it seems funny of me to ask such a question. Loco! But I was so glad to get off that rotten tub that I didn't ask nothing of no one except my pay—and I got shortchanged on that. I have trouble counting these pesos or Whatzit-you-call-'em.

[*He jerks out his wallet.*]

All-a-this-here. In the States that pile of lettuce would make you a plutocrat!—But I bet you this stuff don't add up to fifty dollars American coin. Ha ha!

OFFICER:
Ha ha.

KILROY:

Ha ha!

OFFICER [*making it sound like a death rattle*]:

Ha-ha-ha-ha-ha.

[*He turns and starts into the cantina. Kilroy grabs his arm.*]

KILROY:

Hey!

OFFICER:

What is it you want?

KILROY:

What is the name of this country and this town?

[*The Officer thrusts his elbow in Kilroy's stomach and twists his arm loose with a Spanish curse. He kicks the swinging doors open and enters the cantina.*]

Brass hats are the same everywhere.

[*As soon as the Officer goes, the Street People come forward and crowd about Kilroy with their wheedling cries.*]

STREET PEOPLE:

Dulces, dulces! Lotería! Lotería! Pasteles, café con leche!

KILROY:

No caree, no caree!

[*The Prostitute creeps up to him and grins.*]

ROSITA:

Love? Love?

KILROY:

What did you say?

ROSITA:
Love?

KILROY:

Sorry—I don't feature that. [*to audience*] I have ideals.

[*The Gypsy appears on the roof of her establishment with Esmeralda whom she secures by handcuffs to the iron railing.*]

GYPSY:
Stay there while I give the pitch!

[*She then advances with a portable microphone.*]

Testing! One, two, three, four!

NURSIE [*from offstage*]:
You're on the air!

GYPSY'S LOUDSPEAKER:
Are you perplexed by something? Are you tired out and confused? Do you have a fever?

[*Kilroy looks around for the source of the voice.*]

Do you feel yourself to be spiritually unprepared for the age of exploding atoms? Do you distrust the newspapers? Are you suspicious of governments? Have you arrived at a point on the Camino Real where the walls converge not in the distance but right in front of your nose? Does further progress appear impossible to you? Are you afraid of anything at all? Afraid of your heartbeat? Or the eyes of strangers! Afraid of breathing? Afraid of not breathing? Do you' wish that things could be straight and simple again as they were in your childhood? Would you like to go back to Kindy Garten?

[*Rosita has crept up to Kilroy while he listens. She reaches out to him. At the same time a Pickpocket lifts his wallet.*]

KILROY [*catching the whore's wrist*]:
Keep y'r hands off me, y' dirty ole bag! No caree putas! No loteria, no dulces, nada—so get away! Vamoose! All of you! Quit picking at me!

[*He reaches in his pocket and jerks out a handful of small copper and silver coins which he flings disgustedly down the street. The grotesque people scramble after it with their inhuman cries. Kilroy goes on a few steps—then stops short —feeling the back pocket of his dungarees. Then he lets out a startled cry.*]

Robbed! My God, I've been robbed!

[*The Street People scatter to the walls.*]

Which of you got my wallet? *Which* of you dirty—? Shh–Uh!

[*They mumble with gestures of incomprehension. He marches back to the entrance to the hotel.*]

Hey! Officer! Official!—General!

[*The Officer finally lounges out of the hotel entrance and glances at Kilroy.*]

Tiende? One of them's got my wallet! Picked it out of my pocket while that old whore there was groping me! Don't you comprendo?

OFFICER:
Nobody rob you. You don't have no pesos.

KILROY:
Huh?

OFFICER:

You just dreaming that you have money. You don't ever have money. Nunca! Nada!

[*He spits between his teeth.*]

LOCO ...

[*The Officer crosses to the fountain. Kilroy stares at him, then bawls out:*]

KILROY [*to the Street People*]:

We'll see what the American Embassy has to say about this! I'll go to the American Consul. Whichever of you rotten spivs lifted my wallet is going to jail—calaboose! I hope I have made myself plain. If not, I will make myself plainer!

[*There are scattered laughs among the crowd. He crosses to the fountain. He notices the body of the no longer Survivor, kneels beside it, shakes it, turns it over, springs up and shouts:*]

Hey! This guy is dead!

[*There is the sound of the Streetcleaners' piping. They trundle their white barrel into the plaza from one of the downstage arches. The appearance of these men undergoes a progressive alteration through the play. When they first appear they are almost like any such public servants in a tropical country; their white jackets are dirtier than the musicians' and some of the stains are red. They have on white caps with black visors. They are continually exchanging sly jokes and giggling unpleasantly together. Lord Mulligan has come out upon the terrace and as they pass him, they pause for a moment, point at him, snicker. He is extremely discomfited by this impertinence, touches his chest as if he felt a palpitation and turns back inside.*]

460

[*Kilroy yells to the advancing Streetcleaners.*]

There's a dead man layin' here!

[*They giggle again. Briskly they lift the body and stuff it into the barrel; then trundle it off, looking back at Kilroy, giggling, whispering. They return under the downstage arch through which they entered. Kilroy, in a low, shocked voice:*]

What *is* this place? What kind of a hassle have I got myself into?

LOUDSPEAKER:

If anyone on the Camino is bewildered, come to the Gypsy. A poco dinero will tickle the Gypsy's palm and give her visions!

ABDULLAH [*giving Kilroy a card*]:
If you got a question, ask my mama, the Gypsy!

KILROY:

Man, whenever you see those three brass balls on a street, you don't have to look a long ways for a Gypsy. Now le' me think. I am faced with three problems. One: I'm hungry. Two: I'm lonely. Three: I'm in a place where I don't know what it is or how I got there! First action that's indicated is to—cash in on something—Well . . . let's see . . .

[*Honky-tonk music fades in at this point and the Skid Row façade begins to light up for the evening. There is the Gypsy's stall with its cabalistic devices, its sectional cranium and palm, three luminous brass balls overhanging the entrance to the Loan Shark and his window filled with a vast assortment of hocked articles for sale: trumpets, banjos, fur coats, tuxedos, a gown of scarlet sequins, loops of pearls and rhinestones. Dimly behind this display is a neon sign*]

461

*in three pastel colors, pink, green, and blue. It fades softly
in and out and it says: "Magic Tricks Jokes." There is also
the advertisement of a flea-bag hotel or flophouse called
"Ritz Men Only." This sign is also pale neon or luminous
paint, and only the entrance is on the street floor, the rooms
are above the Loan Shark and Gypsy's stall. One of the
windows of this upper story is practical. Figures appear in
it sometimes, leaning out as if suffocating or to hawk and
spit into the street below. This side of the street should
have all the color and animation that are permitted by the
resources of the production. There may be moments of
dancelike action (a fight, a seduction, sale of narcotics,
arrest, etc.).]*

KILROY [*to the audience from the apron*]:
What've I got to cash in on? My golden gloves? Never! I'll
say that once more, never! The silver-framed photo of my
One True Woman? Never! Repeat that! Never! What else
have I got of a detachable and a negotiable nature? Oh! My
ruby-and-emerald-studded belt with the word CHAMP on it.

[*He whips it off his pants.*]

This is not necessary to hold on my pants, but this is a
precious reminder of the sweet used-to-be. Oh, well. Sometimes a man has got to hock his sweet used-to-be in order to
finance his present situation . . .

[*He enters the Loan Shark's. A Drunken Bum leans out the
practical window of the "Ritz Men Only" and shouts:*]

462

BUM:

O Jack o' Diamonds, you robbed my pockets, you robbed my
pockets of silver and gold!

[*He jerks the window shade down.*]

GUTMAN [*on the terrace*]:
Block Four on the Camino Real!

BLOCK FOUR

There is a phrase of light music as the Baron de Charlus, an elderly foppish sybarite in a light silk suit, a carnation in his lapel, crosses from the Siete Mares to the honky-tonk side of the street. On his trail is a wild-looking young man of startling beauty called Lobo. Charlus is aware of the follower and, during his conversation with A. Ratt, he takes out a pocket mirror to inspect him while pretending to comb his hair and point his moustache. As Charlus approaches, the Manager of the flea-bag puts up a vacancy sign and calls out:

A. RATT:

Vacancy here! A bed at the "Ritz Men Only"! A little white ship to sail the dangerous night in . . .

THE BARON:

Ah, bon soir, Mr. Ratt.

A. RATT:

Cruising?

THE BARON:

No, just—walking!

A. RATT:

That's all you need to do.

THE BARON:

I sometimes find it suffices. You have a vacancy, do you?

A. RATT:

For you?

THE BARON:

And a possible guest. You know the requirements. An iron bed with no mattress and a considerable length of stout

knotted rope. No! Chains this evening, metal chains. I've
been very bad, I have a lot to atone for . . .

A. RATT:

Why don't you take these joy rides at the Siete Mares?

THE BARON [*with the mirror focused on Lobo*]:

They don't have Ingreso Libero at the Siete Mares. Oh, I
don't like places in the haute saison, the alta staggione, and
yet if you go between the fashionable seasons, it's too hot or
too damp or appallingly overrun by all the wrong sort of
people who rap on the wall if canaries sing in your bedsprings
after midnight. I don't know why such people don't stay at
home. Surely a Kodak, a Brownie, or even a Leica works just
as well in Milwaukee or Sioux City as it does in these places
they do on their whirlwind summer tours, and don't look
now, but I think I am being followed!

A. RATT:

Yep, you've made a pickup!

THE BARON:

Attractive?

A. RATT:

That depends on who's driving the bicycle, Dad.

THE BARON:

Ciao, Caro! Expect me at ten.

[*He crosses elegantly to the fountain.*]

A. RATT:

Vacancy here! A little white ship to sail the dangerous night
in!

[*The music changes. Kilroy backs out of the Loan Shark's, belt unsold, engaged in a violent dispute. The Loan Shark is haggling for his golden gloves. Charlus lingers, intrigued by the scene.*]

LOAN SHARK:
I don't want no belt! I want the gloves! Eight-fifty!

KILROY:
No dice.

LOAN SHARK:
Nine, nine-fifty!

KILROY:
Nah, nah, nah!

LOAN SHARK:
Yah, yah, yah.

KILROY:
I say nah.

LOAN SHARK:
I say yah.

KILROY:
The nahs have it.

LOAN SHARK:
Don't be a fool. What can you do with a pair of golden gloves?

KILROY:
I can remember the battles I fought to win them! I can remember that I used to be—CHAMP!

[*Fade in Band Music: "March of the Gladiators"—ghostly cheers, etc.*]

LOAN SHARK:

You can remember that you *used to be*—Champ?

KILROY:

Yes! I used to be—CHAMP!

THE BARON:

Used to be is the past tense, meaning useless.

KILROY:

Not to me, Mister. These are my gloves, these gloves are gold, and I fought a lot of hard fights to win 'em! I broke clean from the clinches. I never hit a low blow, the referee never told me to mix it up! And the fixers never got to me!

LOAN SHARK:

In other words, a sucker!

KILROY:

Yep, I'm a sucker that won the golden gloves!

LOAN SHARK:

Congratulations. My final offer is a piece of green paper with Alexander Hamilton's picture on it. Take it or leave it.

KILROY:

I leave it for you to *stuff* it! I'd hustle my heart on this street, I'd peddle my heart's true blood before I'd leave my golden gloves hung up in a loan shark's window between a rusted trombone and some poor lush's long-ago mildewed tuxedo!

LOAN SHARK:

So you say but I will see you later.

THE BARON:

The name of the Camino is not unreal!

[*The Bum sticks his head out the window and shouts:*]

BUM:
Pa dam, Pa dam, Pa dam!

THE BARON [*continuing the Bum's song*]:
Echoes the beat of my heart!
Pa dam, Pa dam—*hello!*

[*He has crossed to Kilroy as he sings and extends his hand to him.*]

KILROY [*uncertainly*]:
Hey, mate. It's wonderful to see you.

THE BARON:
Thanks, but why?

KILROY:
A normal American. In a clean white suit.

THE BARON:
My suit is pale yellow. My nationality is French, and my normality has been often subject to question.

KILROY:
I still say your suit is clean.

THE BARON:
Thanks. That's more than I can say for your apparel.

KILROY:
Don't judge a book by the covers. I'd take a shower if I could locate the "Y."

THE BARON:
What's the "Y"?

KILROY:
Sort of a Protestant church with a swimmin' pool in it. Some-

times it also has an employment bureau. It does good in the community.

THE BARON:

Nothing in this community does much good.

KILROY:

I'm getting the same impression. This place is confusing to me. I think it must be the aftereffects of fever. Nothing seems real. Could you give me the scoop?

THE BARON:

Serious questions are referred to the Gypsy. Once upon a time. Oh, once upon a time. I used to wonder. Now I simply wander. I stroll about the fountain and hope to be followed. Some people call it corruption. I call it—simplification . . .

BUM [*very softly at the window*]:
I wonder what's become of Sally, that old gal of mine?

[*He lowers the blind.*]

KILROY:
Well, anyhow . . .

THE BARON:
Well, anyhow?

KILROY:
How about the hot spots in this town?

THE BARON:

Oh, the hot spots, ho ho! There's the Pink Flamingo, the Yellow Pelican, the Blue Heron, and the Prothonotary Warbler! They call it the Bird Circuit. But I don't care for such places. They stand three-deep at the bar and look at themselves in the mirror and what they see is depressing. One sailor comes in—they faint! My own choice of resorts is the

Bucket of Blood downstairs from the "Ritz Men Only."—
How about a match?

KILROY:
Where's your cigarette?

THE BARON [*gently and sweetly*]:
Oh, I don't smoke. I just wanted to see your eyes more
clearly . . .

KILROY:
Why?

THE BARON:
The eyes are the windows of the soul, and yours are too gentle
for someone who has as much as I have to atone for.

[*He starts off.*]
Au revoir . . .

KILROY:
—A very unusual type character . . .

[*Casanova is on the steps leading to the arch, looking out
at the desert beyond. Now he turns and descends a few
steps, laughing with a note of tired incredulity. Kilroy
crosses to him.*]

Gee, it's wonderful to see you, a normal American in a—

[*There is a strangulated outcry from the arch under which
the Baron has disappeared.*]

Excuse me a minute!

[*He rushes toward the source of the outcry. Jacques crosses
to the bench before the fountain. Rhubarb is heard through
the arch. Jacques shrugs wearily as if it were just a noisy*]

radio. Kilroy comes plummeting out backward, all the way to Jacques.]

I tried to interfere, but what's th' use?!

JACQUES:
No use at all!

[*The Streetcleaners come through the arch with the Baron doubled up in their barrel. They pause and exchange sibilant whispers, pointing and snickering at Kilroy.*]

KILROY:
Who are they pointing at? At me, Kilroy?

[*The Bum laughs from the window. A. Ratt laughs from his shadowy doorway. The Loan Shark laughs from his.*]

Kilroy is here and he's not about to be there!—If he can help it . . .

[*He snatches up a rock and throws it at the Streetcleaners. Everybody laughs louder and the laughter seems to reverberate from the mountains. The light changes, dims a little in the plaza.*]

Sons a whatever you're sons of! Don't look at me, I'm not about to take no ride in the barrel!

[*The Baron, his elegant white shoes protruding from the barrel, is wheeled up the Alleyway Out. Figures in the square resume their dazed attitudes and one or two Guests return to the terrace of the Siete Mares as—*]

GUTMAN:
Block Five on the Camino Real!

[*He strolls off.*]

BLOCK FIVE

KILROY [*to Jacques*]:
Gee, the blocks go fast on this street!

JACQUES:
Yes. The blocks go fast.

KILROY:
My name's Kilroy. I'm here.

JACQUES:
Mine is Casanova. I'm here, too.

KILROY:
But you been here longer than me and maybe could brief me on it. For instance, what do they do with a stiff picked up in this town?

[*The Guard stares at them suspiciously from the terrace.*

[*Jacques whistles "La Golondrina" and crosses downstage. Kilroy follows.*]

Did I say something untactful?

JACQUES [*smiling into a sunset glow*]:
The exchange of serious questions and ideas, especially between persons from opposite sides of the plaza, is regarded unfavorably here. You'll notice I'm talking as if I had acute laryngitis. I'm gazing into the sunset. If I should start to whistle "La Golondrina" it means we're being overheard by the Guards on the terrace. Now you want to know what is done to a body from which the soul has departed on the Camino Real!—Its disposition depends on what the Street-cleaners happen to find in its pockets. If its pockets are empty as the unfortunate Baron's turned out to be, and as mine are at this moment—the "stiff" is wheeled straight off to the

Laboratory. And there the individual becomes an undistin-
guished member of a collectivist state. His chemical com-
ponents are separated and poured into vats containing the
corresponding elements of countless others. If any of his vital
organs or parts are at all unique in size or structure, they're
placed on exhibition in bottles containing a very foul-smelling
solution called formaldehyde. There is a charge of admission
to this museum. The proceeds go to the maintenance of the
military police.

[*He whistles "La Golondrina" till the Guard turns his back
again. He moves toward the front of the stage.*]

KILROY [*following*]:
—I guess that's—sensible . . .

JACQUES:
Yes, but not romantic. And romance is important. Don't you
think?

KILROY:
Nobody thinks romance is more important than me!

JACQUES:
Except possibly me!

KILROY:
Maybe that's why fate has brung us together! We're buddies
under the skin!

JACQUES:
Travelers born?

KILROY:
Always looking for something!

JACQUES:
Satisfied by nothing!

KILROY:
Hopeful?

JACQUES:
Always!

OFFICER:
Keep moving!

[*They move apart till the Officer exits.*]

KILROY:
And when a joker on the Camino gets fed up with one continual hassle—how does he get *off* it?

JACQUES:
You see the narrow and very steep stairway that passes under what is described in the travel brochures as a "Magnificent Arch of Triumph"?—Well, that's the Way Out!

KILROY:
That's the way out?

[*Kilroy without hesitation plunges right up to almost the top step; then pauses with a sound of squealing brakes. There is a sudden loud wind.*]

JACQUES [*shouting with hand cupped to mouth*]:
Well, how does the prospect please you, Traveler born?

KILROY [*shouting back in a tone of awe*]:
It's too unknown for my blood. Man, I seen nothing like it except through a telescope once on the pier on Coney Island. "Ten cents to see the craters and plains of the moon!"—And here's the same view in three dimensions for nothing!

[*The desert wind sings loudly: Kilroy mocks it.*]

JACQUES:

Are you—ready to cross it?

KILROY:

Maybe sometime with someone but not right now and alone!
How about you?

JACQUES:

I'm not alone.

KILROY:

You're with a party?

JACQUES:

No, but I'm sweetly encumbered with a—lady . . .

KILROY:

It wouldn't do with a lady. I don't see nothing but nothing—
and then more nothing. And then I see some mountains. But
the mountains are covered with snow.

JACQUES:

Snowshoes would be useful!

[*He observes Gutman approaching through the passage at
upper left. He whistles "La Golondrina" for Kilroy's attention and points with his cane as he exits.*]

KILROY [*descending steps disconsolately*]:
Mush, mush.

[*The Bum comes to his window. A. Ratt enters his doorway. Gutman enters below Kilroy.*]

BUM:

It's sleepy time down South!

GUTMAN [*warningly as Kilroy passes him*]:
Block Six in a progress of sixteen blocks on the Camino Real.

475

KILROY [*from the stairs*]:

Man, I could use a bed now.—I'd like to make me a cool pad on this camino now and lie down and sleep and dream of being with someone—friendly . . .

[*He crosses to the "Ritz Men Only."*]

A. RATT [*softly and sleepily*]:

Vacancy here! I got a single bed at the "Ritz Men Only," a little white ship to sail the dangerous night in.

[*Kilroy crosses down to his doorway.*]

KILROY:

—You got a vacancy here?

A. RATT:

I got a vacancy here if you got the one-fifty there.

KILROY:

Ha ha! I been in countries where money was not legal tender. I mean it was legal but it wasn't tender.

[*There is a loud groan from offstage above.*]

—Somebody dying on you or just drunk?

A. RATT:

Who knows or cares in this pad, Dad?

KILROY:

I heard once that a man can't die while he's drunk. Is that a fact or a fiction?

A. RATT:

Strictly a fiction.

VOICE ABOVE:

Stiff in number seven! Call the Streetcleaners!

A. RATT [*with absolutely no change in face or voice*]:
Number seven is vacant.

[*Streetcleaners' piping is heard.*

[*The Bum leaves the window.*]

KILROY:
Thanks, but tonight I'm going to sleep under the stars.

[*A. Ratt gestures "Have it your way" and exits.*

[*Kilroy, left alone, starts downstage. He notices that La
Madrecita is crouched near the fountain, holding something
up, inconspicuously, in her hand. Coming to her he sees that
it's a piece of food. He takes it, puts it in his mouth, tries to
thank her but her head is down, muffled in her rebozo and
there is no way for him to acknowledge the gift. He starts
to cross. Street People raise up their heads in their Pit and
motion him invitingly to come in with them. They call
softly, "Sleep, sleep . . ."*]

GUTMAN [*from his chair on the terrace*]:
Hey, Joe.

[*The Street People duck immediately.*]

KILROY:
Who? Me?

GUTMAN:
Yes, you, Candy Man. Are you disocupado?

KILROY:
—That means—unemployed, don't it?

[*He sees Officers converging from right.*]

477

GUTMAN:

Jobless. On the bum. Carrying the banner!

KILROY:

—Aw, no, aw, no, don't try to hang no vagrancy rap on me!
I was robbed on this square and I got plenty of witnesses to
prove it.

GUTMAN [*with ironic courtesy*]:
Oh?

[*He makes a gesture asking "Where?"*]

KILROY [*coming down to apron left and crossing to the
right*]:

Witnesses! Witness! Witnesses!

[*He comes to La Madrecita.*]

You were a witness!

[*A gesture indicates that he realizes her blindness. Opposite
the Gypsy's balcony he pauses for a second.*]

Hey, Gypsy's daughter!

[*The balcony is dark. He continues up to the Pit. The Street
People duck as he calls down:*]

You were witnesses!

[*An Officer enters with a Patsy outfit. He hands it to
Gutman.*]

GUTMAN:

Here, Boy! Take these.

[*Gutman displays and then tosses on the ground at Kilroy's
feet the Patsy outfit—the red fright wig, the big crimson*]

*nose that lights up and has horn-rimmed glasses attached,
a pair of clown pants that have a huge footprint on the
seat.*]

KILROY:
What is this outfit?

GUTMAN:
The uniform of a Patsy.

KILROY:
I know what a Patsy is—he's a clown in the circus who takes
pratfalls *but I'm no Patsy!*

GUTMAN:
Pick it up.

KILROY:
Don't give me orders. Kilroy is a free agent—

GUTMAN [*smoothly*]:
But a Patsy isn't. Pick it up and put it on, Candy Man. You
are now the Patsy.

KILROY:
So you say but you are completely mistaken.

[*Four Officers press in on him.*]

And don't crowd me with your torpedoes! I'm a stranger
here but I got a clean record in all the places I been, I'm not
in the books for nothin' but vagrancy and once when I was
hungry I walked by a truck-load of pineapples without picking one, because I was brought up good—

[*Then, with a pathetic attempt at making friends with the
Officer to his right.*]

and there was a cop on the corner!

OFFICER:

Ponga selo!

KILROY:

What'd you say? [*Desperately to audience he asks:*] What did he say?

OFFICER:

Ponga selo!

KILROY:

What'd you say?

[*The Officer shoves him down roughly to the Patsy outfit. Kilroy picks up the pants, shakes them out carefully as if about to step into them and says very politely:*]

Why, surely. I'd be delighted. My fondest dreams have come true.

[*Suddenly he tosses the Patsy dress into Gutman's face and leaps into the aisle of the theatre.*]

GUTMAN:

Stop him! Arrest that vagrant! Don't let him get away!

LOUDSPEAKER:

Be on the lookout for a fugitive Patsy. The Patsy has escaped. Stop him, stop that Patsy!

[*A wild chase commences. The two Guards rush madly down either side to intercept him at the back of the house. Kilroy wheels about at the top of the center aisle, and runs back down it, panting, gasping out questions and entreaties to various persons occupying aisle seats, such as:*]

KILROY:

How do I git out? Which way do I go, which way do I get out? Where's the Greyhound depot? Hey, do you know where the Greyhound bus depot is? What's the best way out, if there is any way out? I got to find one. I had enough of this place. I had too much of this place. I'm free. I'm a free man with equal rights in this world! You better believe it because that's news for you and you had better believe it! Kilroy's a free man with equal rights in this world! All right, now, help me, somebody, help me find a way out, I got to find one, I don't like this place! It's not for me and I am not buying any! Oh! Over there! I see a sign that says EXIT. That's a sweet word to me, man, that's a lovely word, EXIT! That's the entrance to paradise for Kilroy! Exit, I'm coming, Exit, I'm coming!

[*The Street People have gathered along the forestage to watch the chase. Esmeralda, barefooted, wearing only a slip, bursts out of the Gypsy's establishment like an animal broken out of a cage, darts among the Street People to the front of the crowd which is shouting like the spectators at the climax of a corrida. Behind her, Nursie appears, a male actor, wigged and dressed austerely as a duenna, crying out in both languages.*]

NURSIE:
Esmeralda! Esmeralda!

GYPSY:
Police!

NURSIE:
Come back here, Esmeralda!

GYPSY:
Catch her, idiot!

NURSIE:
Where is my lady bird, where is my precious treasure?

481

GYPSY:

Idiot! I told you to keep her door locked!

NURSIE:

She jimmied the lock, Esmeralda!

[*These shouts are mostly lost in the general rhubarb of the chase and the shouting Street People. Esmeralda crouches on the forestage, screaming encouragement in Spanish to the fugitive. Abdullah catches sight of her, seizes her wrist, shouting:*]

ABDULLAH:

Here she is! I got her!

[*Esmeralda fights savagely. She nearly breaks loose, but Nursie and the Gypsy close upon her, too, and she is overwhelmed and dragged back, fighting all the way, toward the door from which she escaped.*

[*Meanwhile—timed with the above action—shots are fired in the air by Kilroy's pursuers. He dashes, panting, into the boxes of the theatre, darting from one box to another, shouting incoherently, now, sobbing for breath, crying out:*]

KILROY:

Mary, help a Christian! Help a Christian, Mary!

ESMERALDA:

Yankee! Yankee, jump!

[*The Officers close upon him in the box nearest the stage. A dazzling spot of light is thrown on him. He lifts a little gilded chair to defend himself. The chair is torn from his grasp. He leaps upon the ledge of the box.*]

Jump! Jump, Yankee!

[*The Gypsy is dragging the girl back by her hair.*]

KILROY:

Watch out down there! Geronimo!

[*He leaps onto the stage and crumples up with a twisted ankle. Esmeralda screams demoniacally, breaks from her mother's grasp and rushes to him, fighting off his pursuers who have leapt after him from the box. Abdullah, Nursie and the Gypsy seize her again, just as Kilroy is seized by his pursuers. The Officers beat him to his knees. Each time he is struck, Esmeralda screams as if she received the blow herself. As his cries subside into sobbing, so do hers, and at the end, when he is quite helpless, she is also overcome by her captors and as they drag her back to the Gypsy's she cries to him:*]

ESMERALDA:

They've got you! They've got me!

[*Her mother slaps her fiercely.*]

Caught! Caught! We're caught!

[*She is dragged inside. The door is slammed shut on her continuing outcries. For a moment nothing is heard but Kilroy's hoarse panting and sobbing. Gutman takes command of the situation, thrusting his way through the crowd to face Kilroy who is pinioned by two Guards.*]

GUTMAN [*smiling serenely*]:

Well, well, how do you do! I understand that you're seeking employment here. We need a Patsy and the job is yours for the asking!

KILROY:

I don't. Accept. This job. I been. Shanghied!

[*Kilroy dons Patsy outfit.*]

483

GUTMAN:

Hush! The Patsy doesn't talk. He lights his nose, that's all!

GUARD:

Press the little button at the end of the cord.

GUTMAN:

That's right. Just press the little button at the end of the cord!

[*Kilroy lights his nose. Everybody laughs.*]

GUTMAN:

Again, ha ha! Again, ha ha! Again!

[*The nose goes off and on like a firefly as the stage dims out.*

[*The curtain falls. There is a short intermission.*]

BLOCK SEVEN

*The Dreamer is singing with mandolin, "Noche de Ronde."
The Guests murmur, "cool—cool . . ." Gutman stands on the
podiumlike elevation downstage right, smoking a long thin
cigar, signing an occasional tab from the bar or café. He is
standing in an amber spot. The rest of the stage is filled with
blue dusk. At the signal the song fades to a whisper and
Gutman speaks.*

GUTMAN:

Block Seven on the Camino Real—
I like this hour.

[*He gives the audience a tender gold-toothed smile.*]

The fire's gone out of the day but the light of it lingers . . .
In Rome the continual fountains are bathing stone heroes with
silver, in Copenhagen the Tivoli Gardens are lighted, they're
selling the lottery on San Juan de Latrene . . .

[*The Dreamer advances a little, playing the mandolin
softly.*]

LA MADRECITA [*holding up glass beads and shell necklaces*]:
Recuerdos, recuerdos?

GUTMAN:

And these are the moments when we look into ourselves and
ask with a wonder which never is lost altogether: "Can this
be all? Is there nothing more? Is this what the glittering
wheels of the heavens turn for?"

[*He leans forward as if conveying a secret.*]

—Ask the Gypsy! Un poco dinero will tickle the Gypsy's palm
and give her visions!

[*Abdullah emerges with a silver tray, calling:*]

ABDULLAH:
Letter for Signor Casanova, letter for Signor Casanova!

[*Jacques springs up but stands rigid.*]

GUTMAN:
Casanova, you have received a letter. Perhaps it's the letter with the remittance check in it!

JACQUES [*in a hoarse, exalted voice*]:
Yes! It is! The letter! With the remittance check in it!

GUTMAN:
Then why don't you take it so you can maintain your residence at the Siete Mares and so avoid the more somber attractions of the "Ritz Men Only"?

JACQUES:
My hand is—

GUTMAN:
Your hand is paralyzed? . . . By what? *Anxiety? Apprehension?* . . . Put the letter in Signor Casanova's pocket so he can open it when he recovers the use of his digital extremities. Then give him a shot of brandy on the house before he falls on his face!

[*Jacques has stepped down into the plaza. He looks down at Kilroy crouched to the right of him and wildly blinking his nose.*]

JACQUES:
Yes. I know the Morse code.

[*Kilroy's nose again blinks on and off.*]

Thank you, brother.

[*This is said as if acknowledging a message.*]

I knew without asking the Gypsy that something of this sort
would happen to you. You have a spark of anarchy in your
spirit and that's not to be tolerated. Nothing wild or honest is
tolerated here! It has to be extinguished or used only to light
up your nose for Mr. Gutman's amusement . . .

[*Jacques saunters around Kilroy whistling "La Golondrina."
Then satisfied that no one is suspicious of this encounter . . .*]

Before the final block we'll find some way out of here! Meanwhile, patience and courage, little brother!

[*Jacques feeling he's been there too long starts away giving
Kilroy a reassuring pat on the shoulder and saying:*]

Patience! . . . Courage!

LADY MULLIGAN [*from the Mulligans' table*]:
Mr. Gutman!

GUTMAN:
Lady Mulligan! And how are you this evening, Lord Mulligan?

LADY MULLIGAN [*interrupting Lord Mulligan's rumblings*]:
He's not at all well. This . . . climate is so enervating!

LORD MULLIGAN:
I was so weak this morning . . . I couldn't screw the lid on
my tooth paste!

LADY MULLIGAN:
Raymond, tell Mr. Gutman about those two impertinent
workmen in the square! . . . These two idiots pushing a white
barrel! Pop up every time we step outside the hotel!

LORD MULLIGAN:
—point and giggle at me!

487

LADY MULLIGAN:
Can't they be discharged?

GUTMAN:
They can't be discharged, disciplined nor bribed! All you can
do is pretend to ignore them.

LADY MULLIGAN:
I can't eat! . . . Raymond, stop stuffing!

LORD MULLIGAN:
Shut up!

GUTMAN [*to the audience*]:
When the big wheels crack on this street it's like the fall of
a capital city, the destruction of Carthage, the sack of Rome
by the white-eyed giants from the North! I've seen them fall!
I've seen the destruction of them! Adventurers suddenly
frightened of a dark room! Gamblers unable to choose between odd and even! Con men and pitchmen and plume-
hatted cavaliers turned baby-soft at one note of the Streetcleaners' pipes! When I observe this change, I say to myself:
"Could it happen to ME?"—The answer is "YES!" And
that's what curdles my blood like milk on the doorstep of
someone gone for the summer!

[*A Hunchback Mummer somersaults through his hoop of
silver bells, springs up and shakes it excitedly toward a
downstage arch which begins to flicker with a diamond-
blue radiance; this marks the advent of each legendary
character in the play. The music follows: a waltz from the
time of Camille in Paris.*]

GUTMAN [*downstage to the audience*]:
Ah, there's the music of another legend, one that everyone
knows, the legend of the sentimental whore, the courtesan

488

who made the mistake of love. But now you see her coming into this plaza not as she was when she burned with a fever that cast a thin light over Paris, but changed, yes, faded as lanterns and legends fade when they burn into day!

[*He turns and shouts:*]

Rosita, sell her a flower!

[*Marguerite has entered the plaza. A beautiful woman of indefinite age. The Street People cluster about her with wheedling cries, holding up glass beads, shell necklaces and so forth. She seems confused, lost, half-awake. Jacques has sprung up at her entrance but has difficulty making his way through the cluster of vendors. Rosita has snatched up a tray of flowers and cries out:*]

ROSITA:
Camellias, camellias! Pink or white, whichever a lady finds suitable to the moon!

GUTMAN:
That's the ticket!

MARGUERITE:
Yes, I would like a camellia.

ROSITA [*in a bad French accent*]:
Rouge ou blanc ce soir?

MARGUERITE:
It's always a white one, now . . . but there used to be five evenings out of the month when a pink camellia, instead of the usual white one, let my admirers know that the moon those nights was unfavorable to pleasure, and so they called me—Camille . . .

489

JACQUES:
Mia cara!

[*Imperiously, very proud to be with her, he pushes the Street People aside with his cane.*]

Out of the way, make way, let us through, please!

MARGUERITE:
Don't push them with your cane.

JACQUES:
If they get close enough they'll snatch your purse.

[*Marguerite utters a low, shocked cry.*]

What is it?

MARGUERITE:
My purse is gone! It's lost! My papers were in it!

JACQUES:
Your passport was in it?

MARGUERITE:
My passport and my permiso de residencia!

[*She leans faint against the arch during the following scene.*

[*Abdullah turns to run. Jacques catches him.*]

JACQUES [*seizing Abdullah's wrist*]:
Where did you take her?

ABDULLAH:
Oww!—P'tit Zoco.

JACQUES:
The Souks?

ABDULLAH:
The Souks!

JACQUES:
Which cafés did she go to?

ABDULLAH:
Ahmed's, she went to—

JACQUES:
Did she smoke at Ahmed's?

ABDULLAH:
Two kif pipes!

JACQUES:
Who was it took her purse? Was it *you*? We'll see!

[*He strips off the boy's burnoose. He crouches whimpering, shivering in a ragged slip.*]

MARGUERITE:
Jacques, let the boy go, he didn't take it!

JACQUES:
He doesn't have it on him but knows who does!

ABDULLAH:
No, no, I don't know!

JACQUES:
You little son of a Gypsy! Senta! . . . You know who I am? I am Jacques Casanova! I belong to the Secret Order of the Rose-colored Cross! . . . Run back to Ahmed's. Contact the spiv that took the lady's purse. Tell him to keep it but give her back her papers! There'll be a large reward.

[*He thumps his cane on the ground to release Abdullah*

from the spell. The boy dashes off. Jacques laughs and turns triumphantly to Marguerite.]

LADY MULLIGAN:
Waiter! That adventurer and his mistress must not be seated next to Lord Mulligan's table!

JACQUES [*loudly enough for Lady Mulligan to hear*]:
This hotel has become a mecca for black marketeers and their expensively kept women!

LADY MULLIGAN:
Mr. Gutman!

MARGUERITE:
Let's have dinner upstairs!

WAITER [*directing them to terrace table*]:
This way, M'sieur.

JACQUES:
We'll take our usual table.

[*He indicates one.*]

MARGUERITE:
Please!

WAITER [*overlapping Marguerite's "Please!"*]:
This table is reserved for Lord Byron!

JACQUES [*masterfully*]:
This table is always our table.

MARGUERITE:
I'm not hungry.

JACQUES:
Hold out the lady's chair, cretino!

GUTMAN [*darting over to Marguerite's chair*]:
Permit me!

[*Jacques bows with mock gallantry to Lady Mulligan as he turns to his chair during seating of Marguerite.*]

LADY MULLIGAN:
We'll move to *that* table!

JACQUES:
—You must learn how to carry the banner of Bohemia into the enemy camp.

[*A screen is put up around them.*]

MARGUERITE:
Bohemia has no banner. It survives by discretion.

JACQUES:
I'm glad that you value discretion. *Wine list!* Was it discretion that led you through the bazaars this afternoon wearing your cabochon sapphire and diamond eardrops? You were fortunate that you lost only your purse and papers!

MARGUERITE:
Take the wine list.

JACQUES:
Still or sparkling?

MARGUERITE:
Sparkling.

GUTMAN:
May I make a suggestion, Signor Casanova?

JACQUES:
Please do.

493

GUTMAN:

It's a very cold and dry wine from only ten metres below the snowline in the mountains. The name of the wine is Quando! —meaning when! Such as "When are remittances going to be received?" "When are accounts to be settled?" Ha ha ha! Bring Signor Casanova a bottle of Quando with the compliments of the house!

JACQUES:

I'm sorry this had to happen in—your presence . . .

MARGUERITE:

That doesn't matter, my dear. But why don't you *tell* me when you are short of money?

JACQUES:

I thought the fact was apparent. It is to everyone else.

MARGUERITE:

The letter you were expecting, it still hasn't come?

JACQUES [*removing it from his pocket*]:
It came this afternoon—Here it is!

MARGUERITE:

You haven't opened the letter!

JACQUES:

I haven't had the nerve to! I've had so many unpleasant surprises that I've lost faith in my luck.

MARGUERITE:

Give the letter to me. Let me open it for you.

JACQUES:

Later, a little bit later, after the—**wine . . .** ·

494

MARGUERITE:
Old hawk, anxious old hawk!

[*She clasps his hand on the table; he leans toward her; she kisses her fingertips and places them on his lips.*]

JACQUES:
Do you call that a kiss?

MARGUERITE:
I call it the ghost of a kiss. It will have to do for now.

[*She leans back, her blue-tinted eyelids closed.*]

JACQUES:
Are you tired? Are you tired, Marguerite? You know you should have rested this afternoon.

MARGUERITE:
I looked at silver and rested.

JACQUES:
You looked at silver at Ahmed's?

MARGUERITE:
No, I rested at Ahmed's, and had mint tea.

[*The Dreamer accompanies their speech with his guitar. The duologue should have the style of an antiphonal poem, the cues picked up so that there is scarcely a separation between the speeches, and the tempo quick and the voices edged.*]

JACQUES:
You had mint tea downstairs?

MARGUERITE:
No, upstairs.

JACQUES:

Upstairs where they burn the poppy?

MARGUERITE:

Upstairs where it's cool and there's music and the haggling of the bazaar is soft as the murmur of pigeons.

JACQUES:

That sounds restful. Reclining among silk pillows on a divan, in a curtained and perfumed alcove above the bazaar?

MARGUERITE:

Forgetting for a while where I am, or that I don't know where I am . . .

JACQUES:

Forgetting alone or forgetting with some young companion who plays the lute or the flute or who had silver to show you? Yes. That sounds very restful. And yet you do seem tired.

MARGUERITE:

If I seem tired, it's your insulting solicitude that I'm tired of!

JACQUES:

Is it insulting to feel concern for your safety in this place?

MARGUERITE:

Yes, it is. The implication is.

JACQUES:

What is the implication?

MARGUERITE:

You know what it is: that I am one of those *aging—voluptuaries*—who used to be paid for pleasure but now have to pay!—Jacques, I won't be followed, I've gone too far to be followed!—*What is it?*

[*The Waiter has presented an envelope on a salver.*]

WAITER:
A letter for the lady.

MARGUERITE:
How strange to receive a letter in a place where nobody knows I'm staying! Will you open it for me?

[*The Waiter withdraws. Jacques takes the letter and opens it.*]

Well! What is it?

JACQUES:
Nothing important. An illustrated brochure from some resort in the mountains.

MARGUERITE:
What is it called?

JACQUES:
Bide-a-While.

[*A chafing dish bursts into startling blue flame at the Mulligans' table. Lady Mulligan clasps her hands and exclaims with affected delight, the Waiter and Mr. Gutman laugh agreeably. Marguerite springs up and moves out upon the forestage. Jacques goes to her.*]

Do you know this resort in the mountains?

MARGUERITE:
Yes. I stayed there once. It's one of those places with open sleeping verandahs, surrounded by snowy pine woods. It has rows and rows of narrow white iron beds as regular as tombstones. The invalids smile at each other when axes flash across valleys, ring, flash, ring again! Young voices shout across

valleys Hola! And mail is delivered. The friend that used to write you ten-page letters contents himself now with a post card bluebird that tells you to "Get well quick!"

[*Jacques throws the brochure away.*]

—And when the last bleeding comes, not much later nor earlier than expected, you're wheeled discreetly into a little tent of white gauze, and the last thing you know of this world, of which you've known so little and yet so much, is the smell of an empty icebox.

[*The blue flame expires in the chafing dish. Gutman picks up the brochure and hands it to the Waiter, whispering something.*]

JACQUES:
You won't go back to that place.

[*The Waiter places the brochure on the salver again and approaches behind them.*]

MARGUERITE:
I wasn't released. I left without permission. They sent me this to remind me.

WAITER [*presenting the salver*]:
You dropped this.

JACQUES:
We threw it away!

WAITER:
Excuse me.

JACQUES:
Now, from now on, Marguerite, you must take better care of yourself. Do you hear me?

MARGUERITE:

I hear you. No more distractions for me? No more entertainers in curtained and perfumed alcoves above the bazaar, no more young men that a pinch of white powder or a puff of gray smoke can almost turn to someone devoutly remembered?

JACQUES:
No, from now on—

MARGUERITE:
What "from now on," old hawk?

JACQUES:
Rest. Peace.

MARGUERITE:

Rest in peace is that final bit of advice they carve on grave-stones, and I'm not ready for it! Are you? Are *you* ready for it?

[*She returns to the table. He follows her.*]

Oh, Jacques, when are we going to leave here, how are we going to leave here, you've got to tell me!

JACQUES:
I've told you all I know.

MARGUERITE:
Nothing, you've given up hope!

JACQUES:
I haven't, that's not true.

[*Gutman has brought out the white cockatoo which he shows to Lady Mulligan at her table.*]

GUTMAN [*his voice rising above the murmurs*]:
Her name is Aurora.

499

LADY MULLIGAN:
Why do you call her Aurora?

GUTMAN:
She cries at daybreak.

LADY MULLIGAN:
Only at daybreak?

GUTMAN:
Yes, at daybreak only.

[*Their voices and laughter fade under.*]

MARGUERITE:
How long is it since you've been to the travel agencies?

JACQUES:
This morning I made the usual round of Cook's, American Express, Wagon-lits Universal, and it was the same story. There are no flights out of here till further orders from someone higher up.

MARGUERITE:
Nothing, nothing at all?

JACQUES:
Oh, there's a rumor of something called the Fugitivo, but—

MARGUERITE:
The What!!! ?

JACQUES:
The Fugitivo. It's one of those nonscheduled things that—

MARGUERITE:
When, when, when?

JACQUES:

I told you it was nonscheduled. Nonscheduled means it comes and goes at no predictable—

MARGUERITE:

Don't give me the dictionary! I want to know how does one get on it? Did you bribe them? Did you offer them money? No. Of course you didn't! And I know why! You really don't want to leave here. You *think* you don't want to go because you're brave as an old hawk. But the truth of the matter—the real not the royal truth—is that you're terrified of the Terra Incognita outside that wall.

JACQUES:

You've hit upon the truth. I'm terrified of the unknown country inside or outside this wall or any place on earth without you with me! The only country, known or unknown that I can breathe in, or care to, is the country in which we breathe together, as we are now at this table. And later, a little while later, even closer than this, the sole inhabitants of a tiny world whose limits are those of the light from a rose-colored lamp— beside the sweetly, completely known country of your cool bed!

MARGUERITE:

The little comfort of love?

JACQUES:

Is that comfort so little?

MARGUERITE:

Caged birds accept each other but flight is what they long for.

JACQUES:

I want to stay here with you and love you and guard you

until the time or way comes that we both can leave with honor.

MARGUERITE:

"Leave with honor"? Your vocabulary is almost as out-of-date as your cape and your cane. How could anyone quit this field with honor, this place where there's nothing but the gradual wasting away of everything decent in us . . . the sort of desperation that comes after even desperation has been worn out through long wear! . . . Why have they put these screens around the table?

[*She springs up and knocks one of them over.*]

LADY MULLIGAN:

There! You see? I don't understand why you let such people stay here.

GUTMAN:

They pay the price of admission the same as you.

LADY MULLIGAN:

What price is that?

GUTMAN:

Desperation!—With cash here!

[*He indicates the Siete Mares.*]

Without cash there!

[*He indicates Skid Row.*]

Block Eight on the Camino Real!

BLOCK EIGHT

There is the sound of loud desert wind and a flamenco cry followed by a dramatic phrase of music.

A flickering diamond-blue radiance floods the hotel entrance. The crouching, grimacing Hunchback shakes his hoop of bells which is the convention for the appearance of each legendary figure.

Lord Byron appears in the doorway readied for departure. Gutman raises his hand for silence.

GUTMAN:
You're leaving us, Lord Byron?

BYRON:
Yes, I'm leaving you, Mr. Gutman.

GUTMAN:
What a pity! But this is a port of entry and departure. There are no permanent guests. Possibly you are getting a little restless?

BYRON:
The luxuries of this place have made me soft. The metal point's gone from my pen, there's nothing left but the feather.

GUTMAN:
That may be true. But what can you do about it?

BYRON:
Make a departure!

GUTMAN:
From yourself?

BYRON:
From my present self to myself as I used to be!

GUTMAN:

That's the *furthest* departure a man could make! I guess you're sailing to Athens? There's another war there and like all wars since the beginning of time it can be interpreted as a —struggle for *what?*

BYRON:

—For *freedom!* You may laugh at it, but it still means something to *me!*

GUTMAN:

Of course it does! I'm not laughing a bit, I'm beaming with admiration.

BYRON:

I've allowed myself many distractions.

GUTMAN:

Yes, indeed!

BYRON:

But I've never altogether forgotten my old devotion to the—

GUTMAN:

—To the *what,* Lord Byron?

[*Byron passes nervous fingers through his hair.*]

You can't remember the object of your one-time devotion?

[*There is a pause. Byron limps away from the terrace and goes toward the fountain.*]

BYRON:

When Shelley's corpse was recovered from the sea . . .

[**Gutman beckons the Dreamer who approaches and accompanies Byron's speech.**]

—It was burned on the beach at Viareggio.—I watched the spectacle from my carriage because the stench was revolting . . . Then it—fascinated me! I got out of my carriage. Went nearer, holding a handkerchief to my nostrils!—I saw that the front of the skull had broken away in the flames, and there—

[*He advances out upon the stage apron, followed by Abdullah with the pine torch or lantern.*]

And there was the brain of Shelley, indistinguishable from a cooking stew!—*boiling, bubbling, hissing!*—in the *blackening* —*cracked*—*pot*—of his skull!

[*Marguerite rises abruptly. Jacques supports her.*]

—Trelawney, his friend, Trelawney, threw salt and oil and frankincense in the flames and finally the almost intolerable stench—

[*Abdullah giggles. Gutman slaps him.*]

—was *gone* and the burning was *pure!*—as a man's burning should be . . .

A man's burning *ought* to be pure!—*not* like mine—(a crepe suzette—burned in brandy . . .)

Shelley's burning was finally very *pure!*

But the body, the corpse, split open like a grilled pig!

[*Abdullah giggles irrepressibly again. Gutman grips the back of his neck and he stands up stiff and assumes an expression of exaggerated solemnity.*]

—And then Trelawney—as the ribs of the corpse unlocked— reached into them as a baker reaches quickly into an oven!

[*Abdullah almost goes into another convulsion.*]

—And snatched out—as a baker would a biscuit!—the *heart* of Shelley! Snatched the heart of Shelley out of the blistering corpse!—Out of the purifying—blue flame . . .

[*Marguerite resumes her seat; Jacques his.*]

—And it was *over*!—I thought—

[*He turns slightly from the audience and crosses upstage from the apron. He faces Jacques and Marguerite.*]

—I thought it was a disgusting thing to do, to snatch a man's heart from his body! What can one man do with another man's heart?

[*Jacques rises and strikes the stage with his cane.*]

JACQUES [*passionately*]:
He can do this with it!

[*He seizes a loaf of bread on his table, and descends from the terrace.*]

He can twist it like this!

[*He twists the loaf.*]

He can tear it like this!

[*He tears the loaf in two.*]

He can crush it under his foot!

[*He drops the bread and stamps on it.*]

—*And kick it away—like this!*

[*He kicks the bread off the terrace. Lord Byron turns away from him and limps again out upon the stage apron and speaks to the audience.*]

BYRON:

That's very true, Señor. But a poet's vocation, which used to be my vocation, is to influence the heart in a gentler fashion than you have made your mark on that loaf of bread. He ought to purify it and lift it above its ordinary level. For what is the heart but a sort of—

[*He makes a high, groping gesture in the air.*]

—A sort of—*instrument!*—that translates *noise* into *music, chaos into—order . . .*

[*Abdullah ducks almost to the earth in an effort to stifle his mirth. Gutman coughs to cover his own amusement.*]

—*a mysterious order!*

[*He raises his voice till it fills the plaza.*]

—That was my vocation once upon a time, before it was obscured by vulgar plaudits!—Little by little it was lost among gondolas and palazzos!—masked balls, glittering salons, huge shadowy courts and torch-lit entrances!—Baroque façades, canopies and carpets, candelabra and gold plate among snowy damask, ladies with throats as slender as flower stems, bending and breathing toward me their fragrant breath—

—Exposing their breasts to me!

Whispering, half smiling!—And everywhere marble, the visible grandeur of marble, pink and gray marble, veined and tinted as flayed corrupting flesh,—all these provided agreeable distractions from the rather frightening solitude of a poet. Oh, I wrote many cantos in Venice and Constantinople and in Ravenna and Rome, on all of those Latin and Levantine excursions that my twisted foot led me into—but I wonder about them a little. They seem to improve as the wine in the

507

bottle—dwindles . . . *There is a passion for declivity in this world!*

And lately I've found myself listening to hired musicians behind a row of artificial palm trees—instead of the single—pure-stringed instrument of my heart . . .

Well, then, it's time to leave here!

[*He turns back to the stage.*]

—There is a time for departure even when there's no certain place to go!

I'm going to look for one, now. I'm sailing to Athens. At least I can look up at the Acropolis, I can stand at the foot of it and look up at broken columns on the crest of a hill—if not purity, at least its recollection . . .

I can sit quietly looking for a long, long time in absolute silence, and possibly, yes, *still* possibly—

The old pure music will come to me again. Of course on the other hand I may hear only the little noise of insects in the grass . . .

But I am sailing to Athens! *Make voyages!—Attempt them!—*there's nothing else . . .

MARGUERITE [*excitedly*]:
Watch where he goes!

[*Lord Byron limps across the plaza with his head bowed, making slight, apologetic gestures to the wheedling Beggars who shuffle about him. There is music. He crosses toward the steep Alleyway Out. The following is played with a quiet intensity so it will be in a lower key than the later Fugitivo Scene.*]

Watch him, watch him, see which way he goes. Maybe he knows of a way that we haven't found out.

JACQUES:
Yes, I'm watching him, cara.

[*Lord and Lady Mulligan half rise, staring anxiously through monocle and lorgnon.*]

MARGUERITE:
Oh, my God, I believe he's going up that alley.

JACQUES:
Yes, he is. He has.

LORD and LADY MULLIGAN:
Oh, the fool, the idiot, he's going under the arch!

MARGUERITE:
Jacques, run after him, warn him, tell him about the desert he has to cross.

JACQUES:
I think he knows what he's doing.

MARGUERITE:
I can't look!

[*She turns to the audience, throwing back her head and closing her eyes. The desert wind sings loudly as Byron climbs to the top of the steps.*]

BYRON [*to several porters carrying luggage—which is mainly caged birds*]:
THIS WAY!

[*He exits.*

[*Kilroy starts to follow. He stops at the steps, cringing and*

509

looking at Gutman. Gutman motions him to go ahead. Kilroy rushes up the stairs. He looks out, loses his nerve and sits—blinking his nose. Gutman laughs as he announces—]

GUTMAN:
Block Nine on the Camino Real!

[He goes into the hotel.]

BLOCK NINE

Abdullah runs back to the hotel with the billowing flambeau.
A faint and faraway humming sound becomes audible . . .
Marguerite opens her eyes with a startled look. She searches
the sky for something. A very low percussion begins with the
humming sound, as if excited hearts are beating.

MARGUERITE:
Jacques! I hear something in the sky!

JACQUES:
I think what you hear is—

MARGUERITE [*with rising excitement*]:
—No, it's a plane, a great one, I see the lights of it, now!

JACQUES:
Some kind of fireworks, cara.

MARGUERITE:
Hush! LISTEN!

[*She blows out the candle to see better above it. She rises,*
peering into the sky.]

I see it! I see it! There! It's circling over us!

LADY MULLIGAN:
Raymond, Raymond, sit down, your face is flushed!

HOTEL GUESTS [*overlapping*]:
—What is it?
—The FUGITIVO!
—THE FUGITIVO! THE FUGITIVO!
—Quick, get my jewelry from the hotel safe!
—Cash a check!

—Throw some things in a bag! I'll wait here!
—Never mind luggage, we have our money and papers!
—Where is it now?
—There, there!
—It's turning to land!
—To go like this?
—Yes, go anyhow, just go anyhow, just go!
—Raymond! Please!
—Oh, it's rising again!
—Oh, it's—*SHH! MR. GUTMAN!*

[*Gutman appears in the doorway. He raises a hand in a commanding gesture.*]

GUTMAN:

Signs in the sky should not be mistaken for wonders!

[*The Voices modulate quickly.*]

Ladies, gentlemen, please resume your seats!

[*Places are resumed at tables, and silver is shakily lifted. Glasses are raised to lips, but the noise of concerted panting of excitement fills the stage and a low percussion echoes frantic heart beats.*

[*Gutman descends to the plaza, shouting furiously to the Officer.*]

Why wasn't I told the Fugitivo was coming?

[*Everyone, almost as a man, rushes into the hotel and reappears almost at once with hastily collected possessions. Marguerite rises but appears stunned.*

[*There is a great whistling and screeching sound as the aerial transport halts somewhere close by, accompanied by rainbow splashes of light and cries like children's on a*

512

*roller coaster. Some incoming Passengers approach the stage
down an aisle of the theatre, preceded by Redcaps with luggage.*]

PASSENGERS:
—What a heavenly trip!
—The scenery was thrilling!
—It's so quick!
—The only way to travel! Etc., etc.

[*A uniformed man, the Pilot, enters the plaza with a
megaphone.*]

PILOT [*through the megaphone*]:
Fugitivo now loading for departure! Fugitivo loading immediately for departure! Northwest corner of the plaza!

MARGUERITE:
Jacques, it's the Fugitivo, it's the nonscheduled thing you
heard of this afternoon!

PILOT:
All out-going passengers on the Fugitivo are requested to
present their tickets and papers immediately at this station.

MARGUERITE:
He said "outgoing passengers"!

PILOT:
Outgoing passengers on the Fugitivo report immediately at
this station for customs inspection.

MARGUERITE [*with a forced smile*]:
Why are you just standing there?

JACQUES [*with an Italian gesture*]:
Che cosa possa fare!

513

MARGUERITE:
Move, move, do something!

JACQUES:
What!

MARGUERITE:
Go to them, ask, find out!

JACQUES:
I have no idea what the damned thing is!

MARGUERITE:
I do, I'll tell you! It's a way to escape from this abominable place!

JACQUES:
Forse, forse, non so!

MARGUERITE:
It's a way *out* and *I'm* not going to miss it!

PILOT:
Ici la Douane! Customs inspection here!

MARGUERITE:
Customs. That means luggage. Run to my room! Here! Key! Throw a few things in a bag, my jewels, my furs, but hurry! Vite, vite, vite! I don't believe there's much time! No, everybody is—

[*Outgoing Passengers storm the desk and table.*]

—Clamoring for tickets! There must be limited space! Why don't you do what I tell you?

[*She rushes to a man with a rubber stamp and a roll of tickets.*]

514

Monsieur! Señor! Pardonnez-moi! I'm going, I'm going out! I want my ticket!

PILOT [*coldly*]:
Name, please.

MARGUERITE:
Mademoiselle—Gautier—but I—

PILOT:
Gautier? Gautier? We have no Gautier listed.

MARGUERITE:
I'm—*not* listed! I mean I'm—traveling under another name.

TRAVEL AGENT:
What name are you traveling under?

[*Prudence and Olympe rush out of the hotel half dressed, dragging their furs. Meanwhile Kilroy is trying to make a fast buck or two as a Redcap. The scene gathers wild momentum, is punctuated by crashes of percussion. Grotesque mummers act as demon custom inspectors and immigration authorities, etc. Baggage is tossed about, ripped open, smuggled goods seized, arrests made, all amid the wildest importunities, protests, threats, bribes, entreaties; it is a scene for improvisation.*]

PRUDENCE:
Thank God I woke up!

OLYMPE:
Thank God I wasn't asleep!

PRUDENCE:
I knew it was nonscheduled but I *did* think they'd give you time to get in your girdle.

OLYMPE:
Look who's trying to crash it! I know damned well *she* don't have a reservation!

PILOT [*to Marguerite*]:
What name did you say, Mademoiselle? Please! People are waiting, you're holding up the line!

MARGUERITE:
I'm so confused! Jacques! What name did you make my reservation under?

OLYMPE:
She has no reservation!

PRUDENCE:
I have, I got mine!

OLYMPE:
I got mine!

PRUDENCE:
I'm next!

OLYMPE:
Don't push *me*, you old bag!

MARGUERITE:
I was here first! I was here before anybody! Jacques, quick! Get my money from the hotel safe!

[*Jacques exits.*]

AGENT:
Stay in line!

[*There is a loud warning whistle.*]

PILOT:

Five minutes. The Fugitivo leaves in five minutes. Five, five
minutes only!

[*At this announcement the scene becomes riotous.*]

TRAVEL AGENT:
Four minutes! The Fugitivo leaves in four minutes!

[*Prudence and Olympe are shrieking at him in French. The
warning whistle blasts again.*]

Three minutes, the Fugitivo leaves in three minutes!

MARGUERITE [*topping the turmoil*]:
Monsieur! Please! I was here first, I was here before anybody! Look!

[*Jacques returns with her money.*]

I have thousands of francs! Take whatever you want! Take
all of it, it's yours!

PILOT:
Payment is only accepted in pounds sterling or dollars. Next,
please.

MARGUERITE:
You don't accept francs? They do at the hotel! They accept
my francs at the Siete Mares!

PILOT:
Lady, don't argue with me, I don't make the rules!

MARGUERITE [*beating her forehead with her fist*]:
Oh, God, Jacques! Take these back to the cashier!

[*She thrusts the bills at him.*]

517

Get them changed to dollars or—*Hurry! Tout de suite!* I'm—
going to faint . . .

JACQUES:
But Marguerite—

MARGUERITE:
Go! Go! Pleàse!

PILOT:
Closing, we're closing now! The Fugitivo leaves in two
minutes!

[*Lord and Lady Mulligan rush forward.*]

LADY MULLIGAN:
Let Lord Mulligan through.

PILOT [*to Marguerite*]:
You're standing in the way.

[*Olympe screams as the Customs Inspector dumps her
jewels on the ground. She and Prudence butt heads as they
dive for the gems: the fight is renewed.*]

MARGUERITE [*detaining the Pilot*]:
Oh, look, Monsieur! Regardez ça! My diamond, a solitaire—
two carats! Take that as security!

PILOT:
Let me go. The Loan Shark's across the plaza!

[*There is another warning blast. Prudence and Olympe
seize hat boxes and rush toward the whistle.*]

MARGUERITE [*clinging desperately to the Pilot*]:
You don't understand! Señor Casanova has gone to change
money! He'll be here in a second. And I'll pay five, ten, twenty

518

times the price of—*JACQUES! JACQUES! WHERE ARE YOU?*

VOICE [*back of auditorium*]:
We're closing the gate!

MARGUERITE:
You can't close the gate!

PILOT:
Move, Madame!

MARGUERITE:
I won't move!

LADY MULLIGAN:
I tell you, Lord Mulligan is the Iron & Steel man from Cobh!
Raymond! They're closing the gate!

LORD MULLIGAN:
I can't seem to get through!

GUTMAN:
Hold the gate for Lord Mulligan!

PILOT [*to Marguerite*]:
Madame, stand back or I will have to use force!

MARGUERITE:
Jacques! Jacques!

LADY MULLIGAN:
Let us through! We're clear!

PILOT:
Madame! Stand back and let these passengers through!

MARGUERITE:
No, No! I'm first! I'm next!

LORD MULLIGAN:
Get her out of our way! That woman's a whore!

LADY MULLIGAN:
How dare you stand in our way?

PILOT:
Officer, take this woman!

LADY MULLIGAN:
Come on, Raymond!

MARGUERITE [*as the Officer pulls her away*]:
Jacques! Jacques! Jacques!

[*Jacques returns with changed money.*]

Here! Here is the money!

PILOT:
All right, give me your papers.

MARGUERITE:
—My papers? Did you say my papers?

PILOT:
Hurry, hurry, your passport!

MARGUERITE:
—Jacques! He wants my papers! Give him my papers, Jacques!

JACQUES:
—The lady's papers are lost!

MARGUERITE [*wildly*]:
No, no, no, THAT IS NOT TRUE! HE WANTS TO KEEP ME HERE! HE'S LYING ABOUT IT!

520

JACQUES:
Have you forgotten that your papers were stolen?

MARGUERITE:
I gave you my papers, I gave you my papers to keep, you've got my papers.

[*Screaming, Lady Mulligan breaks past her and descends the stairs.*]

LADY MULLIGAN:
Raymond! Hurry!

LORD MULLIGAN [*staggering on the top step*]:
I'm sick! I'm sick!

[*The Streetcleaners disguised as expensive morticians in swallowtail coats come rapidly up the aisle of the theatre and wait at the foot of the stairway for the tottering tycoon.*]

LADY MULLIGAN:
You cannot be sick till we get on the Fugitivo!

LORD MULLIGAN:
Forward all cables to Guaranty Trust in Paris.

LADY MULLIGAN:
Place de la Concorde.

LORD MULLIGAN:
Thank you! All purchases C.O.D. to Mulligan Iron & Steel Works in Cobh—Thank you!

LADY MULLIGAN:
Raymond! Raymond! Who are these men?

LORD MULLIGAN:
I know these men! I recognize their faces!

521

LADY MULLIGAN:
Raymond! They're the Streetcleaners!

[*She screams and runs up the aisle screaming repeatedly, stopping halfway to look back. The two Streetcleaners seize Lord Mulligan by either arm as he crumples.*]

Pack Lord Mulligan's body in dry ice! Ship Air Express to Cobh care of Mulligan Iron & Steel Works, in Cobh!

[*She runs sobbing out of the back of the auditorium as the whistle blows repeatedly and a Voice shouts.*]

I'm coming! I'm coming!

MARGUERITE:
Jacques! Jacques! Oh, God!

PILOT:
The Fugitivo is leaving, all aboard!

[*He starts toward the steps. Marguerite clutches his arm.*]

Let go of me!

MARGUERITE:
You can't go without me!

PILOT:
Officer, hold this woman!

JACQUES:
Marguerite, let him go!

[*She releases the Pilot's arm and turns savagely on Jacques. She tears his coat open, seizes a large envelope of papers and rushes after the Pilot who has started down the steps over the orchestra pit and into a center aisle of the house. Timpani build up as she starts down the steps, screaming—*]

MARGUERITE:

Here! I have them here! Wait! I have my papers now, I have
my papers!

[*The Pilot runs cursing up the center aisle as the Fugitivo
whistle gives repeated short, shrill blasts; timpani and dis-
sonant brass are heard.*

[*Outgoing Passengers burst into hysterical song, laughter,
shouts of farewell. These can come over a loudspeaker at
the back of the house.*]

VOICE IN DISTANCE:

Going! Going! Going!

MARGUERITE [*attempting as if half paralyzed to descend the
steps*]:

NOT WITHOUT ME, NO, NO, NOT WITHOUT ME!

[*Her figure is caught in the dazzling glacial light of the
follow-spot. It blinds her. She makes violent, crazed gestures,
clinging to the railing of the steps; her breath is loud and
hoarse as a dying person's, she holds a bloodstained handkerchief to her lips.*

[*There is a prolonged, gradually fading, rocketlike roar as
the Fugitivo takes off. Shrill cries of joy from departing
passengers; something radiant passes above the stage and
streams of confetti and tinsel fall into the plaza. Then there
is a great calm, the ship's receding roar diminished to the
hum of an insect.*]

GUTMAN [*somewhat compassionately*]:

Block Ten on the Camino Real.

BLOCK TEN

There is something about the desolation of the plaza that suggests a city devastated by bombardment. Reddish lights flicker here and there as if ruins were smoldering and wisps of smoke rise from them.

LA MADRECITA [*almost inaudibly*]:
Donde?

THE DREAMER:
Aquí. Aquí, Madrecita.

MARGUERITE:
Lost! Lost! Lost! Lost!

[*She is still clinging brokenly to the railing of the steps. Jacques descends to her and helps her back up the steps.*]

JACQUES:
Lean against me, cara. Breathe quietly, now.

MARGUERITE:
Lost!

JACQUES:
Breathe quietly, quietly, and look up at the sky.

MARGUERITE:
Lost . . .

JACQUES:
These tropical nights are so clear. There's the Southern Cross. Do you see the Southern Cross, Marguerite?

[*He points through the proscenium. They are now on the bench before the fountain; she is resting in his arms.*]

And there, over there, is Orion, like a fat, golden fish swimming north in the deep clear water, and we are together, breathing quietly together, leaning together, quietly, quietly together, completely, sweetly together, not frightened, now, not alone, but completely quietly together . . .

[*La Madrecita, led into the center of the plaza by her son, has begun to sing very softly; the reddish flares dim out and the smoke disappears.*]

All of us have a desperate bird in our hearts, a memory of—some distant mother with—wings . . .

MARGUERITE:
I would have—left—without you . . .

JACQUES:
I know, I know!

MARGUERITE:
Then how can you—still—?

JACQUES:
Hold you?

[*Marguerite nods slightly.*]

Because you've taught me that part of love which is tender. I never knew it before. Oh, I had—mistresses that circled me like moons! I scrambled from one bed chamber to another bed chamber with shirttails always aflame, from girl to girl, like buckets of coal oil poured on a conflagration! But never loved until now with the part of love that's tender . . .

MARGUERITE:
—We're used to each other. That's what you think is love . . . You'd better leave me now, you'd better go and let me go because there's a cold wind blowing out of the mountains and over the desert and into my heart, and if you stay with me now, I'll say cruel things, I'll wound your vanity, I'll taunt you with the decline of your male vigor!

JACQUES:
Why does disappointment make people unkind to each other?

MARGUERITE:
Each of us is very much alone.

JACQUES:
Only if we distrust each other.

MARGUERITE:
We have to distrust each other. It is our only defense against betrayal.

JACQUES:
I think our defense is love.

MARGUERITE:
Oh, Jacques, we're used to each other, we're a pair of captive hawks caught in the same cage, and so we've grown used to each other. That's what passes for love at this dim, shadowy end of the Camino Real . . .

What are we sure of? Not even of our existence, dear comforting friend! And whom can we ask the questions that torment us? "What is this place?" "Where are we?"—a fat old man who gives sly hints that only bewilder us more, a fake of a Gypsy squinting at cards and tea leaves. What else are we offered? The never-broken procession of little events that assure us that we and strangers about us are still going on! Where? Why? and the perch that we hold is unstable! We're threatened with eviction, for this is a port of entry and departure, there are no permanent guests! And where else have we to go when we leave here? Bide-a-While? "Ritz Men Only"? Or under that ominous arch into Terra Incognita? We're lonely. We're frightened. We hear the Streetcleaners' piping not far away. So now and then, although we've wounded each other time and again—we stretch out hands to each other in the dark that we can't escape from— we huddle together for some dim-communal comfort—and that's what passes for love on this terminal stretch of the road that used to be royal. What is it, this feeling between us? When you feel my exhausted weight against your shoulder— when I clasp your anxious old hawk's head to my breast, what is it we feel in whatever is left of our hearts? Something, yes, something—delicate, unreal, bloodless! The sort of violets that could grow on the moon, or in the crevices of those far away mountains, fertilized by the droppings of carrion birds. Those birds are familiar to us. Their shadows inhabit the plaza. I've heard them flapping their wings like old charwomen beating worn-out carpets with gray brooms . . .

But tenderness, the violets in the mountains—can't break the rocks!

JACQUES:
The violets in the mountains can break the rocks if you believe in them and allow them to grow!

[*The plaza has resumed its usual aspect. Abdullah enters through one of the downstage arches.*]

ABDULLAH:
Get your carnival hats and noisemakers here! Tonight the moon will restore the virginity of my sister!

MARGUERITE [*almost tenderly touching his face*]:
Don't you know that tonight I am going to betray you?

JACQUES:
—Why would you do that?

MARGUERITE:
Because I've outlived the tenderness of my heart. Abdullah,

527

come here! I have an errand for you! Go to Ahmed's and deliver a message!

ABDULLAH:
I'm working for Mama, making the Yankee dollar! Get your carnival hats and—

MARGUERITE:
Here, boy!

[*She snatches a ring off her finger and offers it to him.*]

JACQUES:
—Your cabochon sapphire?

MARGUERITE:
Yes, my cabochon sapphire!

JACQUES:
Are you mad?

MARGUERITE:
Yes, I'm mad, or nearly! The specter of lunacy's at my heels tonight!

[*Jacques drives Abdullah back with his cane.*]

Catch, boy! The other side of the fountain! Quick!

[*The guitar is heard molto vivace. She tosses the ring across the fountain. Jacques attempts to hold the boy back with his cane. Abdullah dodges in and out like a little terrier, laughing. Marguerite shouts encouragement in French. When the boy is driven back from the ring, she snatches it up and tosses it to him again, shouting:*]

Catch, boy! Run to Ahmed's! Tell the charming young man that the French lady's bored with her company tonight! Say that the French lady missed the Fugitivo and wants to forget she missed it! Oh, and reserve a room with a balcony so I can watch your sister appear on the roof when the moonrise makes her a virgin!

[*Abdullah skips shouting out of the plaza. Jacques strikes the stage with his cane. She says, without looking at him:*]

Time betrays us and we betray each other.

JACQUES:
Wait, Marguerite.

MARGUERITE:
No! I can't! The wind from the desert is sweeping me away!

[*A loud singing wind sweeps her toward the terrace, away from him. She looks back once or twice as if for some gesture of leave-taking but he only stares at her fiercely, striking the stage at intervals with his cane, like a death march. Gutman watches, smiling, from the terrace, bows to Marguerite as she passes into the hotel. The drum of Jacques' cane is taken up by other percussive instruments, and almost unnoticeably at first, weird-looking celebrants or carnival mummers creep into the plaza, silently as spiders descending a wall.*]

[*A sheet of scarlet and yellow rice paper bearing some cryptic device is lowered from the center of the plaza. The percussive effects become gradually louder. Jacques is oblivious to the scene behind him, standing in front of the plaza, his eyes closed.*]

GUTMAN:
Block Eleven on the Camino Real.

BLOCK ELEVEN

GUTMAN:

The Fiesta has started. The first event is the coronation of the King of Cuckolds.

[*Blinding shafts of light are suddenly cast upon Casanova on the forestage. He shields his face, startled, as the crowd closes about him. The blinding shafts of light seem to strike him like savage blows and he falls to his knees as—*

[*The Hunchback scuttles out of the Gypsy's stall with a crown of gilded antlers on a velvet pillow. He places it on Jacques' head. The celebrants form a circle about him chanting.*]

JACQUES:

What is this?—a crown—

GUTMAN:

A crown of horns!

CROWD:

Cornudo! Cornudo! Cornudo! Cornudo! Cornudo!

GUTMAN:

Hail, all hail, the King of Cuckolds on the Camino Real!

[*Jacques springs up, first striking out at them with his cane. Then all at once he abandons self-defense, throws off his cape, casts away his cane, and fills the plaza with a roar of defiance and self-derision.*]

JACQUES:

Si, si, sono cornudo! Cornudo! Cornudo! Casanova is the King of Cuckolds on the Camino Real! Show me crowned to the world! Announce the honor! Tell the world of the honor bestowed on Casanova, Chevalier·de Seingalt! Knight

530

of the Golden Spur by the Grace of His Holiness the Pope
. . . Famous adventurer! Con man Extraordinary! Gambler!
Pitchman par excellence! Shill! Pimp! Spiv! *And—great—
lover* . . .

[*The Crowd howls with applause and laughter but his voice
rises above them with sobbing intensity.*]

Yes, I said GREAT LOVER! The greatest lover wears the
longest horns on the Camino! GREAT! LOVER!

GUTMAN:

Attention! Silence! The moon is rising! The restoration is
about to occur!

[*A white radiance is appearing over the ancient wall of the
town. The mountains become luminous. There is music.
Everyone, with breathless attention, faces the light.*

[*Kilroy crosses to Jacques and beckons him out behind the
crowd. There he snatches off the antlers and returns him his
fedora. Jacques reciprocates by removing Kilroy's fright
wig and electric nose. They embrace as brothers. In a Chap-
linesque dumb-play, Kilroy points to the wildly flickering
three brass balls of the Loan Shark and to his golden gloves:
then with a terrible grimace he removes the gloves from
about his neck, smiles at Jacques and indicates that the two
of them together will take flight over the wall. Jacques
shakes his head sadly, pointing to his heart and then to the
Siete Mares. Kilroy nods with regretful understanding of a
human and manly folly. A Guard has been silently approaching them in a soft-shoe dance. Jacques whistles "La
Golondrina." Kilroy assumes a very nonchalant pose. The
Guard picks up curiously the discarded fright wig and
electric nose. Then glancing suspiciously at the pair, he
advances. Kilroy makes a run for it. He does a baseball*

531

slide into the Loan Shark's welcoming doorway. The door slams. The Cop is about to crash it when a gong sounds and Gutman shouts:]

GUTMAN:
SILENCE! ATTENTION! THE GYPSY!

GYPSY [*appearing on the roof with a gong*]:
The moon has restored the virginity of my daughter Esmeralda!

[*The gong sounds.*]

STREET PEOPLE:
Ahh!

GYPSY:
The moon in its plenitude has made her a virgin!

[*The gong sounds.*]

STREET PEOPLE:
Ahh!

GYPSY:
Praise her, celebrate her, give her suitable homage!

[*The gong sounds.*]

STREET PEOPLE:
Ahh!

GYPSY:
Summon her to the roof!

[*She shouts:*]

ESMERALDA!

[*Dancers shout the name in rhythm.*]

RISE WITH THE MOON, MY DAUGHTER! CHOOSE
THE HERO!

[*Esmeralda appears on the roof in dazzling light. She seems
to be dressed in jewels. She raises her jeweled arms with a
harsh flamenco cry.*]

ESMERALDA:
OLE!

DANCERS:
OLE!

[*The details of the Carnival are a problem for director and
choreographer but it has already been indicated in the script
that the Fiesta is a sort of serio-comic, grotesque-lyric "Rites
of Fertility" with roots in various pagan cultures.*

[*It should not be overelaborated or allowed to occupy much
time. It should not be more than three minutes from the
appearance of Esmeralda on the Gypsy's roof till the return
of Kilroy from the Loan Shark's.*

[*Kilroy emerges from the pawn shop in grotesque disguise, a
turban, dark glasses, a burnoose and an umbrella or sun-
shade.*]

KILROY [*to Jacques*]:

So long, pal, I wish you could come with me.

[*Jacques clasps his cross in Kilroy's hands.*]

ESMERALDA:
Yankee!

KILROY [*to the audience*]:
So long, everybody. Good luck to you all on the Camino! I

hocked my golden gloves to finance this expedition. I'm going. Hasta luega. I'm going. I'm gone!

ESMERALDA:
Yankee!

[*He has no sooner entered the plaza than the riotous women strip off everything but the dungarees and skivvy which he first appeared in.*]

KILROY [*to the women*]:
Let me go. Let go of me! Watch out for my equipment!

ESMERALDA:
Yankee! Yankee!

[*He breaks away from them and plunges up the stairs of the ancient wall. He is halfway up them when Gutman shouts out:*]

GUTMAN:
Follow-spot on that gringo, light the stairs!

[*The light catches Kilroy. At the same instant Esmeralda cries out to him:*]

ESMERALDA:
Yankee! Yankee!

GYPSY:
What's goin' on down there?

[*She rushes into the plaza.*]

KILROY:
Oh, no, I'm on my way out!

ESMERALDA:
Espere un momento!

[*The Gypsy calls the police, but is ignored in the crowd.*]

KILROY:
Don't tempt me, baby! I hocked my golden gloves to finance this expedition!

ESMERALDA:
Querido!

KILROY:
Querido means sweetheart, a word which is hard to resist but I must resist it.

ESMERALDA:
Champ!

KILROY:
I used to be Champ but why remind me of it?

ESMERALDA:
Be Champ again! Contend in the contest! Compete in the competition!

GYPSY [*shouting*]:
Naw, naw, not eligible!

ESMERALDA:
Pl-eeeeeeze!

GYPSY:
Slap her, Nursie, she's flippin'.

[*Esmeralda slaps Nursie instead.*]

ESMERALDA:
Hero! Champ!

KILROY:
I'm not in condition!

ESMERALDA:

You're still the Champ, the undefeated Champ of the golden gloves!

KILROY:

Nobody's called me that in a long, long time!

ESMERALDA:

Champ!

KILROY:

My resistance is crumbling!

ESMERALDA:

Champ!

KILROY:

It's crumbled!

ESMERALDA:

Hero!

KILROY:

GERONIMO!

[*He takes a flying leap from the stairs into the center of the plaza. He turns toward Esmeralda and cries:*]

DOLL!!

[*Kilroy surrounded by cheering Street People goes into a triumphant eccentric dance which reviews his history as fighter, traveler and lover.*

[*At finish of the dance, the music is cut off, as Kilroy lunges, arm uplifted toward Esmeralda, and cries:*]

KILROY:

Kilroy the Champ!

ESMERALDA:

KILROY the Champ!

[*She snatches a bunch of red roses from the stunned Nursie and tosses them to Kilroy.*]

CROWD [*sharply*]:

OLE!

[*The Gypsy, at the same instant, hurls her gong down, creating a resounding noise.*

[*Kilroy turns and comes down toward the audience, saying to them:*]

KILROY:

Y'see?

[*Cheering Street People surge toward him and lift him in the air. The lights fade as the curtain descends.*]

CROWD [*in a sustained yell*]:

OLE!

[*The curtain falls. There is a short intermission.*]

BLOCK TWELVE

The stage is in darkness except for a spotlight which picks out Esmeralda on the Gypsy's roof.

ESMERALDA:

Mama, what happened? —Mama, the lights went out!— Mama, where are you? It's so dark I'm scared!—MAMA!

[*The lights are turned on displaying a deserted plaza. The Gypsy is seated at a small table before her stall.*]

GYPSY:

Come on downstairs, Doll. The mischief is done. You've chosen your hero!

GUTMAN [*from the balcony of the Siete Mares*]:
Block Twelve on the Camino Real.

NURSIE [*at the fountain*]:
Gypsy, the fountain is still dry!

GYPSY:

What d'yuh expect? There's nobody left to uphold the old traditions! You raise a girl. She watches television. Plays bebop. Reads *Screen Secrets.* Comes the Big Fiesta. The moonrise makes her a virgin—which is the neatest trick of the week! And what does she do? Chooses a Fugitive Patsy for the Chosen Hero! Well, show him in! Admit the joker and get the virgin ready!

NURSIE:
You're going through with it?

GYPSY:

Look, Nursie! I'm operating a legitimate joint! This joker'll get the same treatment he'd get if he breezed down the

Camino in a blizzard of G-notes! Trot, girl! Lubricate your
means of locomotion!

[*Nursie goes into the Gypsy's stall. The Gypsy rubs her hands
together and blows on the crystal ball, spits on it and gives
it the old one-two with a "shammy" rag . . . She mutters
"Crystal ball, tell me all . . . crystal ball tell me all" . . . as:*

[*Kilroy bounds into the plaza from her stall . . . a rose
between his teeth.*]

GYPSY:
Siente se, por favor.

KILROY:
No comprendo the lingo.

GYPSY:
Put it down!

NURSIE [*offstage*]:
Hey, Gypsy!

GYPSY:
Address me as Madam!

NURSIE [*entering*]:
Madam! Winchell has scooped you!

GYPSY:
In a pig's eye!

NURSIE:
The Fugitivo has "*fftt . . .*"!

GYPSY:
In Elizabeth, New Jersey . . . ten fifty seven P.M. . . . Eastern
Standard Time—while you were putting them kiss-me-quicks
in your hair-do! Furthermore, my second exclusive is that the

539

solar system is drifting toward the constellation of Hercules: *Skiddoo!*

[*Nursie exits. Stamping is heard offstage.*]

Quiet, back there! God damn it!

NURSIE [*offstage*]:
She's out of control!

GYPSY:
Give her a double-bromide!

[*To Kilroy:*]

Well, how does it feel to be the Chosen Hero?

KILROY:
I better explain something to you.

GYPSY:
Save your breath. You'll need it.

KILROY:
I want to level with you. Can I level with you?

GYPSY [*rapidly stamping some papers*]:
How could you help but level with the Gypsy?

KILROY:
I don't know what the hero is chosen for

[*Esmeralda and Nursie shriek offstage.*]

GYPSY:
Time will brief you . . . Aw, I hate paper work! . . . NURS-EHH!

[*Nursie comes out and stands by the table.*]

This filing system is screwed up six ways from next Sunday . . . File this crap under crap!—

[*To Kilroy:*]

The smoking lamp is lit. Have a stick on me!

[*She offers him a cigarette.*]

KILROY:
No thanks.

GYPSY:
Come on, indulge yourself. You got nothing to lose that won't be lost.

KILROY:
If that's a professional opinion, I don't respect it.

GYPSY:
Resume your seat and give me your full name.

KILROY:
Kilroy.

GYPSY [*writing all this down*]:
Date of birth and place of that disaster?

KILROY:
Both unknown.

GYPSY:
Address?

KILROY:
Traveler.

GYPSY:
Parents?

KILROY:

Anonymous.

GYPSY:

Who brought·you up?

KILROY:

I was brought up and down by an eccentric old aunt in Dallas.

GYPSY:

Raise both hands simultaneously and swear that you have not come here for the purpose of committing an immoral act.

ESMERALDA [*from offstage*]:
Hey, Chico!

GYPSY:

QUIET! Childhood diseases?

KILROY:

Whooping cough, measles and mumps.

GYPSY:

Likes and dislikes?

KILROY:

I like situations I can get out of. I don't like cops and—

GYPSY:

Immaterial! Here! Signature on this!

[*She hands him a blank.*]

KILROY:

What is it?

GYPSY:

You always sign something, don't you?

KILROY:

Not till I know what it is.

GYPSY:

It's just a little formality to give a tone to the establishment and make an impression on our out-of-town trade. Roll up your sleeve.

KILROY:

What for?

GYPSY:

A shot of some kind.

KILROY:

What kind?

GYPSY:

Any kind. Don't they always give you some kind of a shot?

KILROY:

"They"?

GYPSY:

Brass hats, Americanos!

[*She injects a hypo.*]

KILROY:

I am no guinea pig!

GYPSY:

Don't kid yourself. We're all of us guinea pigs in the laboratory of God. Humanity is just a work in progress.

KILROY:

I don't make it out.

GYPSY:

Who does? The Camino Real is a funny paper read backward!

[*There is weird piping outside. Kilroy shifts on his seat. The Gypsy grins.*]

Tired? The altitude makes you sleepy?

KILROY:

It makes me nervous.

GYPSY:

I'll show you how to take a slug of tequila! It dilates the capillaries. First you sprinkle salt on the back of your hand. Then lick it off with your tongue. Now then you toss the shot down!

[*She demonstrates.*]

—And then you bite into the lemon. That way it goes down easy, but what a bang! —You're next.

KILROY:

No, thanks, I'm on the wagon.

GYPSY:

There's an old Chinese proverb that says, "When your goose is cooked you might as well have it cooked with plenty of gravy."

[*She laughs.*]

Get up, baby. Let's have a look at yuh!—You're not a bad-looking boy. Sometimes working for the Yankee dollar isn't a painful profession. Have you ever been attracted by older women?

KILROY:

Frankly, no, ma'am.

GYPSY:

Well, there's a first time for everything.

KILROY:

That is a subject I cannot agree with you on.

GYPSY:

You think I'm an old bag?

[*Kilroy laughs awkwardly. The Gypsy slaps his face.*]

Will you take the cards or the crystal?

KILROY:

It's immaterial.

GYPSY:

All right, we'll begin with the cards.

[*She shuffles and deals.*]

Ask me a question.

KILROY:

Has my luck run out?

GYPSY:

Baby, your luck ran out the day you were born. Another question.

KILROY:

Ought I to leave this town?

GYPSY:

It don't look to me like you've got much choice in the matter ... Take a card.

545

[*Kilroy takes one.*]

GYPSY:
Ace?

KILROY:
Yes, ma'am.

GYPSY:
What color?

KILROY:
Black.

GYPSY:
Oh, oh—That does it. How big is your heart?

KILROY:
As big as the head of a baby.

GYPSY:
It's going to **break.**

KILROY:
That's what I was afraid of.

GYPSY:
The Streetcleaners are waiting for you outside the door.

KILROY:
Which door, the front one? I'll slip out the back!

GYPSY:
Leave us face it frankly, your number is up! You must've known a long time that the name of Kilroy was on the Streetcleaners' list.

KILROY:
Sure. But not on top of it!

GYPSY:

It's always a bit of a shock. Wait a minute! Here's good news. The Queen of Hearts has turned up in proper position.

KILROY:

What's that mean?

GYPSY:

Love, baby!

KILROY:

Love?

GYPSY:

The Booby Prize! —Esmeralda!

[*She rises and hits a gong. A divan is carried out. The Gypsy's Daughter is seated in a reclining position, like an odalisque, on this low divan. A spangled veil covers her face. From this veil to the girdle below her navel, that supports her diaphanous bifurcated skirt, she is nude except for a pair of glittering emerald snakes coiled over her breasts. Kilroy's head moves in a dizzy circle and a canary warbles inside it.*]

KILROY:

WHAT'S—WHAT'S *HER* SPECIALTY?—Tea leaves?

[*The Gypsy wags a finger.*]

GYPSY:

You know what curiosity did to the tomcat!—Nursie, give me my glamor wig and my forty-five. I'm hitting the street! I gotta go down to Walgreen's for change.

KILROY:

What change?

GYPSY:

The change from that ten-spot you're about to give me.

NURSIE:

Don't argue with her. She has a will of iron.

KILROY:

I'm not arguing!

[*He reluctantly produces the money.*]

But let's be *fair* about this! I hocked my golden gloves for this sawbuck!

NURSIE:

All of them Yankee bastids want something for nothing!

KILROY:

I want a receipt for this bill.

NURSIE:

No one is gypped at the Gypsy's!

KILROY:

That's wonderful! How do I know it?

GYPSY:

It's in the cards, it's in the crystal ball, it's in the tea leaves! Absolutely no one is gypped at the Gypsy's!

[*She snatches the bill. The wind howls.*]

Such changeable weather! I'll slip on my summer furs! Nursie, break out my summer furs!

NURSIE [*leering grotesquely*]:
Mink or sable?

GYPSY:
Ha ha, that's a doll! Here! Clock him!

548

[*Nursie tosses her a greasy blanket, and the Gypsy tosses Nursie an alarm clock. The Gypsy rushes through the beaded string curtains.*]

Adios! Ha ha!!

[*She is hardly offstage when two shots ring out. Kilroy starts.*]

ESMERALDA [*plaintively*]:
Mother has such an awful time on the street.

KILROY:
You mean that she is insulted on the street?

ESMERALDA:
By strangers.

KILROY [*to the audience*]:
I shouldn't think acquaintances would do it.

[*She curls up on the low divan. Kilroy licks his lips.*]

—You seem very different from—this afternoon . . .

ESMERALDA:
This afternoon?

KILROY:
Yes, in the plaza when I was being roughed up by them gorillas and you was being dragged in the house by your Mama!

[*Esmeralda stares at him blankly.*]

You don't remember?

ESMERALDA:
I never remember what happened before the moonrise makes me a virgin.

KILROY:
—That—comes as a shock to you, huh?

ESMERALDA:
Yes. It comes as a shock.

KILROY [*smiling*]:
You have a little temporary amnesia they call it!

ESMERALDA:
Yankee . . .

KILROY:
Huh?

ESMERALDA:
I'm glad I chose you. I'm glad that you were chosen.

[*Her voice trails off.*]

I'm glad. I'm very glad . . .

NURSIE:
Doll!

ESMERALDA:
—What is it, Nursie?

NURSIE:
How are things progressing?

ESMERALDA:
Slowly, Nursie—

[*Nursie comes lumbering in.*]

NURSIE:
I want some light reading matter.

ESMERALDA:

He's sitting on *Screen Secrets.*

KILROY [*jumping up*]:

Aw. Here.

[*He hands her the fan magazine. She lumbers back out, coyly.*]

—I—I feel——self-conscious . .

[*He suddenly jerks out a silver-framed photo.*]

—D'you—like pictures?

ESMERALDA:

Moving pictures?

KILROY:

No, a—motionless—snapshot!

ESMERALDA:

Of you?

KILROY:

Of my—real—true woman . . . She was a platinum blonde the same as Jean Harlow. Do you remember Jean Harlow? No, you wouldn't remember Jean Harlow. It shows you are getting old when you remember Jean Harlow.

[*He puts the snapshot away.*]

. . . They say that Jean Harlow's ashes are kept in a little private cathedral in Forest Lawn . . . Wouldn't it be wonderful if you could sprinkle them ashes over the ground like seeds, and out of each one would spring another Jean Harlow? And when spring comes you could just walk out and pick them off the bush! . . . You don't talk much.

ESMERALDA:
You want me to *talk*?

KILROY:
Well, that's the way we do things in the States. A little vino, some records on the Victrola, some quiet conversation—and then if both parties are in a mood for romance . . . Romance—

ESMERALDA:
Music!

[*She rises and pours some wine from a slender crystal decanter as music is heard.*]

They say that the monetary system has got to be stabilized all over the world.

KILROY [*taking the glass*]:
Repeat that, please. My radar was not wide open.

ESMERALDA:
I said that *they* said that—uh, skip it! But we couldn't care less as long as we keep on getting the Yankee dollar . . . plus federal tax!

KILROY:
That's for surely!

ESMERALDA:
How do you feel about the class struggle? Do you take sides in that?

KILROY:
Not that I—

ESMERALDA:
Neither do we because of the dialectics.

KILROY:

Who! Which?

ESMERALDA:

Languages with accents, I suppose. But Mama don't care as long as they don't bring the Pope over here and put him in the White House.

KILROY:

Who would do that?

ESMERALDA:

Oh, the Bolsheviskies, those nasty old things with whiskers! *Whiskers scratch!* But little moustaches tickle . . .

[*She giggles.*]

KILROY:

I always got a smooth shave . . .

ESMERALDA:

And how do you feel about the Mumbo Jumbo? Do you think they've got the Old Man in the bag yet?

KILROY:

The Old Man?

ESMERALDA:

God. We don't think so. We think there has been so much of the Mumbo Jumbo it's put Him to sleep!

[*Kilroy jumps up impatiently.*]

KILROY:

This is not what I mean by a quiet conversation. I mean this is no where! *No where!*

ESMERALDA:

What sort of talk do you want?

KILROY:
Something more—intimate sort of! You know, like—

ESMERALDA:
—Where did you get those eyes?

KILROY:
PERSONAL! Yeah . . .

ESMERALDA:
Well,—where did you get those eyes?

KILROY:
Out of a dead codfish!

NURSIE [*shouting offstage*]:
DOLL!

[*Kilroy springs up, pounding his left palm with his right fist.*]

ESMERALDA:
What?

NURSIE:
Fifteen minutes!

KILROY:
I'm no hot-rod mechanic.

[*To the audience:*]

I bet she's out there holding a stop watch to see that I don't overstay my time in this place!

ESMERALDA [*calling through the string curtains*]:
Nursie, go to bed, Nursie!

KILROY [*in a fierce whisper*]:
That's right, go to bed, Nursie!!

[*There is a loud crash offstage.*]

ESMERALDA:

—Nursie has gone to bed . . .

[*She drops the string curtains and returns to the alcove.*]

KILROY [*with vast relief*]:

—Ahhhhhhhhhh . . .

ESMERALDA:

What've you got your eyes on?

KILROY:

Those green snakes on you—what do you wear them for?

ESMERALDA:

Supposedly for protection, but really for fun.

[*He crosses to the divan.*]

What are you going to do?

KILROY:

I'm about to establish a beachhead on that sofa.

[*He sits down.*]

How about—lifting your veil?

ESMERALDA:

I can't lift it.

KILROY:

Why not?

ESMERALDA:

I promised Mother I wouldn't.

KILROY:

I thought your mother was the broad-minded type.

ESMERALDA:

Oh, she is, but you know how mothers are. You can lift it for me, if you say pretty please.

KILROY:

Aww——

ESMERALDA:

Go on, say it! Say pretty please!

KILROY:

No!!

ESMERALDA:

Why not?

KILROY:

It's silly.

ESMERALDA:

Then you can't lift my veil!

KILROY:

Oh, all right. Pretty please.

ESMERALDA:

Say it again!

KILROY:

Pretty please.

ESMERALDA:

Now say it once more like you meant it.

[*He jumps up. She grabs his hand.*]

Don't go away.

KILROY:

You're making a fool out of me.

ESMERALDA:

I was just teasing a little. Because you're so cute. Sit down again, please—*pretty* please!

[*He falls on the couch.*]

KILROY:

What is that wonderful perfume you've got on?

ESMERALDA:

Guess!

KILROY:

Chanel Number Five?

ESMERALDA:

No.

KILROY:

Tabu?

ESMERALDA:

No.

KILROY:

I give up.

ESMERALDA:

It's *Noche en Acapulco*! I'm just dying to go to Acapulco. I wish that you would take me to Acapulco.

[*He sits up.*]

What's the matter?

KILROY:

You Gypsies' daughters are invariably reminded of something without which you cannot do—just when it looks like everything has been fixed.

557

ESMERALDA:

That isn't nice at all. I'm not the gold-digger type. Some girls see themselves in silver foxes. I only see myself in Acapulco!

KILROY:

At Todd's Place?

ESMERALDA:

Oh, no, at the Mirador! Watching those pretty boys dive off the Quebrada!

KILROY:

Look again, baby. Maybe you'll see yourself in Paramount Pictures or having a Singapore Sling at a Statler bar!

ESMERALDA:

You're being sarcastic?

KILROY:

Nope. Just realistic. All of you Gypsies' daughters have hearts of stone, and I'm not whistling "Dixie"! But just the same, the night before a man dies, he says, "Pretty please—will you let me lift your veil?"—while the Streetcleaners wait for him right outside the door!—Because to be warm for a little longer is life. And love?—that's a four-letter word which is sometimes no better than one you see printed on fences by kids playing hooky from school!—Oh, well—what's the use of complaining? You Gypsies' daughters have ears that only catch sounds like the snap of a gold cigarette case! Or, pretty please, baby,—we're going to Acapulco!

ESMERALDA:

Are we?

KILROY:

See what I mean?

[*To the audience:*]

Didn't I tell you?!

[*To Esmeralda:*]

Yes! In the morning!

ESMERALDA:
Ohhhh! I'm dizzy with joy! My little heart is going pitty-pat!

KILROY:
My big heart is going boom-boom! Can I lift your veil now?

ESMERALDA:
If you will be gentle.

KILROY:
I would not hurt a fly unless it had on leather mittens.

[*He touches a corner of her spangled veil.*]

ESMERALDA:
Ohhh . . .

KILROY:
What?

ESMERALDA:
Ohhhhhh!!

KILROY:
Why! What's the matter?

ESMERALDA:
You are not being gentle!

KILROY:
I *am* being gentle.

ESMERALDA:
You are *not* being gentle.

KILROY:
What was I being, then?

ESMERALDA:
Rough!

KILROY:
I am *not* being rough.

ESMERALDA:
Yes, you *are* being rough. You have to be gentle with me because you're the first.

KILROY:
Are you kidding?

ESMERALDA:
No.

KILROY:
How about all of those other fiestas you've been to?

ESMERALDA:
Each one's the first one. That is the wonderful thing about Gypsies' daughters!

KILROY:
You can say that again!

ESMERALDA:
I don't like you when you're like that.

KILROY:
Like what?

ESMERALDA:

Cynical and sarcastic.

KILROY:

I am sincere.

ESMERALDA:

Lots of boys aren't sincere.

KILROY:

Maybe they aren't but I am.

ESMERALDA:

Everyone says he's sincere, but everyone isn't sincere. If everyone was sincere who says he's sincere there wouldn't be half so many insincere ones in the world and there would be lots, lots, lots more really sincere ones!

KILROY:

I think you have got something there. But how about Gypsies' daughters?

ESMERALDA:

Huh?

KILROY:

Are they one hundred per cent in the really sincere category?

ESMERALDA:

Well, yes, and no, mostly no! But some of them are for a while if their sweethearts are gentle.

KILROY:

Would you believe I am sincere and gentle?

ESMERALDA:

I would believe that you believe that you are . . . For a while . . .

561

KILROY:

Everything's for a while. For a while is the stuff that dreams are made of, Baby! Now?—Now?

ESMERALDA:

Yes, now, but be gentle!—*gentle* ...

[*He delicately lifts a corner of her veil. She utters a soft cry. He lifts it further. She cries out again. A bit further ... He turns the spangled veil all the way up from her face.*]

KILROY:

I am sincere.

ESMERALDA:

I am sincere.

KILROY:

I am sincere.

ESMERALDA:

I am sincere.

KILROY:

I am sincere.

ESMERALDA:

I am sincere.

KILROY:

I am sincere.

ESMERALDA:

I am sincere.

[*Kilroy leans back, removing his hand from her veil. She opens her eyes.*]

Is that all?

KILROY:
I am tired.

ESMERALDA:
—Already?

[*He rises and goes down the steps from the alcove.*]

KILROY:
I am tired, and full of regret ...

ESMERALDA:
Oh!

KILROY:
It wasn't much to give my golden gloves for.

ESMERALDA:
You pity yourself?

KILROY:
That's right, I pity myself and everybody that goes to the Gypsy's daughter. I pity the world and I pity the God who made it.

[*He sits down.*]

ESMERALDA:
It's always like that as soon as the veil is lifted. They're all so ashamed of having degraded themselves, and their hearts have more regret than a heart can hold!

KILROY:
Even a heart that's as big as the head of a baby!

ESMERALDA:
You don't even notice how pretty my face is, do you?

KILROY:
You look like all Gypsies' daughters, no better, no worse. But

as long as you get to go to Acapulco, your cup runneth over with ordinary contentment.

ESMERALDA:
—I've never been so insulted in all my life!

KILROY:
Oh, yes, you have, baby. And you'll be insulted worse if you stay in this racket. You'll be insulted so much that it will get to be like water off *a duck's back!*

[*The door slams. Curtains are drawn apart on the Gypsy. Esmeralda lowers her veil hastily. Kilroy pretends not to notice the Gypsy's entrance. She picks up a little bell and rings it over his head.*]

Okay, Mamacita! I am aware of your presence!

GYPSY:
Ha-ha! I was followed three blocks by some awful man!

KILROY:
Then you caught him.

GYPSY:
Naw, he ducked into a subway! I waited fifteen minutes outside the men's room and he never came out!

KILROY:
Then you went in?

GYPSY:
No! I got myself a sailor!—The streets are brilliant! . . . Have you all been good children?

[*Esmeralda makes a whimpering sound.*]

The pussy will play while the old mother cat is away?

KILROY:

Your sense of humor is wonderful, but how about my change, Mamacita?

GYPSY:

What change are you talking about?

KILROY:

Are you boxed out of your mind? The change from that ten-spot you trotted over to Walgreen's?

GYPSY:

Ohhhhh—

KILROY:

Oh, what?

GYPSY [*counting on her fingers*]:

Five for the works, one dollar luxury tax, two for the house percentage and two more pour la service!—makes ten! Didn't I tell you?

KILROY:

—What kind of a deal is this?

GYPSY [*whipping out a revolver*]:

A rugged one, Baby!

ESMERALDA:

Mama, don't be unkind!

GYPSY:

Honey, the gentleman's friends are waiting outside the door and it wouldn't be nice to detain him! Come on—Get going—Vamoose!

KILROY:

Okay, Mamacita! Me voy!

[*He crosses to the beaded string curtains, turns to look back at the Gypsy and her daughter. The piping of the Street-cleaners is heard outside.*]

Sincere?—Sure! That's the wonderful thing about Gypsies' daughters!

[*He goes out. Esmeralda raises a wondering fingertip to one eye. Then she cries out:*]

ESMERALDA:
Look, Mama! Look, Mama! A tear!

GYPSY:
You have been watching television too much . . .

[*She gathers the cards and turns off the crystal ball as—*

[*Light fades out on the phony paradise of the Gypsy's.*]

GUTMAN:
Block Thirteen on the Camino Real.

[*He exits.*]

BLOCK THIRTEEN

In the blackout the Streetcleaners place a barrel in the center and then hide in the Pit.

Kilroy, who enters from the right, is followed by a spotlight. He sees the barrel and the menacing Streetcleaners and then runs to the closed door of the Siete Mares and rings the bell. No one answers. He backs up so he can see the balcony and calls:

KILROY:

Mr. Gutman! Just gimme a cot in the lobby. I'll do odd jobs in the morning. I'll be the Patsy again. I'll light my nose sixty times a minute. I'll take pratfalls and assume the position for anybody that drops a dime on the street . . . Have a heart! Have just a LITTLE heart. Please!

[*There is no response from Gutman's balcony. Jacques enters. He pounds his cane once on the pavement.*]

JACQUES:

Gutman! Open the door!—*GUTMAN! GUTMAN!*

[*Eva, a beautiful woman, apparently nude, appears on the balcony.*]

GUTMAN [*from inside*]:

Eva darling, you're exposing yourself!

[*He appears on the balcony with a portmanteau.*]

JACQUES:

What are you doing with my portmanteau?

GUTMAN:

Haven't you come for your luggage?

JACQUES:
Certainly not! I haven't checked out of here!

GUTMAN:
Very few do . . . but residences are frequently terminated.

JACQUES:
Open the door!

GUTMAN:
Open the letter with the remittance check in it!

JACQUES:
In the morning!

GUTMAN:
Tonight!

JACQUES:
Upstairs in my room!

GUTMAN:
Downstairs at the entrance!

JACQUES:
I won't be intimidated!

GUTMAN [*raising the portmanteau over his head*]:
What?!

JACQUES:
Wait!—

[*He takes the letter out of his pocket.*]

Give me some light.

[*Kilroy strikes a match and holds it over Jacques' shoulder.*]

Thank you. What does it say?

GUTMAN:
—Remittances?

KILROY [*reading the letter over Jacques' shoulder*]:
—*discontinued* . . .

[*Gutman raises the portmanteau again.*]

JACQUES:
Careful, I have—

[*The portmanteau lands with a crash.*

[*The Bum comes to the window at the crash. A. Ratt comes out to his doorway at the same time.*]

—fragile—mementos . . .

[*He crosses slowly down to the portmanteau and kneels as . . .*

[*Gutman laughs and slams the balcony door. Jacques turns to Kilroy. He smiles at the young adventurer.*]

—"And so at last it has come, the distinguished thing!"

[*A. Ratt speaks as Jacques touches the portmanteau.*]

A. RATT
Hey, Dad—Vacancy here! A bed at the "Ritz Men Only." A little white ship to sail the dangerous night in.

JACQUES:
Single or double?

A. RATT
There's only singles in this pad.

JACQUES [*to Kilroy*]:
Match you for it.

KILROY:

What the hell, we're buddies, we can sleep spoons!· If we can't sleep, we'll push the washstand against the door and sing old popular songs till the crack of dawn! . . . "Heart of my heart, I love that melody!" . . . You bet your life I do.

[*Jacques takes out a pocket handkerchief and starts to grasp the portmanteau handle.*]

—It looks to me like you could use a redcap and my rates are nonunion!

[*He picks up the portmanteau and starts to cross toward the "Ritz Men Only." He stops at right center.*]

Sorry, buddy. Can't make it! The altitude on this block has affected my ticker! And in the distance which is nearer than further, I hear—the Streetcleaners'—piping!

[*Piping is heard.*]

JACQUES:
COME ALONG!

[*He lifts the portmanteau and starts on.*]

KILROY:
NO. Tonight! I prefer! To sleep! Out! Under! The stars!

JACQUES [*gently*]:
I understand, Brother!

KILROY [*to Jacques as he continues toward the "Ritz Men Only"*]:

Bon Voyage! I hope that you sail the dangerous night to the sweet golden port of morning!

JACQUES [*exiting*]:
Thanks, Brother!

KILROY:
Excuse the *corn!* I'm sincere!

BUM:
Show me the way to go home! ...

GUTMAN [*appearing on the balcony with white parakeet*]:
Block Fourteen on the Camino Real.

BLOCK FOURTEEN

At opening, the Bum is still at the window.

The Streetcleaners' piping continues a little louder. Kilroy climbs, breathing heavily, to the top of the stairs and stands looking out at Terra Incognita as ...

Marguerite enters the plaza through alleyway at right. She is accompanied by a silent Young Man who wears a domino.

MARGUERITE:

Don't come any further with me. I'll have to wake the night porter. Thank you for giving me safe conduct through the Medina.

[*She has offered her hand. He grips it with a tightness that makes her wince.*]

Ohhhh . . . I'm not sure which is more provocative in you, your ominous silence or your glittering smile or—

[*He's looking at her purse.*]

What do you want? . . . Oh!

[*She starts to open the purse. He snatches it. She gasps as he suddenly strips her cloak off her. Then he snatches off her pearl necklace. With each successive despoilment, she gasps and retreats but makes no resistance. Her eyes are closed. He continues to smile. Finally, he rips her dress and runs his hands over her body as if to see if she had anything else of value concealed on her.*]

—What else do I have that you want?

THE YOUNG MAN [*contemptuously*]:
Nothing.

[*The Young Man exits through the cantina, examining his loot. The Bum leans out his window, draws a deep breath and says:*]

BUM:
Lonely.

MARGUERITE [*to herself*]:
Lonely . . .

KILROY [*on the steps*]:
Lonely . . .

[*The Streetcleaners' piping is heard.*

[*Marguerite runs to the Siete Mares and rings the bell. Nobody answers. She crosses to the terrace. Kilroy, meanwhile, has descended the stairs.*]

MARGUERITE:
Jacques!

[*Piping is heard.*]

KILROY:
Lady?

MARGUERITE:
What?

KILROY:
—*I'm—safe* . . .

MARGUERITE:
I wasn't expecting that music tonight, were you?

[*Piping.*]

KILROY:
It's them Streetcleaners.

MARGUERITE:
I know.

[*Piping.*]

KILROY:
You better go on in, lady.

MARGUERITE:
No.

KILROY:
GO ON IN!

MARGUERITE:
NO! I want to stay out here and I do what I want to do!

[*Kilroy looks at her for the first time.*]

Sit down with me please.

KILROY:
They're coming for me. The Gypsy told me I'm on top of their list. Thanks for. Taking my. Hand.

[*Piping is heard.*]

MARGUERITE:
Thanks for taking mine.

[*Piping.*]

KILROY:
Do me one more favor. Take out of my pocket a picture. My fingers are. Stiff.

MARGUERITE:
This one?

KILROY:

My one. True. Woman.

MARGUERITE:

A silver-framed photo! Was she really so fair?

KILROY:

She was so fair and much fairer than they could tint that picture!

MARGUERITE:

Then you have been on the street when the street was royal.

KILROY:

Yeah . . . when the street was royal!

[*Piping is heard. Kilroy rises.*]

MARGUERITE:

Don't get up, don't leave me!

KILROY:

I want to be on my feet when the Streetcleaners come for me!

MARGUERITE:

Sit back down again and tell me about your girl.

[*He sits.*]

KILROY:

Y'know what it is you miss most? When you're separated. From someone. You lived. With. And loved? It's waking up in the night! With that—warmness beside you!

MARGUERITE:

Yes, that *warmness* beside you!

KILROY:

Once you get used to that. *Warmness!* It's a hell of a lonely feeling to wake up without it! Specially in some dollar-a-night hotel room on Skid! A hot-water bottle won't do. And a stranger. Won't do. It has to be some one you're used to. And that you. *KNOW LOVES* you!

[*Piping is heard.*]

Can you see them?

MARGUERITE:
I see no one but you.

KILROY:
I looked at my wife one night when she was sleeping and that was the night that the medics wouldn't okay me for no more fights . . . Well . . . My wife was sleeping with a smile like a child's. I kissed her. She didn't wake up. I took a pencil and paper. I wrote her. Good-bye!

MARGUERITE:
That was the night she would have loved you the most!

KILROY:
Yeah, *that* night, but what about *after* that night? Oh, lady . . . Why should a beautiful girl tie up with a broken-down champ?—The earth still turning and her obliged to turn with it, not out—of dark into light but out of light into dark? Naw, naw, naw, naw!—Washed up!—Finished!

[*Piping.*]

. . . that ain't a word that a man can't look at . . . There ain't no words in the language a man can't look at . . . and know just what they mean. And be. And act. And *go!*

[*He turns to the waiting Streetcleaners.*]

Come on! . . . Come on! . . . COME ON, YOU SONS OF
BITCHES! KILROY IS HERE! HE'S READY!

[*A gong sounds.*

[*Kilroy swings at the Streetcleaners. They circle about him
out of reach, turning him by each of their movements. The
swings grow wilder like a boxer. He falls to his knees still
swinging and finally collapses flat on his face.*

[*The Streetcleaners pounce but La Madrecita throws herself
protectingly over the body and covers it with her shawl.*

[*Blackout.*]

MARGUERITE:
Jacques!

GUTMAN [*on balcony*]:
Block Fifteen on the Camino Real.

BLOCK FIFTEEN

*La Madrecita is seated; across her knees is the body of Kilroy.
Up center, a low table on wheels bears a sheeted figure. Beside
the table stands a Medical Instructor addressing Students and
Nurses, all in white surgical outfits.*

INSTRUCTOR:
This is the body of an unidentified vagrant.

LA MADRECITA:
This was thy son, America—and now mine.

INSTRUCTOR:
He was found in an alley along the Camino Real.

LA MADRECITA:
Think of him, now, as he was before his luck failed him.
Remember his time of greatness, when he was not faded, not
frightened.

INSTRUCTOR:
More light, please!

LA MADRECITA:
More light!

INSTRUCTOR:
Can everyone see clearly!

LA MADRECITA:
Everyone must see clearly!

INSTRUCTOR:
There is no external evidence of disease.

LA MADRECITA:
He had clear eyes and the body of a champion boxer.

INSTRUCTOR:

There are no marks of violence on the body.

LA MADRECITA:

He had the soft voice of the South and a pair of golden gloves.

INSTRUCTOR:

His death was apparently due to natural causes.

[*The Students make notes. There are keening voices.*]

LA MADRECITA:

Yes, blow wind where night thins! He had many admirers!

INSTRUCTOR:

There are no legal claimants.

LA MADRECITA:

He stood as a planet among the moons of their longing, haughty with youth, a champion of the prize-ring!

INSTRUCTOR:

No friends or relatives having identified him—

LA MADRECITA:

You should have seen the lovely monogrammed robe in which he strode the aisles of the colosseums!

INSTRUCTOR:

After the elapse of a certain number of days, his body becomes the property of the State—

LA MADRECITA:

Yes, blow wind where night thins—for laurel is not everlasting . . .

INSTRUCTOR:

And now is transferred to our hands for the nominal sum of five dollars.

LA MADRECITA:
This was thy son,—and now mine ...

INSTRUCTOR:
We will now proceed with the dissection. Knife, please!

LA MADRECITA:
Blow wind!

[*Keening is heard offstage.*]

Yes, blow wind where night thins! You are his passing bell
and his lamentation.

[*More keening is heard.*]

Keen for him, all maimed creatures, deformed and mutilated
—his homeless ghost is your own!

INSTRUCTOR:
First we will open up the chest cavity and examine the heart
for evidence of coronary occlusion.

LA MADRECITA:
His heart was pure gold and as big as the head of a baby.

INSTRUCTOR:
We will make an incision along the vertical line.

LA MADRECITA:
Rise, ghost! Go! Go bird! "Humankind cannot bear very
much reality."

[*At the touch of her flowers, Kilroy stirs and pushes himself
up slowly from her lap. On his feet again, he rubs his eyes
and looks around him.*]

VOICES [*crying offstage*]:
Olé! Olé! Olé!

580

KILROY:

Hey! Hey, somebody! Where am I?

[*He notices the dissection room and approaches.*]

INSTRUCTOR [*removing a glittering sphere from a dummy corpse*]:

Look at this heart. It's as big as the head of a baby.

KILROY:

My heart!

INSTRUCTOR:

Wash it off so we can look for the pathological lesions.

KILROY:

Yes, siree, that's my heart!

GUTMAN:

Block Sixteen!

[*Kilroy pauses just outside the dissection area as a Student takes the heart and dips it into a basin on the stand beside the table. The Student suddenly cries out and holds aloft a glittering gold sphere.*]

INSTRUCTOR:

Look! This heart's solid gold!

BLOCK SIXTEEN

KILROY [*rushing forward*]:
That's mine, you bastards!

[*He snatches the golden sphere from the Medical Instructor.
The autopsy proceeds as if nothing had happened as the
spot of light on the table fades out, but for Kilroy a ghostly
chase commences, a dreamlike re-enactment of the chase
that occurred at the end of Block Six. Gutman shouts from
his balcony:*]

GUTMAN:
Stop, thief, stop, corpse! That gold heart is the property of
the State! Catch him, catch the golden-heart robber!

[*Kilroy dashes offstage into an aisle of the theatre. There is
the wail of a siren: the air is filled with calls and whistles,
roar of motors, screeching brakes, pistol-shots, thundering
footsteps. The dimness of the auditorium is transected by
searching rays of light—but there are no visible pursuers.*]

KILROY [*as he runs panting up the aisle*]:
This is my heart! It don't belong to no State, not even the
U.S.A. Which way is out? Where's the Greyhound depot?
Nobody's going to put my heart in a bottle in a museum and
charge admission to support the rotten police! Where are
they? Which way are they going? Or coming? Hey, somebody, help me get out of here! Which way do I—which way
—which way do I—*go! go! go! go! go!*

[*He has now arrived in the balcony.*]

Gee, I'm lost! I don't know where I am! I'm all turned
around, I'm *confused,* I don't understand—what's—happened,
it's like a—*dream,* it's—just like a—dream . . . *Mary! Oh,
Mary! Mary!*

[*He has entered the box from which he leapt in Block Two.*

[*A clear shaft of light falls on him. He looks up into it, crying:*]

Mary, help a Christian!! Help a Christian, Mary!—It's like a dream . . .

[*Esmeralda appears in a childish nightgown beside her gauze-tented bed on the Gypsy's roof. Her Mother appears with a cup of some sedative drink, cooing . . .*]

GYPSY:
Beddy-bye, beddy-bye, darling. It's sleepy-time down South and up North, too, and also East and West!

KILROY [*softly*]:
Yes, it's—like a—*dream* . . .

[*He leans panting over the ledge of the box, holding his heart like a football, watching Esmeralda.*]

GYPSY:
Drink your Ovaltine, Ducks, and the sandman will come on tiptoe with a bag full of dreams . . .

ESMERALDA:
I want to dream of the Chosen Hero, Mummy.

GYPSY:
Which one, the one that's coming or the one that is gone?

ESMERALDA:
The *only* one, *Kilroy*! *He* was *sincere*!

KILROY:
That's *right*! *I was*, for a while!

583

GYPSY:

How do you know that Kilroy was sincere?

ESMERALDA:

He said so.

KILROY:

That's the truth, I *was*!

GYPSY:

When did he say that?

ESMERALDA:

When he lifted my veil.

GYPSY:

Baby, they're always sincere when they lift your veil; it's one of those natural reflexes that don't mean a thing.

KILROY [*aside*]:

What a cynical old bitch that Gypsy mama is!

GYPSY:

And there's going to be lots of other fiestas for you, baby doll, and lots of other chosen heroes to lift your little veil when Mamacita and Nursie are out of the room.

ESMERALDA:

No, Mummy, never, I mean it!

KILROY:

I *believe* she means it!

GYPSY:

Finish your Ovaltine and say your Now-I-Lay-Me.

[*Esmeralda sips the drink and hands her the cup.*]

KILROY [*with a catch in his voice*]:
I had one true woman, which I can't go back to, but now I've found another.

[*He leaps onto the stage from the box.*]

ESMERALDA [*dropping to her knees*]:
Now I lay me down to sleep, I pray the Lord my soul to keep.
If I should die before I wake, I pray the Lord my soul to take.

GYPSY:
God bless Mummy!

ESMERALDA:
And the crystal ball and the tea leaves.

KILROY:
Pssst!

ESMERALDA:
What's that?

GYPSY:
A tomcat in the plaza.

ESMERALDA:
God bless all cats without pads in the plaza tonight.

KILROY:
Amen!

[*He falls to his knees in the empty plaza.*]

ESMERALDA:
God bless all con men and hustlers and pitchmen who hawk their hearts on the street, all two-time losers who're likely to lose once more, the courtesan who made the mistake of love, the greatest of lovers crowned with the longest horns, the poet who wandered far from his heart's green country and possibly

will and possibly won't be able to find his way back, look
down with a smile tonight on the last cavaliers, the ones with
the rusty armor and soiled white plumes, and visit with understanding and something that's almost tender those fading
legends that come and go in this plaza like songs not clearly
remembered, oh, sometime and somewhere, let there be something to mean the word *honor* again!

QUIXOTE [*hoarsely and loudly, stirring slightly among his
verminous rags*]:
Amen!

KILROY:
Amen . . .

GYPSY [*disturbed*]:
—That will do, now.

ESMERALDA:
And, oh, God, let me dream tonight of the Chosen Hero!

GYPSY:
Now, sleep. Fly away on the magic carpet of dreams!

[*Esmeralda crawls into the gauze-tented cot. The Gypsy
descends from the roof.*]

KILROY:
Esmeralda! My little Gypsy sweetheart!

ESMERALDA [*sleepily*]:
Go away, cat.

[*The light behind the gauze is gradually dimming.*]

KILROY:
This is no cat. This is the chosen hero of the big fiesta, Kilroy,

the champion of the golden gloves with his gold heart cut
from his chest and in his hands to give you!

ESMERALDA:

Go away. Let me dream of the Chosen Hero.

KILROY:

What a hassle! Mistook for a cat! What can I do to convince
this doll I'm real?

[*Three brass balls wink brilliantly.*]

—Another transaction seems to be indicated!

[*He rushes to the Loan Shark's. The entrance immediately
lights up.*]

My heart is gold! What will you give me for it?

[*Jewels, furs, sequined gowns, etc., are tossed to his feet. He
throws his heart like a basketball to the Loan Shark,
snatches up the loot and rushes back to the Gypsy's.*]

Doll! Behold this loot! I gave my golden heart for it!

ESMERALDA:

Go away, cat ...

[*She falls asleep. Kilroy bangs his forehead with his fist,
then rushes to the Gypsy's door, pounds it with both fists.
The door is thrown open and the sordid contents of a large
jar are thrown at him. He falls back gasping, spluttering,
retching. He retreats and finally assumes an exaggerated
attitude of despair.*]

KILROY:

Had for a button! Stewed, screwed and tattooed on the
Camino Real! Baptized, finally, with the contents of a slop-
jar!—Did anybody say the deal was rugged?!

[*Quixote stirs against the wall of Skid Row. He hawks and spits and staggers to his feet.*]

GUTMAN:
Why, the old knight's awake, his dream is over!

QUIXOTE [*to Kilroy*]:
Hello! Is that a fountain?

KILROY:
—Yeah, but—

QUIXOTE:
I've got a mouthful of old chicken feathers . . .

[*He approaches the fountain. It begins to flow. Kilroy falls back in amazement as the Old Knight rinses his mouth and drinks and removes his jacket to bathe, handing the tattered garment to Kilroy.*]

QUIXOTE [*as he bathes*]:
Qué pasa, mi amigo?

KILROY:
The deal is rugged. D'you know what I mean?

QUIXOTE:
Who knows better than I what a rugged deal is!

[*He produces a toothbrush and brushes his teeth.*]

—Will you take some advice?

KILROY:
Brother, at this point on the Camino I will take anything which is offered!

QUIXOTE:
Don't! Pity! Your! Self!

[*He takes out a pocket mirror and grooms his beard and moustache.*]

The wounds of the vanity, the many offenses our egos have to endure, being housed in bodies that age and hearts that grow tired, are better accepted with a tolerant smile—like *this!* —You *see?*

[*He cracks his face in two with an enormous grin.*]

GUTMAN:
Follow-spot on the face of the ancient knight!

QUIXOTE:
Otherwise what you become is a bag full of curdled cream— *leche mala,* we call it!—attractive to nobody, least of all to yourself!

[*He passes the comb and pocket mirror to Kilroy.*]

Have you got any plans?

KILROY [*a bit uncertainly, wistfully*]:
Well, I was thinking of—going *on* from—*here!*

QUIXOTE:
Good! Come with me.

KILROY [*to the audience*]:
Crazy old bastard.

[*Then to the Knight:*]

Donde?

QUIXOTE [*starting for the stairs*]:
Quien sabe!

[*The fountain is now flowing loudly and sweetly. The Street People are moving toward it with murmurs of wonder. Marguerite comes out upon the terrace.*]

KILROY:

Hey, there's—!

QUIXOTE:

Shhh! Listen!

[*They pause on the stairs.*]

MARGUERITE:

Abdullah!

[*Gutman has descended to the terrace.*]

GUTMAN:

Mademoiselle, allow me to deliver the message for you. It would be in bad form if I didn't take some final part in the pageant.

[*He crosses the plaza to the opposite façade and shouts "Casanova!" under the window of the "Ritz Men Only."*]

[*Meanwhile Kilroy scratches out the verb "is" and prints the correction "was" in the inscription on the ancient wall.*]

Casanova! Great lover and King of Cuckolds on the Camino Real! The last of your ladies has guaranteed your tabs and is expecting you for breakfast on the terrace!

[*Casanova looks first out of the practical window of the flophouse, then emerges from its scabrous doorway, haggard, unshaven, crumpled in dress but bearing himself as erectly as ever. He blinks and glares fiercely into the brilliant morning light.*

[*Marguerite cannot return his look, she averts her face with a look for which anguish would not be too strong a term, but at the same time she extends a pleading hand toward him. After some hesitation, he begins to move toward her, striking the pavement in measured cadence with his cane, glancing once, as he crosses, out at the audience with a wry smile that makes admissions that would be embarrassing to a vainer man than Casanova now is. When he reaches Marguerite she gropes for his hand, seizes it with a low cry and presses it spasmodically to her lips while he draws her into his arms and looks above her sobbing, dyed-golden head with the serene, clouded gaze of someone mortally ill as the mercy of a narcotic laps over his pain.*

[*Quixote raises his lance in a formal gesture and cries out hoarsely, powerfully from the stairs:*]

QUIXOTE:
The violets in the mountains have broken the rocks!

[*Quixote goes through the arch with Kilroy.*]

GUTMAN [*to the audience*]:
The Curtain Line has been spoken!

[*To the wings:*]

Bring it down!

[*He bows with a fat man's grace as—*

[*The curtain falls.*]

591

New Directions Paperbooks—A Partial Listing

For complete listing request free catalog from
New Directions, 80 Eighth Avenue, New York 10011

†Bilingual